A TOWPATH GUIDE TO THE

Staffordshire and Worcestershire Canal

A TOWPATH GUIDE TO THE
Staffordshire and Worcestershire Canal

J. IAN LANGFORD
B.Sc.Eng.(Lond.), Ph.D.(Wales), M.I.E.E.
Chartered Engineer
Senior Research Associate in the University of Birmingham

With illustrations by
ROBERT MAY
Staff Photographer, Birmingham Evening Mail

GOOSE AND SON
PUBLISHERS

Goose and Son Publishers Limited,
Salisbury House, Station Road,
Cambridge, CB1 2LA,
England

Trade Distribution:
Goose and Son Publishers Limited,
Warner House, Folkestone, Kent,
England

First Published 1974

ISBN 0 900404 22 1

Composed in 11/12 Monotype Garamond
Text printed letterpress by Latimer Trend & Company Ltd Plymouth
Illustrations printed litho by Tinlings (1973) Ltd. Prescot, Lancs.
Cover printed letterpress by Bristol Typesetting Co. Ltd.
Bound in Great Britain by Tinlings (1973) Ltd.

Contents

Acknowledgements

The main contributor to this book, and the inspiration for it, has been the Staffordshire & Worcestershire Canal, which for two centuries has been faithfully recording its own story. Much information was imparted freely, though some secrets were withheld for the time being, perhaps for ever.

Many people have contributed to the work, either by sending material or by patiently answering questions at personal interviews. I am particularly indebted to the employees of British Waterways Board, the present custodians of the canal, who supplied information: Messrs Len P. Wall and Brian P. Haskins, Area Engineers responsible for the southern and northern sections of the Staffs & Worcs; Messrs Charlie Merrick of Slade Heath, Bert Hardman of Wightwick (now retired), Jim Hodgson of the Hyde and George Wood and his wife, Margaret, of Greensforge, who all work or have worked on the canal; and Mr Philip Morgan, Foreman of the Stourport section, whose knowledge of the basins there is unrivalled. Of the boatmen who have been or who still are associated with the canal, Messrs Ernie Thomas of Calf Heath, Tom Heritage of Langley and Cliff Sherwood of the N.B. *Bellatrix*, Kinver, have between them provided the story of life on the Staffs & Worcs since the beginning of the century. Mr Denis W. Grosvenor of the Central Electricity Generating Board kindly supplied details of coal traffic on the Stourport 'Light Run' and Mr J. P. Barnes, Manager of Barnhurst works, made available his history of sewage treatment at Wolverhampton.

7

The first edition 6in. maps of the Ordnance Survey provided the framework around which the strip maps and indeed much of the guide were devised. I am greatly indebted to the Department of Geography, University of Birmingham, for access to these and many other early maps and plans; to Mr D. W. Oliver of that department for his assistance on numerous occasions; and to Professor F. W. Shotton, Department of Geology, whose advice and comments on the geological notes in this guide were invaluable. I also received valuable assistance from Mr Colin Gall of Stafford when carrying out surveys of the northern section of the canal; and the dossier on canalside pubs, compiled by Mr Gordon Bennett of the Staffs & Worcs Canal Society, and kindly made available by him, was most helpful. Mr Alan T. Smith, Chairman of the Society, provided much of the information on cruising facilities, as well as suggesting sources of material and taking a keen general interest in the work.

I should especially like to thank Lord Hatherton for permission to use material from diaries written by the first Lord, Edward Littleton; also Mr Sam Prince, Bailiff to the Teddesley estate, for the loan of the diaries, and Mr J. H. Parker Oxspring for providing a masterly account of the origins of the canal. For information on associated transport systems I have relied on the expertise of Messrs J. Stanley Webb (Kinver Light Railway), Eric S. Tonks (Courtaulds Siding) and Michael Hale (all other railways).

No words of mine could adequately portray the beauty, serenity and historical interest of the Staffs & Worcs Canal. For this I have relied on Mr Robert May, Staff Photographer with the *Birmingham Evening Mail*, who has returned to the canal time and again to capture the spirit of the waterway in all its moods. I am also greatly indebted to the Editor of the *Evening Mail* for permission to reproduce the majority of illustrations in this book. In addition, my thanks are due to the following for providing photographs: Waterways Museum (British Waterways Board), Stoke Bruerne (Plate 68 and company seal); V. W. Smallshire (Plates 40, 48, 53, 59 and 60); J. S. Webb (Plate 47); David Richards (Plates 41, 51 and 54); Dudley Library (Plate 39); Birmingham Reference Library (Plates 14, 26, 69, 71 and 79); W. D. Cain/Kidderminster Library (Plate 64); University of Birmingham Library (Plate 81); B. A. Hardman (Plate 82).

ACKNOWLEDGEMENTS

Finally, this book would not have been possible without the continual encouragement and support of my wife. Her critical reading of the text and helpful suggestions were of inestimable value at every stage.   J. IAN LANGFORD

Foreword

LORD HATHERTON

It is most fitting that this meticulous work by Dr Ian Langford, the first of a series, should be completed in this bicentenary year of the Staffordshire & Worcestershire Canal, after so much diligent research into every facet of these wonderful waterways which are an important part of our heritage.

As an engineer, Ian Langford has given us more than a towpath guide. He has provided us with a study of their construction with the advantage of his own engineering knowledge, consequently giving us a deeper understanding of the many structures and geological aspects, coupled with historical facts, not only territorial, but also of individuals deeply involved in the building of our waterways. He has given us anecdotes about people from the past which will span two hundred years for the canal user of today, and cannot fail to stir the canal enthusiast with a sense of history.

In compiling this first book of the series, Ian Langford has not spared himself in his research for this most unselfish work, to provide both present and future canal users with not only a fuller knowledge of the canals, the estates they pass through, the owners then and now, and their influence on the construction, but also that their enjoyment may be increased by confirming what they have read, and interpreting what they see.

Readers will no doubt look forward with great interest to future sequels to this volume. I feel proud to be associated with his work, and to add my name to those of my ancestors mentioned in this book.

House of Lords, October 1972

11

Preface

Water has a fascination for young and old alike. When it forms a highway, steeped in history and available for all to enjoy, its charm is even more irresistible. For mile after mile the story of a canal unfolds, bridge by bridge and lock by lock. The problems encountered by the early pioneers, the influence of the waterway on communities along its banks and the rise and decline in commercial traffic are all recorded. The Towpath Guides tell this story so that canal users can increase their enjoyment of the waterway system, whether they travel on foot, cycle or boat, 'bridge hop' by car or just sit at the end of a fishing line. Canals are living history. In an age when our environment is changing rapidly and not always for the better, canals are almost unique in providing a link with the past and at the same time contributing to the 'Recreational Revolution' of the present. Through the canals themselves, the Towpath Guides trace the story of each waterway from its inception to the present period of transition.

The traveller will be better able to interpret what he sees along a canal if he knows something of the company who created and ran it and the life of the people who worked the boats. A brief history of each canal company is included in the Guides, but many excellent and detailed books on the subject have already been written. Those unfamiliar with the development of the canal system or the story of trading upon it are recommended to read some of the works listed in the Bibliography before setting out on their journey. The choice of route and nature of the works along a canal depend on the geography of the area and this in turn is

related to the rocks which lie under it. An elementary knowledge
of the geology of the area can add much to one's enjoyment of a
canal and a short account has also been included.

A system of strip maps of varying scale has been adopted to
indicate where items of interest may be found, since this allows
for the changing density of material between, say, rural and urban
sections. This is not ideal for cruising purposes, but it is assumed
that the traveller has with him a 1in. Ordnance map (or the
1:50,000 scale map that is replacing it), or better still, the 2½in.
series. Distances are given at frequent intervals and are measured
from each end of the canal. Wherever possible these have been
related to mile posts or taken from the Canal Company's tables,
except when the latter are obviously in error.

Many of the Towpath Guides are based on excursion notes
provided for the Navigable Waterways of the Midlands course,
held annually at Pendrell Hall College, near Wolverhampton.
This course at the residential Adult Education Centre of Staffordshire County Council has been extremely popular for over a
decade and many miles of Midland waterway have been covered
during excursions in the *Cactus*, a traditional boat of the
narrow canals.

Most canals are at present owned by British Waterways Board
and boats using them require a licence. A permit should also be
obtained for walking or cycling along the towing path, and this
may be had from the Board at low cost, though there is a public
right-of-way along some sections. There are few car parks along
canals, aside from private ones at pubs, marinas and boatyards.
This may change in years to come, but in the meantime parking
near canals can be hazardous. Many bridges were intended to
carry only carts, horses and pedestrians, and are often narrow,
particularly on the earlier waterways. Although 'bridge hopping'
by car is becoming a popular pastime, in the interests of safety it
is often advisable to park at some distance from the canal.

Finally, although locks, bridges, wharves and other works tell
the story of a canal, their message is not always clear and contemporary documents to make it so are not always available.
Throughout the Guides, the distinction has been made between
what can only be inferred and what is fairly certain. Inference
implies an opinion on the part of the writer and occasionally

14

information comes to light which shows this to be erroneous. In this respect the Guides perhaps differ from what are normally regarded as 'works of reference', but it was felt worthwhile to include the non-factual as well as the factual, if only to illustrate how one sets about 'reading' canals and their works.

J. Ian Langford

Birmingham,
April 1974

Illustrations

All illustrations are copyright as follows:

B.A.H. B. A. Hardman

B.R.L. Birmingham Reference Library

B.W.B. British Waterways Board

D.L. Dudley Library

D.R. David Richards

J.S.W. J. Stanley Webb

R.M. Robert May

U.B.L. University of Birmingham Library

V.W.S. V. W. Smallshire

W.D.C. W. D. Cain/Kidderminster Library

Overleaf: Kidderminster lock in 1959, showing Mill wharf, SUCCo. (LM&SR) warehouse and cottages, all now demolished. The top gate has S&WCCo. paddle gear and that on the bottom gate is of BCN pattern. (R.M.)

Plate 1 (above): Brindley's elegant roving bridge (No. 109) at Great Haywood, spanning the junction between the Staffs and Worcs and Grand Trunk (Trent and Mersey) canals. (R.M.) **Plate 2** (below): Basin, wharf and corn mill at Haywood junction. (R.M.) **Plate 3** (opposite): A rope-worn bollard at Haywood. (R.M.)

Plate 4 (above) : The early 19th century Toll office in 'Chapel' style at Haywood. (R.M.)
Plate 5 (below) : The low arches of Brindley's Trent aqueduct at Haywood, with parapet added at a later date. (R.M.) **Plate 6** (opposite) : The Broad Water, Tixall. (R.M.)

Plate 7 (above) : The late Tudor gatehouse at Tixall ; all that remains of the old hall. (R.M.)
Plate 8 (below) : The Bottle Lodge, Tixall. (R.M.)

Plate 9 (above) : Tixall lock, with wooden S&WCCo. paddle posts, lock cottage and Old Hill bridge (No. 107). (R.M.) **Plate 10** (below) : Beauty in brick and stone ; Brindley's turnover bridge at Milford (No. 105), unchanged after 200 years. (R.M.)

Plate 11 (above): Old wharves, the Royal Brine Baths, and Green bridge at Stafford, the end of the disused Sow Navigation. (R.M.) Plate 12 (below): Warehouses at Radford Wharf, demolished in 1972, and the much altered Radford bridge (No. 98). (R.M.)

Plate 13 (above): Filance bridge (No. 84) and the 'Cross Keys', Penkridge, a pub popular among boatmen, past and present. (R.M.)
Plate 14: Loading gantry at Littleton Colliery basin, Otherton, c. 1920 (B.R.L.)

Plate 15 (above left): 'Long and Short' masonry of Rodbaston bridge (No. 80), typical of Brindley's lock bridges. (R.M.) **Plate 16** (left): Boggs lock, typical tail of a lock without a bridge. (R.M.) **Plate 17** (above): Old engine house and culvert at Gailey 'New' reservoirs. (R.M.) **Plate 18** (top right): Gailey Round House, *c.* 1805, and lock, showing strapping post, stud, and cranked bottom-gate beams. (R.M.) **Plate 19** (right): Industry at Four Ashes, from Calf Heath bridge (No. 77). (R.M.)

Plate 20: The late Ernie Thomas, boatman, at Calf Heath Marina. (R.M.)

Plate 21: Telford's roving/accommodation bridge, *c.* 1830 at Autherley, the junction between Staffs and Worcs and Birmingham and Liverpool Junction canals. (R.M.)

Plate 22 (above) : Oxley railway viaducts and sewage aqueduct. (R.M.)

Plate 23 (below) : Aldersley roving bridge (1772) ; B.C.N. style. (R.M.)

Plate 24 (above) : The junction with the Birmingham Canal at Aldersley and the bottom lock of the Wolverhampton '21'. (R.M.) Plate 25 (below) : Tettenhall Old and New bridges (No. 61 and No. 62). (R.M.) Plate 26 (top right) : A. J. Butler, Company Secretary, Engineer and General Manager, c. 1905 to 1937. (B.R.L.) Plate 27 (bottom right) : High and dry at Compton Bridge (No. 59), after Wightwick breach of 9th September 1972. (R.M.)

Plate 28 (above) : Breach near Wightwick Mill lock that occurred when the Smestow brook overflowed into the canal. (R.M.) **Plate 29** (below) : Dimmingsdale storage reservoir (No. 8). (R.M.)

Plate 30 (right) : Aw bridge (No. 49). (R.M.) Plate 31 (below) Aw bridge (No. 49) ; detail of rope-worn split bridge at the tail of the lock. (R.M.)

Plate 32 (top left): Toll office and middle lock of the flight of three locks at the Bratch, Wombourn. (R.M.) Plate 33 (bottom left): sculptured history; timeless scene at Bratch bridge (No. 47). (R.M.) Plate 34 (right): The unusual bridge at Bumble Hole (No. 46) and lock cottage. (R.M.) Plate 35 (below): Roundel bridge (No. 45) showing skewed extension and the 'Round Oak'. (R.M.)

Plate **36** (left): Botterham bridge (No. 42) and the lower lock of the 'riser' or two-lock staircase. (R.M.)
Plate **37** (right): Swindon lock, showing S&WCCo. and BCN paddle gear and re-hung top gate, and the strip mill on the site of the Swindon ironworks. (R.M.) Plate **38** (below): George and Margaret Wood, former employees of the S&WCCo., at Greensforge lock. (R.M.)

Plate 39 (above): The 'Agenoria', built in 1829 by Messrs. Foster, Rastrick and Co., Stourbridge, and used on the Shutt End (Kingswinford) Railway for 35 years. (D.L.) Plate 40 (below): The Earl of Dudley's Greensforge (Ashwood) basin in the mid-1920s. (V.W.S.) Plate 41 (top right): The basin today; Ashwood Marina. (D.R.) Plate 42 (bottom right): Flatheridge roving bridge (No. 36) *c.* 1829 (R.M.)

Plate **43** (above): The tail of Gothersley lock. (R.M.) Plate **44** (left): The remains of the Round House, *c.* 1805, Gothersley ironworks wharf. (R.M.) Plate **45** (top right): Prestwood or Trickett's bridge (No. 34); a perfect example of Brindley's bridges. (R.M.) Plate **46** (bottom right): The old boathouse of the Foley's estate at Prestwood (the 'Devil's Den') and stop narrows. (R.M.)

Plate 47 (above) : Stewponey bridge (No. 32), warehouse and toll office and the original Kinver Light Railway bridge, *c.* 1905. (J.S.W.) **Plate 48** (below) : The Kinver Light Railway at The Beeches, near Dunsley tunnel. (V.W.S.)

Plate 49 (above): Lee and Boulton's Hyde Ironworks, *c.* 1870. (U.B.L.)
Plate 50 (below): Hyde lock and former ironworks house. (R.M.)

Plate 51 (above): Hyde bridge (No. 30) and lock cottage. (D.R.) **Plate 52** (right): The circular weir and warehouse at Kinver wharf. (R.M.) **Plate 53** (below): Kinver terminus of the Kinver Light Railway (V.W.S.)

Plate 54 (below) : Fishing at Whittington. (D.R.) **Plate 55** (right) : Hanging Rock ; the spectacular outcrop of Bunter Pebble Beds near Austcliff bridge (No. 24). (R.M.)

Plate 59 (above) : Mill Wharf, Kidderminster, in the mid-1920s; the distribution point for coal from the Earl of Dudley's Baggeridge colliery (V.W.S.)   Plate 60 (below) : The above wharf, with coal boats from Greensforge basin and the Canal Company steam dredger. (V.W.S.)   Plate 61 (opposite) : Kidderminster wharf, warehouse, crane and church in 1972. (R.M.)

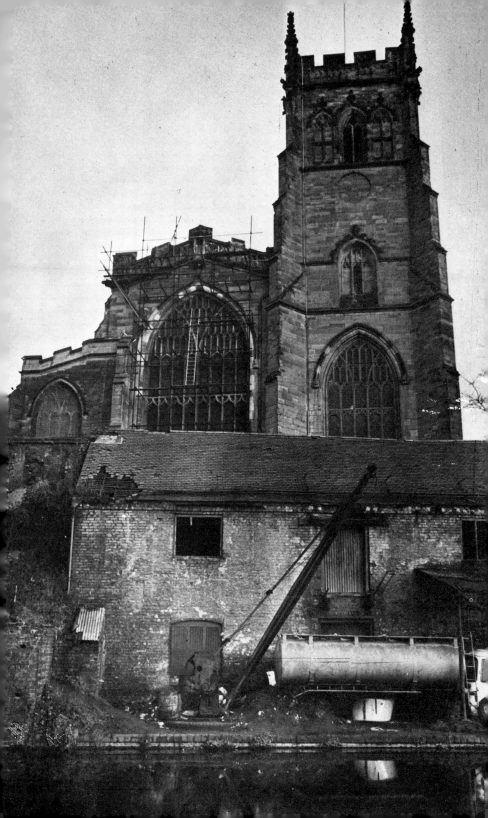

Plate 62 (top left): The twenty-four yard 'tunnel' (No. 16) at Kidderminster. (R.M.)
Plate 63 (far left): The Kidderminster 'canyon'; old carpet warehouses. (R.M.)
Plate 64 (left): The split accommodation at Caldwell (No. 12) before demolition of the lock cottage. (W.D.C.) **Plate 65** (above): The split iron footbridge at the tail of Falling Sands (Oldington) lock. (R.M.) **Plate 66** (right): Pratt's Wharf (Stour) lock in 1972; with the remains of the wooden S&WCCo. paddle gear. (R.M.)

Plate 67 (above) : Stourport (York Street) lock ; 1853 toll office and former maintenance yard of the Canal Company (now the boatyard of Canal Pleasurecraft). (R.M.)

Plate 69 (below) : Stourport barge locks, the 'Tontine Hotel' and the Severn and Canal Carrying Company trows in the early years of the present century. (B.R.L.)

Plate 68 (above) : Sheriff's view of Stourport in 1776, showing original layout of the basins, warehouses, locks and river basin, and the 'Tontine Hotel'. (B.W.B.)
Plate 70 (below) : The 'Tontine Hotel' and the lower barge lock in 1972. (R.M.)

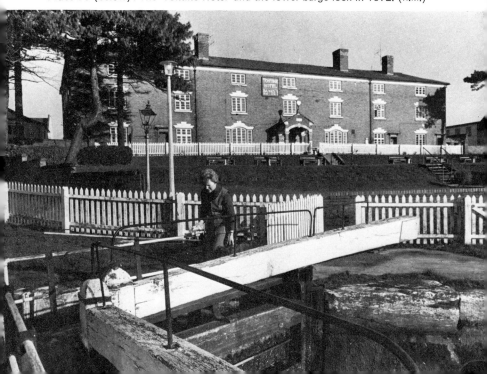

Plate 71 (top left) : The entrance to Stourport narrow locks early in the present century. (B.R.L.) **Plate 72** (bottom left) : The end of the line; the junction between the Staffs and Worcs Canal and the Severn Navigation on the site of the old river basin. (R.M.) **Plate 73** (above) : The Clock Warehouse from the Middle (Upper) basin. (R.M.) **Plate 74** (below) : Old cottages at Severnside, Stourport. (R.M.)

Plate 75 (left): The effects of mining subsidence on Cat's (Catch) or Four Crosses bridge (No. 6) on the Hatherton Branch. (R.M.) Plate 76 (bottom left): Bridge (No. 8), Hatherton Branch. (R.M.) Plate 77 (right): The use of an abandoned canal as a water channel; Hatherton Branch between bridge (No. 8) and Wedge's Mill. (R.M.) Plate 78 (below): Lock cottage and Bridgtown top lock at Walkmill, Hatherton Branch. (R.M.)

Plate 79 (top left): Hawkins's basin and Cannock Old Coppice colliery, *c.* 1920. (B.R.L.)

Plate 80 Seven bridge plates of the Staffs and Worcs Canal. *c.* 1835. (R.M.)

Plate 81 Part of Bradshaw's 'Map of Canals, Navigable Rivers, Rail Roads, etc. in the Midland Counties', published in 1830. (U.B.L.)
Plate 82 (overleaf): Canal Company Bye-Laws. (B.A.H.)

STAFFORDSHIRE & WORCESTERSHIRE CANAL NAVIGATION
BYE-LAWS.

BYE-LAWS.

1.

NO PERSON TO DAMAGE ANY BRIDGE, BANK, LOCK, TOLL BOARD, OR OTHER WORKS, OR ANY HEDGE, QUICKSET, OR OTHER FENCE, ANY TREE OR GATE, BELONGING TO THIS COMPANY, UNDER A PENALTY NOT EXCEEDING **FORTY SHILLINGS,** IN ADDITION TO THE AMOUNT OF THE ACTUAL DAMAGE.

2.

NO PERSON TO TURN INTO THE NAVIGATION, OR ANY WATERCOURSE RUNNING INTO THE SAME, ANY NOXIOUS OR POLLUTING LIQUID, UNDER A PENALTY NOT EXCEEDING **FIVE POUNDS.**

3.

ANY BOATMAN OR OTHER PERSON REFUSING TO LOAD OR UNLOAD HIS BOAT UPON ANY OF THE WHARVES BELONGING TO THE COMPANY, IN SUCH MANNER AND UNDER SUCH REGULATIONS AS THE WHARFINGER OR OTHER PERSON APPOINTED BY THE COMPANY SHALL, FOR THE PROPER CONVENIENCE AND ACCOMMODATION OF THE TRAFFIC, DIRECT, SHALL FOR EVERY SUCH OFFENCE FORFEIT AND PAY A SUM NOT EXCEEDING **TEN SHILLINGS.**

4.

ANY BOATMAN THROWING WATER OR CARGO OUT OF HIS BOAT WHILE PASSING OVER ANY AQUEDUCT OR THROUGH ANY LOCK, SHALL FOR EVERY SUCH OFFENCE FORFEIT AND PAY A SUM NOT EXCEEDING **TEN SHILLINGS.**

5.

EVERY PERSON HAVING THE CARE OF ANY BOAT AND, NOT MOORING IT AT EACH END WHILST LYING IN THE CANAL, OR IN ANY BASIN THEREOF; AND EVERY PERSON WILFULLY UNMOORING ANY BOAT, OR LEAVING IT UNMOORED WHILST SO LYING, SHALL FORFEIT AND PAY A SUM NOT EXCEEDING **TEN SHILLINGS.**

6.

ANY BOATMAN WHO SHALL FAIL TO COMPLY WITH ANY SPECIAL REGULATION, ISSUED FROM TIME TO TIME BY THE COMPANY, WITH REGARD TO PASSING THROUGH ANY LOCK, FOR THE BETTER WORKING OF ANY PARTICULAR TRAFFIC, OR FOR THE SAVING OF WATER, SHALL FORFEIT AND PAY A SUM NOT EXCEEDING **TEN SHILLINGS.**

7.

BOATMEN, WHEN THEY MEET ON THE TOWING PATH OF THE CANAL, MUST DRIVE THEIR HORSES ON THE LEFT SIDE OF THE TOWING PATH, AS IS USUAL ON TURNPIKE ROADS, AND THE HORSE NEXT THE HEDGE, OR FURTHEST FROM THE CANAL, MUST DROP THE LINE, IN ORDER THAT THE HORSE NEXT THE CANAL MAY PASS OVER IT. UNDER A PENALTY FOR THE NEGLECT THEREOF NOT EXCEEDING **TEN SHILLINGS.**

8.

NO BOATMAN WILL BE PERMITTED TO NAVIGATE WITHOUT A RUDDER OR WITHOUT A COMPETENT PERSON ON BOARD TO STEER (AND IN CASE OF TWO BOATS HAULED TOGETHER, ON EACH SUCH BOAT), OR WITHOUT A PERSON TO ATTEND TO THE HORSE, UNDER A PENALTY NOT EXCEEDING **TEN SHILLINGS.**

9.

NO ARTICLES ARE TO BE LOADED OR DISCHARGED, WITHOUT PERMISSION, WHILE THE BOAT IS IN ANY LOCK, BRIDGEWAY, STOP PLACE, TUNNEL, OR AQUEDUCT, OR SO NEAR THERETO AS TO OBSTRUCT THE PASSAGE THEREOF, UNDER A PENALTY NOT EXCEEDING **TEN SHILLINGS.**

10.

NO BOAT TO BE PLACED OR PERMITTED TO LIE SO AS TO OBSTRUCT THE PASSAGE OF THE CANAL, UNDER A PENALTY NOT EXCEEDING **TEN SHILLINGS** FOR EVERY HOUR SUCH OBSTRUCTION SHALL CONTINUE.

11.

EVERY PERSON WHO SHALL IMPEDE THE SERVANTS OF THE NAVIGATION IN RAISING OR REMOVING A BOAT SUNK, OR PLACED SO AS TO OBSTRUCT THE NAVIGATION, SHALL FORFEIT AND PAY FOR EACH OFFENCE A SUM NOT EXCEEDING **FORTY SHILLINGS.**

12.

NO PERSON TO MOOR ANY BOAT TO ANY PADDLE POST OR LOCK GATE, OR NEAR TO THE ENTRANCE TO ANY LOCK, BRIDGE, OR AQUE DUCT, OR TO WIND OR COIL A ROPE ROUND OR FASTEN THE SAME TO ANY PART OR ANY LOCK GATE UNDER A PENALTY NOT EXCEEDING **FORTY SHILLINGS.**

13.

ANY PERSON DEPOSITING ANY ARTICLES OR THINGS, OR LEAVING ANY CART, CARRIAGE, OR BARROW ON THE TOWING PATH, SO AS TO OBSTRUCT THE NAVIGATION OF THE CANAL, OR ALLOWING HORSES OR OTHER ANIMALS TO PASS OR STRAY ALONG ANY PART OF THE SAID TOWING PATH, SHALL, FOR EACH OFFENCE FORFEIT AND PAY A SUM NOT EXCEEDING **FORTY SHILLINGS.**

14.

NO PERSON SHALL RIDE, LEAD, OR DRIVE ANY HORSE, OR OTHER ANIMAL (NOT ACTUALLY EMPLOYED IN HAULING A BOAT), OR DRIVE OR CONDUCT ANY CART OR OTHER VEHICLE ON THE TOWING PATH, UNLESS LEGALLY ENTITLED TO DO SO, UNDER A PENALTY FOR EACH OFFENCE NOT EXCEEDING **FORTY SHILLINGS.**

15.

NO PERSON SHALL PLACE ON THE TOWING PATH OR IN THE CANAL ANY DEAD ANIMAL, ASHES, RUBBISH, OR OTHER MATTER; OR DROWN ANY ANIMAL IN THE CANAL, OR RAKE IN THE CANAL FOR IRON, COAL, OR OTHER THINGS, UNDER A PENALTY FOR EACH OFFENCE NOT EXCEEDING **FORTY SHILLINGS.**

16.

NO PERSON SHALL TRESPASS OR LOITER ON THE TOWING PATH, WHARVES, OR OTHER PROPERTY OF THE COMPANY, OR USE THE SAME FOR ANY OTHER PURPOSE THAN THAT OF THE TRAFFIC ON THE CANAL, FOR EACH OFFENCE NOT EXCEEDING **FORTY SHILLINGS.**

17.

ANY BOATMAN SUFFERING ANY DOG TO GO LOOSE UPON THE TOWING PATH, OR ON THE LANDS ADJOINING, SHALL FORFEIT AND PAY FOR EACH OFFENCE A SUM NOT EXCEEDING **FORTY SHILLINGS.**

18.

NO PERSON SHALL BATHE IN THE CANAL, WITHOUT PERMISSION, UNDER A PENALTY FOR EACH OFFENCE NOT EXCEEDING **TEN SHILLINGS.**

19.

EVERY PERSON WHO SHALL USE ANY THREATENING OR ABUSIVE LANGUAGE TO ANY TOLL COLLECTOR, AGENT, OR OTHER SERVANT OF THE COMPANY, IN THE EXECUTION OF HIS DUTY, SHALL FORFEIT AND PAY FOR EACH OFFENCE A SUM NOT EXCEEDING **FORTY SHILLINGS.**

Company's Offices.
87, Darlington Street, Wolverhampton.

PENALTIES.

BY THE COMPANY'S ACTS OF PALIAMENT.

20.

EVERY MASTER, OWNER, AND MANAGER OF EVERY BOAT WHO SHALL NEGLECT OR REFUSE TO GIVE TO THE COLLECTORS A JUST AND TRUE ACCOUNT, IN WRITING, SIGNED BY HIM, OF THE QUANTITIES OF GOODS IN EACH BOAT, FROM WHENCE BROUGHT, AND WHERE THEY IN TEND TO LAND THE SAME, OR SHALL DELIVER ANY PART OF THE GOODS AT ANY OTHER PLACE THAN IS MENTIONED IN SUCH ACCOUNT, SHALL FORFEIT AND PAY THE SUM OF **TEN SHILLINGS FOR EVERY TON** OF GOODS, WHICH SHALL BE IN SUCH BOAT OR WHICH SHALL BE DELIVERED OUT, AS THE CASE MAY BE, OVER AND ABOVE THE RATES AND DUTIES PAYABLE FOR THE SAME. (6 Geo. III., c. 97. sec. 47)

21.

EVERY OWNER, MASTER, OR OTHER PERSON HAVING THE RULE OR COMMAND OF ANY BOAT WHO SHALL NEGLECT OR NEGLECT TO PUT HIS NAME IN LARGE PAINTED WHITE CAPITAL LETTERS ON EACH OF THE OUTSIDES OF EVERY SUCH BOAT, HIGHER THAN THE SAME SHALL SINK INTO THE WATER WHEN FULL LOADED, OR SHALL ALTER, DEFACE, ERASE, OR DESTROY, ANY LETTER DESCRIBING SUCH NAME, OR SHALL REFUSE TO HAVE HIS OR HER BOAT MEASURED AT THE EXPENSE OF THE COMPANY, WHENEVER REQUIRED, NOT EXCEEDING FOUR TIMES IN ANY ONE YEAR, SHALL FOR EVERY SUCH OFFENCE FORFEIT AND PAY THE SUM OF **FORTY SHILLINGS.** (Section 63)

22.

EVERY PERSON HAVING THE CARE OF A BOAT AND WHO SHALL WILFULLY OBSTRUCT THE SAME IN ANY PART OF THE CANAL SO AS TO OBSTRUCT ANOTHER IN PASSING, AND SHALL NOT IMMEDIATELY, UPON REQUEST, MOVE THE SAME, SHALL FORFEIT FOR EVERY SUCH OFFENCE A SUM NOT EXCEEDING **TEN SHILLINGS,** NOR LESS THAN **FIVE SHILLINGS** FOR EVERY HOUR SUCH OBSTRUCTION SHALL CONTINUE. (Section 66)

23.

EVERY PERSON WHO SHALL FLOAT ANY TIMBER UPON THE CANAL, OR SHALL LOAD ANY BOAT WITH TIMBER AND SUFFER SUCH TIMBER TO LIE OVER THE SIDES OF SUCH BOAT, OR SHALL OVERLOAD ANY BOAT OR OTHER VESSEL, AND PUT SUCH BOAT INTO THE CANAL, SO AS BY SUCH OVERLOADING TO OBSTRUCT THE PASSAGE OF ANY OTHER BOAT, AND SHALL NOT IMMEDIATELY, UPON NOTICE, HAUL SUCH BOAT BACK INTO SUCH PLACE AS SHALL BE PROPER OR MADE FOR BOATS TO PASS EACH OTHER, SHALL FORFEIT AND PAY FOR EVERY SUCH OFFENCE THE SUM OF **FIVE POUNDS.** (Section 67)

24.

EVERY PERSON WHO SHALL THROW ANY BALLAST, GRAVEL, STONES, OR RUBBISH INTO ANY PART OF THE CANAL OR ANY TRENCHES OR WATERCOURSES MADE OR MAINTAINED UNDER THE ACT, SHALL FOR EVERY SUCH OFFENCE FORFEIT A SUM NOT EXCEED ING **FIVE POUNDS** (Section 68)

25.

NO BOATMAN OR OTHER PERSON SHALL SUFFER THE WATER TO REMAIN IN ANY LOCK LONGER THAN IS NECESSARY FOR HIS BOAT TO PASS THROUGH SUCH LOCK, AND EVERY SUCH PERSON GOING DOWN THE CANAL SHALL SHUT THE LOWER GATES BEFORE HE SHALL DRAW THE CLOWS OF THE UPPER GATES, AND SHALL SHUT THE UPPER GATES BEFORE HE SHALL DRAW THE CLOWS OF THE LOWER GATES; AND IN GOING UP THE CANAL SHALL, WHEN HIS BOAT HAS PASSED THE LOCK, SHUT THE UPPER GATES AND AFTERWARDS DRAW THE CLOWS OF THE LOWER GATES, UNLESS THERE SHALL BE THEN A BOAT COMING DOWN IN SIGHT OF THE LOCK, IN WHICH CASE THE LOWER GATES SHALL BE LEFT SHUT AND THE UPPER GATES OPEN; AND WHEN THERE SHALL BE A SCARCITY OF WATER, THE BOAT GOING UP, IF WITHIN SIGHT AND NOT MORE THAN 300 YARDS BELOW A LOCK, SHALL PASS THROUGH THE LOCK BEFORE THE BOAT COMING DOWN, AND THEN THE BOAT NEXT ABOVE SHALL COME DOWN, AND IF THERE ARE MORE THAN ONE BOAT BELOW AND ABOVE SUCH AT THE SAME TIME, WITHIN 300 YARDS, THEY SHALL GO UP AND DOWN BY TURNS. EVERY PERSON OFFENDING IN ANY OF THESE PAR TICULARS SHALL FORFEIT THE SUM OF **FORTY SHILLINGS.** (Section 69)

26.

EVERY PERSON NAVIGATING A BOAT AND WHO (NOT BEING QUALIFIED UNDER THE GAME LAWS) SHALL CARRY ON BOARD AND USE ANY FOWLING NET, GUN, OR OTHER INSTRUMENT FOR TAKING OR DESTROYING FISH OR GAME, SHALL ON CONVICTION, FOR EVERY SUCH OFFENCE FORFEIT AND PAY THE SUM OF **FIVE POUNDS.** (Section 76)

27.

EVERY MASTER OR OTHER PERSON HAVING THE COMMAND OF ANY BOAT, WHO SHALL SUFFER OR PERMIT ANY PERSON, (NOT BEING DULY QUALIFIED) TO HAVE, CARRY ON BOARD AND MAKE USE OF ANY FISH ING NET, GUN, OR OTHER INSTRUMENT FOR TAKING OR DESTROYING FISH OR GAME, SHALL ON CONVICTION FOR EVERY SUCH OFFENCE FORFEIT AND PAY THE SUM OF **FIVE POUNDS.** (Section 76)

28.

EVERY PERSON WHO SHALL WANTONLY, CARELESSLY OR NEGLI GENTLY OPEN ANY LOCK OR PADDLE OR SUFFER ANY BOAT TO STRIKE OR RUN UPON ANY BRIDGE OR LOCK, OR SHALL WILFULLY FLUSH OR DRAW OFF THE WATER FROM ANY PART OF THE CANAL, OR SHALL LEAVE ANY CLOUGH OPEN, AND RUNNING AFTER A BOAT SHALL HAVE PASSED ANY LOCK, OR SHALL DRAW ANY PADDLE, VALVE, OR CLOUGH SO AS TO WASTE THE WATER, OR SHALL FULLY AND MALICIOUSLY DO ANY OTHER ACT TO THE PREJUDICE OF THE NAVIGATION SHALL, ON CONVICTION, FORFEIT AND PAY, FOR EVERY SUCH OFFENCE ANY SUM NOT EXCEEDING **FIVE POUNDS,** NOR LESS THAN **TWENTY SHILLINGS.** (10 Geo. III., c. 103, Sec. 19).

29.

ANY PERSON WHO SHALL PULL DOWN, OR BREAK OR DEFACE ANY BOARD PUT UP OR AFFIXED FOR THE PURPOSE OF PUBLISHING ANY BYE-LAWS OR PENALTY, OR SHALL OBLITERATE ANY OF THE LETTERS OR FIGURES THEREON, SHALL FORFEIT FOR EVERY SUCH OFFENCE A SUM NOT EXCEEDING **FIVE POUNDS.** (6 Vic. c. 5, Sec. 37).

30.

ANY PERSON WHO SHALL WITHOUT REASONABLE EXCUSE REFUSE OR NEGLECT TO APPEAR WHEN SUMMONED AS A WITNESS BEFORE JUSTICES TOUCHING ANY OFFENCE COMMITTED AGAINST THIS ACT, OR SHALL REFUSE TO BE EXAMINED UPON OATH, OR TO GIVE EVIDENCE, SHALL FOR EVERY SUCH OFFENCE FORFEIT A SUM NOT EXCEEDING **FIVE POUNDS.** (Sec. 43).

A. J. BUTLER,

CLERK TO THE COMPANY.

I

Introduction

There are two reasons for choosing the Staffordshire & Worcestershire Canal as the subject of the first of this series of Towpath Guides. It was the first link to be forged in the chain of narrow canals that threads its way through central England, and today it is much the same as when it was built two centuries ago. The Staffs & Worcs is one of the best examples of the work of the great canal pioneer James Brindley and his assistants at the dawn of the canal era. The canal avoids towns and passes through undisturbed countryside for most of its length. Evidence of the methods of construction and the problems encountered by the builders, and early approaches to the design of canals can be seen to this day. As well as describing a waterway that is a fascinating study in itself, this guide also serves as an introduction to subsequent accounts of contemporary and later canals.

From the early days, the waterway was known officially as the 'Staffordshire and Worcestershire Canal Navigation', though this name was rarely used except by the Company. Although it did not pass through the town, it was the 'Wolverhampton Canal' for a while, and in later days, men who worked the southern part knew it as the 'Stour Cut'. However, the name used in this guide and the one by which the canal is generally known is the 'Staffs & Worcs', pronounced 'Staffs & Worcester'.

The canal was an afterthought in a far-seeing scheme for linking the ports of Liverpool, Hull and Bristol by an artificial waterway. In the middle of the 18th century, when Britain was beginning to change from a predominantly agricultural nation to an industrial one, these were the principal ports. Unfortunately, nature had decreed that the main deposits of coal, iron and other ingredients essential to industry should occur inland and rarely had she taken the trouble to provide a river near at hand that could be made navigable. The idea of linking the ports by a system of artificial waterways had been in the minds of Midland industrialists for some time, as their pack horses staggered through the mire to places like Bewdley, Winsford and Wilden Ferry, when two significant events enabled the pipe dream to become a reality. One was the building of the Sankey (St Helens) Navigation, begun in 1755. This was by no means the first artificial canal, but its effect locally was dramatic and it paved the way for the canal era. The second was the appearance of James Brindley on the scene. Brindley was a man of humble origins who had an innate genius for civil engineering and is rightly regarded as the father of the English canal system. Although there was a reluctance at first to provide the vast sums of money needed to build canals from one end of the country to the other, at least there was an engineer capable of carrying out the work. A first cautious step towards a national network was made by Earl Gower of Trentham, Thomas Anson of Shugborough and Thomas Broade in 1758. These men commissioned Brindley to survey the line of a canal running parallel with the river Trent, from Stoke to Wilden Ferry, about 12 miles above Nottingham. This was the beginning of the Trent & Mersey Canal, or the Grand Trunk, as Brindley preferred to call it. A few years later, the proposed line was extended to the rivers Weaver and Mersey and a number of other schemes were put forward, the most notable being one by Sir Richard Whitworth of Batchacre Grange, Staffordshire. Sir Richard's proposals followed a rather different line and included a branch to join the Severn at Atcham, near Shrewsbury. There was talk of a connection between the rivers Severn and Thames, but no mention was made of the Staffs & Worcs in all these plans and counter plans.

While these plans were being made in the early 1760s, the Duke of Bridgewater was constructing a private canal from his mines at Worsley to the centre of Manchester. Men then realised that canals could be built without too much difficulty and were at last prepared to provide the necessary capital, even though the Duke had run heavily into debt through his canal. After years of deliberation, the Grand Trunk at last became a reality at the famous meeting at Wolseley bridge, near Rugeley, held on 30th December 1765. Earl Gower presided and Brindley was there to describe the Grand Trunk scheme, but the Staffs & Worcs was not on the agenda. However, the seeds must have been sown, for less than a month later, Aris's *Birmingham Gazette* reported that, 'A scheme is on foot for making a Navigable Canal from Red-stone's Ferry, on the River Severn, through Kidderminster to Autherley, near Wolverhampton, and from thence down to the River Penk, in order to join the Canal intended to be made from Wilden Ferry to Liverpool, near Shudborough, which will open a Communication between the Ports of Bristol, Liverpool and Hull, and be attended with great Advantage to those Ports, as well as to the Trade and Commerce of the Kingdom in General.' This report appeared on Monday, 20th January 1766 and in the same issue of the *Gazette*, a notice exorted all interested landowners, merchants and manufacturers to meet 'at the House of Thomas Badger, known by the Sign of the Red Lion in Wolverhampton, in the County of Stafford, on Wednesday the 29th January 1766 at 11 o'clock in the Forenoon, in order to consider of the most effectual Means of carrying the same into Execution, for the Advantage of the Landed, and Benefit of the Commercial Interest'. In this way the Staffordshire & Worcestershire Canal was born, not as a result of years of careful survey and planning, but as an afterthought following the enthusiastic launching of the Grand Trunk.

Although proposals for the canal were put forward by a group of little-known businessmen from Wolverhampton, headed by James Perry who eventually became the Company's first treasurer, they immediately found favour. A further meeting was held and a notice was inserted in six issues of the weekly *Gazette*, starting on 24th March, stating that an application was to be made for an Act to construct the canal. This same notice gives a more detailed account of the line to be taken by the canal. It was to start 'at or near a Place called Stour's Mouth' and was to go 'through or near Kidderminster, to or near Kinfare, Prestwood, Orton, Tettenhall, Coven, Brewood and Penkridge, to or near Shufborough'. This is a description of the route actually taken by the canal, and Brindley and his assistants must have surveyed the line with great expedition. Although no time was wasted in making the survey, it was carried out skilfully and with great care. The canal is remarkably straight for most of the way and, though use was made of natural features throughout, it only follows river valleys where it was advantageous to do so. Brindley had no accurate maps and he relied on his 'eye' for canal country as he rode along the proposed route on his grey mare. Occasionally he made mistakes, but the Staffs & Worcs is a tribute to his prowess as a civil engineer, as we shall see as we travel along the canal.

Many influential people joined Perry's group as soon as the announcement appeared in the *Gazette*. The list of people who provided capital for the project is headed by Earl Gower himself and includes many owners of land along or near the proposed line, such as the Earl of Stamford, Sir Richard Wrottesley, Sir Edward Littleton, Moreton Wallhouse, Thomas Clifford, Thomas Anson and several members of the Molineux family. Of these, Littleton became closely involved in the running of the canal, but indirectly it was Wallhouse who shaped the destiny of the Staffs & Worcs. His son Edward was the great-nephew of Sir Edward Littleton, who inherited the Teddesley estates when Sir Edward died. In 1835 he became the first Lord Hatherton and was chairman of the Company for many years. The prosperity of the Staffs & Worcs, particularly during the age of railways when many canal companies were in serious difficulty, was largely due to the efforts of Lord Hatherton.

The Parliamentary Act for the Staffs & Worcs Canal was passed on 14th May 1766, on the same day as that for the Trent & Mersey. These two canals formed the basis of the country's canal network and the passing of their Acts may be said to have heralded the canal era. Powers to raise £70,000 were given the Staffordshire & Worcestershire Canal Company (S&WCCo.) and the Act stated that the southern terminal of the canal was to be 'at some Place between Bewdley and Titton Brook'. Bewdley was an important port on the Severn and the reference to it may have been to avoid opposition from inhabitants of the town. Brindley certainly did not have any intention of ending the Staffs & Worcs there. Another odd clause in the Act describes in minutest detail the last mile or so of canal at the northern end, where the land surrounding the proposed line was owned by Clifford and Anson.

The description hints of rivalry between the two families rather than the result of a careful survey, for a second Act was obtained in 1770 to allow the Company to alter the line through the two estates. It seems that the canal would have been in danger of being flooded at frequent intervals if the original proposals had been carried out.

As with the majority of canal schemes, the original estimate of the cost was totally inadequate and the second Act authorised the raising of a further £30,000, making the total cost of the Staffs & Worcs about £100,000. Even in those days, major engineering works were beset by inflation. The extra capital was required 'by reason of the great Increase in the Value of Lands and Wages of Artificers and Labourers and from other unforseen Expenses and Circumstances'!

Work on the canal started on the southern portion with Brindley as surveyor and the canal between Wolverhampton and the Severn was almost complete when the 1770 Act was passed. Good progress had also been made on the summit level and work still to be done was mainly confined to the northern end. This sequence indicates careful planning, for the Company could start trading as soon as a connection was made with the Severn, whereas there was less urgency to complete the northern section. Progress on the Grand Trunk was slow and troubles with the tunnel at Harecastle delayed its opening until 1777. The following notice inviting traders to use the partly-finished Staffs & Worcs appeared in the *Birmingham Gazette* on Monday, 1st April 1771: 'To all Merchants, Traders, and Others. The Proprietors of this Undertaking hereby give Notice, that this Canal is now open from the River Severn near Stour's Mouth in the County of Worcester to Compton near Wolverhampton in the County of Stafford, and that Wharfs and Warehouses are made and erected, and Wharfingers fixed, to receive and forward Goods, at the following places, viz: At Stourport (hitherto called Newport), at Kidderminster, at Stewponey and at Compton, 23 miles from the River Severn.'

No time was lost in completing the rest of the waterway and it was reported open throughout at a committee meeting on 28th May 1772. It had taken six years to build the 46¼ miles of the Staffs & Worcs, no mean achievement when one remembers that the art of canal building was in its infancy. Although Brindley had gained experience on the Bridgewater Canal, he had not tackled a lock before he started work on the Staffs & Worcs, and many other problems were encountered for the first time. His first lock is said to be at Compton, also the first of 31 locks that take the canal through 292ft down to the Severn. The summit level between Compton and Gailey is 10 miles long and this is followed by a fall of 101ft and 12 locks to the Trent & Mersey at Haywood. By later standards, there were few serious obstacles along the line of the canal, though there are four large aqueducts over rivers and many smaller ones across minor streams. About one hundred over-bridges were built to Brindley's design, many of which still survive, and there are three short tunnels. Further information on engineering works is given in Appendix III.

While the Staffs & Worcs and Trent & Mersey were in the making, Brindley was also working on canals to link them with the Thames, adding London to the list of ports that would eventually be reached from the Midlands. These canals were promoted by the Coventry and Oxford companies and the entire system formed a cross, intersecting not far from Wolesley bridge, where it may be said to have all started. This is usually called 'Brindley's Cross', for Brindley surveyed most of the constituent canals and was engineer to the companies that promoted them. However, the only arm of the Cross that the great engineer lived to see completed was the Staffs & Worcs, as he died on 27th September 1772 at the early age of 56 years.

Although James Brindley was surveyor and engineer of the Staffs & Worcs, he delegated detailed work to his assistants Hugh Henshall, Samuel Simcock and particularly Thomas Dadford, senior. In this guide, works attributed to Brindley may have been carried out by one of these assistants, but there is no doubt that the design was his and that he supervised the canal's progress.

The completion of the canal is a convenient point at which to leave the story of the Company that built it. The subsequent history of the Company of Proprietors of the Staffordshire and Worcestershire Canal Navigation is interwoven with the fortunes of neighbouring concerns and a good account of it is given in Hadfield's *Canals of the West Midlands*. The story of the canal itself unfolds as we journey along it through the pages of this guide. The canal was 'out of date' very soon after it was built, but trade was not seriously affected and the Company prospered until the Staffs & Worcs passed to the nation in 1948. The lack of major improvement means that today we can follow in the footsteps of Brindley and his fellow pioneers of the canal system. As we travel the beautiful southern portion, it is as well to remember that ten years after acquiring the canal, the custodians of our waterways recommended that the Staffs & Worcs should not be kept navigable. Fortunately, common sense prevailed, the danger passed, and today the Staffordshire & Worcestershire Canal is part of our heritage, ranking high in the list of recreational amenities of the West Midlands.

2

Round and about Stafford

HAYWOOD TO RADFORD

Miles
from
Haywood

Miles
to
Stourport

0   *Haywood Junction (Bridge No. 109) (Plates 1-4)*   46⅛

The Staffs & Worcs Canal leaves the Grand Trunk (Trent & Mersey) at Haywood Junction and few canals start on their way in such a perfect setting. As the traveller turns from the Grand Trunk Canal, in front of him are wharves and warehouses, an old toll house and a corn mill, all framed by the most elegant of Brindley's bridges. Created at the dawn of the canal era, this meeting place of waterways from the Irish Sea, the Bristol Channel and the North Sea became one of the busiest junctions of the system. How many boats must have passed this way for their grit-laden towlines to have made such deep furrows in the brickwork and bollards (Plate 3)? Since the working boats departed, weeds have taken over and Haywood has quietly decayed, but something of the former glory of Haywood has survived for it to become equally important during the second canal era.

The great variety of bridges along the Staffs & Worcs tell the story of the canal as well as any Company records. Haywood bridge (Plate 1), the most striking feature of the junction, is unique and at the same time typical of the many built by James Brindley and his assistants. It is, of course, a 'roving bridge', carrying the towing path of the Trent & Mersey across the canal. Examples of the harmonious marriage of brick and stone by the canal engineers two centuries ago are plentiful on the Staffs & Worcs, but none compare with the beautiful proportions and wide span of Haywood bridge. The arch itself consists of a double ring of brickwork surrounded by a course of dressed sandstone blocks

24

or dripstone. Where it occurs on other bridges the outer arch is supported on each side by springer stones, but these do not appear on No. 109. This use of stonework is purely ornamental and, like the keystone, serves no structural purpose. For centuries dripstones or string courses had been incorporated in buildings to prevent rainwater from damaging the masonry. Canal building was in its infancy when the Staffs & Worcs was started in 1766 and it may be that Brindley applied traditional methods in the early days and later adapted them to suit canals as he gained experience. Perhaps these features were simply to improve the appearance of the bridges, but for whatever reason, he included them in his specification for all arches along the canal. The dripstone, brick arch and springers are there to this day as Brindley's trademark on all original bridges.

The splayed wing-walls at parapet level on No. 109 are another typical feature of these bridges and the brickwork is supported on blocks of local Keuper Sandstone. The red bricks used in the bridge were made from an impure pebbly clay. Deposits of good quality clay were often inaccessible until the canals were built and the early canal builders had to make do with local materials. From a close look at the brickwork it is usually possible to distinguish between original works on the canal and later additions or repairs. (The more durable engineering bricks made from Etruria Marl could be used as soon as canals penetrated the Staffordshire coalfields.) These examples of Brindley's handiwork are best seen on the more remote sections of the canal, but occasional details are still visible on bridges that have been widened or otherwise altered.

Another attractive detail of the canal, and one which is unique, is the use of oval cast-iron plates giving the name and number of each bridge (Plate 80). The plates were not placed there when the canal was built, as is often supposed, but date from about 1835. Several bridges were added early in the 19th century and there were of course 109 of them when the numbering was carried out. Bradshaw's map of 1830 shows 104 and the number soon increased as railways reached the Midlands. Only a few have since been added and today there are about 120 bridges across the canal. Many original plates have disappeared, but authentic replacements are being fitted and those that survive are being given a much needed coat of paint.

The wharf at Haywood was formerly owned and operated by the Canal Company, and boats on both the Staffs & Worcs and Trent & Mersey canals used it. Although the scene is still essentially the same, a few minor changes have been made. A small warehouse near the Trent & Mersey has been demolished and replaced by a water point and bins for the disposal of refuse. The wharfhouse has been modernised, no doubt a necessary step to make it habitable by today's standards, but it is a pity that the two-storey octagonal bay overlooking the wharf could not have been retained. Situated at the centre of the canal system with a choice of several routes for holidays lasting one or two weeks, Haywood is an ideal spot for a cruising base. Although boats have moored here for several years and N.B. *Cactus* has plied from Haywood for day trips during the summer months, the lack of safe access from the lane to Tixall restricted more ambitious development. This difficulty has now been overcome by the building of a new bridge to replace No. 75 on the Trent & Mersey and the yard has been acquired by Anglo-Welsh Narrow Boats. The hiring of cruisers started in March 1972, two hundred years after the canal opened for commercial traffic. Anglo-Welsh established their first base, at Market Harborough, in 1965 and later opened bases at Trevor on the Llangollen Canal and Wooten Wawen on the Stratford. The Company favours steel-hulled boats built on traditional lines and the service offered is of a very high standard. At Haywood the cruising base has halted the decay and brought the junction to life again.

There were a hundred or more water mills along the line of the Staffs & Worcs and the corn mill at Haywood is one of the few still in use, though it is no longer water powered. Most of the mills existed long before the canal came into being and their presence was a mixed blessing. Although they provided a source of trade, the owners were jealous of their water rights and canal companies often had difficulty in securing alternative supplies. Haywood corn mill did not inconvenience the S&WCCo. in this way, as it obtained its water from the Trent and in any case the northern end of the canal is at its lowest level here, but Brindley had to build a substantial stone aqueduct over the tail race.

The canal narrows where it crosses the aqueduct, providing a convenient place for keeping a tally of boats entering and leaving the canal. The toll office adjoining the narrows has a small window where the clerk would issue or check toll tickets. There are also two unusual iron-framed windows of Georgian Gothic that would be more at home in an early 19th-century chapel than alongside a canal. The window in the end wall represents something of an ironfounder's *tour de force*, with little regard for the unfortunate glazier! The office was last used in the early 1930s.

There were several toll offices along the canal and the one at Bratch locks, Wombourn, is the oldest of those which survive, probably dating from the late 18th century. The early offices were octagonal in section and had simple iron-framed windows and a distinctive central stone chimney that appears to have been purely ornamental. Another example of this type of office was to be found next to Stourport barge locks until it was demolished in the 1950s. The toll office at Haywood appears to be of later date than the Bratch office. The only one actually bearing a date is next to Stourport (York Street) lock and this was built in 1853.

Near the Haywood office are two wooden bollards where boats moored while in the narrows or waiting to be gauged. Initial gauging of boats was carried out when they were built or extensively repaired. This was usually done in a weigh dock, the average freeboard being measured with the boat empty and loaded with iron weights up to full capacity. On the Staffs & Worcs this was carried out at Stourport. The information was entered in a register and a copy was kept in all toll offices where the boat would be working. At Haywood a boat would stop in the narrows and the toll clerk would measure the 'dry inches' at four points, sometimes marked by metal plates, with his gauging stick. (The practice of recording the 'wet inches' or draught was also used.) The average of four readings would then be used to determine the toll to be paid. This performance was repeated every time the boat passed from one canal to another and sometimes at intermediate points.

Next to the toll office is a rack carrying a set of planks and in the narrows are the stop-grooves where the planks are inserted to isolate this section of canal. The aqueduct is followed by an embankment and a breach here could cause serious damage to the canal and surrounding countryside, with the loss of a considerable quantity of water. Until about twenty years ago the entire canal system was divided into short sections, each with a lengthsman in charge to deal with routine maintenance. He usually lived on his section and his duties included running surplus water to waste through storm-water sluices after heavy rain. He also inspected the banks regularly for weak points on vulnerable sections. A breach often starts as the merest trickle through holes made by animals, subsidence or erosion, and a diligent lengthsman would report the matter before a major disaster occurred. A serious breach was about the worst calamity that could befall a canal company and, in spite of the precautions, they did occur from time to time. As working boats were withdrawn and revenue declined, so it became necessary to reduce maintenance costs and lengthsmen were replaced by gangs operating from a central depot. This system works well enough for most of the time, but the cost of repairing a breach on the scale of the one that occurred in September 1971 on the Bridgewater Canal would have paid the wages of many lengthsmen for several years.

Few of the isolated cottages of the lengthsmen and lock keepers remain and the sections in which many of them took great pride have become overgrown. However, the canal is now inspected regularly by a team of volunteer lengthsmen, a scheme pioneered by the Staffordshire & Worcestershire Canal Society and subsequently operated on other waterways. A report on the condition of the canal, towpath and other works is submitted monthly to British Waterways Board and limited maintenance is undertaken. The tools of trade of the original lengthsmen can still be seen along the canal. The storm-water sluices are similar to the ground paddles of locks and they occur at intervals along the towing path, though few are now used. Planks were inserted at bridges or aqueducts to isolate sections of canal and usually there is a rack nearby for the stop-planks, but the activities of vandals nowadays means that these are normally stored elsewhere.

At Haywood there is in fact everything one would expect to find at an important junction with one notable exception. There is no canalside public house, but perhaps boatmen* were not

---

* Carriers on the canals were always 'the men who worked the boats' and never 'boatmen', but the latter is used here for brevity.

encouraged to stop here overnight. The nearest pub is the 'Clifford Arms' in Great Haywood village, not far from Haywood lock on the Trent & Mersey. Also near the lock is the picturesque Essex bridge in Shugborough park. This is reputed to have had forty-two arches and to have been built in the 16th century to enable Robert Devereux of Chartley, the 2nd Earl of Essex, to go hunting on Milford Common. The bridge actually looks some-what older and the present thirteen arches span the river Trent quite adequately. The footpath over the bridge leads to Shug-borough Hall, formerly the home of the Anson family and now the Staffordshire County Museum. The house itself is well worth a visit and there is a good industrial history collection that in-cludes a number of Staffordshire locomotives. Canals are not well represented, bearing in mind the important part they played in the industrial development of the county, but a couple of paintings in the hall show working boats passing the park in the early days of the Staffs & Worcs.

$\frac{1}{8}$ *Trent Aqueduct (Plate 5)* 46

The canal crosses the river Trent by a low four-arch aqueduct. Not far from the tail race of Haywood mill. Here we have an instance of the pioneering work of Brindley, although the first impression is perhaps that of a somewhat solid and uninteresting structure. Carrying a canal across a sizeable river like the Trent must have presented a formidable obstacle two hundred years ago, but our engineer set about the task with the characteristic sim-plicity that earned him the nickname 'Schemer Brindley'. Two arches would adequately contain the normal flow of the Trent at Haywood, but the aqueduct has four. The technique used by Brindley was to construct one or more arches on dry land next to the river and to excavate a new channel. The river was then diverted and more arches were built in the old bed. The extra arches carried surplus water in times of flood and a weir was often built upstream to regulate the flow and reduce the pressure on the masonry. This was not necessary at Haywood, of course, since the mill weir was already in existence, and Brindley may in fact have taken advantage of the tail race to carry some of the water while the aqueduct was being built. Earthworks, abandoned channels and other aids to construction can often be seen around these early aqueducts.

The entire facing of the aqueduct is of Keuper Sandstone, but otherwise it has the familiar features of Brindley's 'standard' bridges. The arches are identical to the one over the mill race and both have later parapets of brindled engineering bricks, laid in Flemish bond. Parapets were evidently regarded as an unnecessary expense in the early days of the canal era. The famous etching of Brindley's aqueduct at the crossing of the river Irwell by the Bridgewater Canal at Barton quite clearly shows a row of coping stones at towpath level. Perhaps the introduction of the high-speed 'fly-boats' and 'packets' early in the 19th century prompted the Canal Company to erect parapets on its aqueducts.

The canal follows a low embankment between the Trent aqueduct and bridge No. 108. This is a rarety on the Staffs & Worcs, as it is on many of Brindley's canals, for he preferred to follow the natural contour and avoid major engineering works as far as possible. As with the aqueduct, this stretch provides a further clue to his methods of canal construction. The embankment was raised by scooping earth from the river meadows, leaving parallel trenches on each side of the canal that still drain the low-lying land. It was many years before material from cuttings was used to build embankments, as happened on Telford's Birmingham & Liverpool Junction Canal, for example. Brindley's method was still being used when the approach to the Teme aqueduct on the Kingston, Leominster & Stourport Canal was being built at the turn of the 18th century. Here the excavations are in the form of a series of regular arcs and, as at Haywood, it looks as though some mechanical device was used.

⅜   *Swivel (Cavan's) Bridge (No. 108) and Tixall Broad*   45¾

The name of No. 108 implies that originally this was an opening bridge. The present one is built of brindled engineering brick, laid in English bond, and is probably slightly later than the parapet of Trent aqueduct. It is perhaps worth noting that the style of brickwork rarely gives a clue to the date of a building, since various bonds had been in use for many years. The type and size of the bricks and the general appearance of a wall are usually more reliable guides to age. There is no sign of a plate on No.

108, so it was rebuilt after 1835, and all traces of the earlier swing bridge have disappeared. As far as we know, there were only two swing bridges on the Staffs & Worcs. Although these would have been a great hindrance to traffic, the other one, just north of Kidderminster, was not removed until the end of the last century.

The Staffs & Worcs is never monotonous. Around the next corner it opens out into a wide expanse of water that is more akin to the Norfolk Broads than a narrow canal. Not surprisingly, this is known as the Broad Water or Tixall Broad (Plate 6).* It is a beautiful stretch of canal at any time, but particularly in the spring when the yellow 'flags' are in bloom and wildfowl are nesting in the rushes. Beauty, they say, is skin deep, and lurking a few inches below the surface at present are several feet of black silt. Boaters are lured from the channel at their peril! The reason for this oddity is said to be that Thomas Clifford of Tixall Hall, whose family arms are commemorated in Haywood village, was willing to tolerate the canal provided it did not spoil the view from the hall. As a rule, promoters of canals did not have the same difficulties as the railway builders in securing land, probably because the land-owners were often shareholders. However, in this case Brindley had to make a concession and 'landscape' almost a mile of waterway.

There was once a Tudor mansion at Tixall, but all that remains are the stately ruins of the gatehouse among the trees beyond the Broad and the curious 'bottle' lodge near Tixall farm (*Plates 7-8*). In August 1586 Mary Queen of Scots visited the gatehouse, albeit unwillingly, during her imprisonment about 4 miles away at Chartley, home of the young Earl of Essex. She was there from December 1585 to September 1586 and it was the intrigue of Walsingham and his confederates at Chartley that led to her trial and execution at Fotheringay castle in Northamptonshire.

Tixall itself was the scene of a different drama enacted in these turbulent times. When the gatehouse was built by Sir Walter Aston in 1580, the hall was the headquarters of a group pledged to persecute and uproot Catholics, and Walter was in fact knighted by Elizabeth I for his part in it. A century later the pendulum had swung the other way and the hall had become the local centre for Catholicism. Walter's descendant, Lord Aston, ended up in the Tower of London after being betrayed by his renegade bailiff,

* The name 'Tixall Wide' is also used nowadays.

31

Stephen Dugdale. Shortly after 1750 the estate passed, through marriage, to Thomas Clifford and Tixall soon figured prominently in the story of the Staffs & Worcs.

The best local building material was provided by the Lower Keuper Sandstone that outcrops over a wide area in Tixall Park. Freestone blocks up to 15ft in length could be obtained and during the canal era the yellowish-buff Tixall stone was used extensively, for bridges, locks and other works. Stone for many original features at the northern end of the Staffs & Worcs came from a quarry about ½ mile to the west of the canal and later the estate became riddled with old workings. Marl was also excavated at Tixall and this may well have been the source of clay for some of the bricks used in constructing the canal. However, the use of Tixall stone was not confined to canal works. The old gatehouse was built of it and so were Sandwell Hall, West Bromwich, and St George's church, Birmingham.

The aqueducts at Haywood show Brindley's prowess as an engineer and at Tixall Broad there is an example of his skill as a surveyor. The land to the south consists of silt and mud brought down by the Sow and its tributaries and is flooded from time to time. On the north and at a slightly higher level is an old river terrace, now above the flood plain. Between bridges 108 and 107 Brindley took the canal along the edge of the gravel terrace.

1⅜   *Old Hill Bridge (No. 107) & Tixall Lock (Plate 9)*   44¾

The Broad Water does not attain the dimensions of a normal canal until the first lock is reached. Originally called Marshall's lock, then Old Hill and now Tixall, it has a rise of only 4ft to keep pace with the natural gradient of the Sow valley. The canal above the lock then stays on one level for about 4½ miles. A few changes have been made to the lock since Brindley's day, but some of the massive hanging stones that support the gates may be original, and an old one on the bank adjoining the lock gives an idea of their size.

The design of the narrow lock, with a single top gate and two mitred bottom gates, is attributed to Brindley and the first to be built is said to be at Compton on this canal. Without exception narrow locks on the Staffs & Worcs are 75ft long and 7ft 2in.

wide, with a depth of 4ft 6in. on the sill. This gauge was adopted, with minor variations, throughout the Midland canal system. The locks were filled by two ground and two gate paddles and emptied by two gate paddles. A few years ago it was the practice to remove paddles from the top gates to reduce maintenance costs and conserve water, at the same time greatly increasing the time taken for the lock to fill. Fortunately, a gate paddle is being fitted again as gates are replaced.

Tixall lock still has some of the wooden paddle posts and inclined paddles installed by the Canal Company. These posts have rounded tops and are protected by iron straps to reduce abrasion from towlines. Other examples occur along the canal and a complete set of S&WCCo. paddle gear survives at Wolverley Court lock, but many paddles are now vertical and of a pattern based on the type used on the Birmingham system. (Some in fact have been taken from that system and have 'BCN' cast in the paddle posts.) This type of paddle, after serving its purpose for two centuries, is now being replaced by enclosed hydraulic gear which has the merit of being cleaner and easier to operate, but it remains to be seen whether it will give such trouble-free service.

The earlier part of the lock cottage is built of Tixall stone, perhaps to conform with other buildings on the Clifford estate. A second cottage of brick was added in the 19th century, probably to house a wharf clerk, but the earlier doorway is now blocked and the two form a single residence. Not so many years ago this was the home of Ephraim Talbot, a well-known 'character' of the canals who has been immortalised by de Maré with such worthies as the Duke of Bridgewater and James Brindley. Time moved backwards for half a century or more during a conversation with Ephraim. Unlike most lock cottages along the canal, the one at Tixall is still inhabited and the gardens around the lock are well looked after.

The hill from which No. 107 gets its name may well be old, but the bridge was built a mere 150 years or so ago on the foundations of an earlier one. The contrast between the original pebbly brickwork and the better quality of bricks used in the present bridge is most marked. Although the first bridges were mainly built of brick, stone was sometimes used for the wing walls and No. 107 is an example of this practice.

C

Above and below the lock are the sites of wharves. The one on the towpath side has the remains of a 'hovel'* and the other, on the opposite side near the head of the lock, was once equipped with a crane. There is no habitation here, aside from the lock cottage and a farm, so why did such a remote spot warrant two wharves? It must be remembered that in the days before the railways, canals were the cheapest and often the most convenient form of transport over long distances. Every village, hamlet, estate and farm along the canals had its own wharf. Provisions, coal, lime and building materials were unloaded there, boats returned with flour from the mills or produce and timber from the estates and passengers embarked on the swift packet boats for all parts of the country. The contribution made by our canals towards the industrial revolution is well known, but what is not so obvious is the way in which they influenced rural life in the early 19th century. Sometimes a community moved away from the church and village green and became centred on the canal, but this did not occur at Tixall. Here the wharves served the estate and their main purpose was for the shipment of Tixall stone. Although there is usually little left of these rural wharves, other than rotting timbers and crumbling masonry, an occasional warehouse, group of cottages or pub can still be seen here and there.

Behind the lock cottage and on the opposite side of the river Sow is the battlemented portal of the railway tunnel through Shugborough Park. This was on the Trent Valley Railway, opened in 1847 to provide a more direct route between London and the North than that taken by the Grand Junction. The tunnel was built about 16 years after one of the Ansons, Thomas William, had been created 1st Earl of Lichfield. An earlier Anson had built an extraordinary collection of temples, triumphal arches and monuments around the park and Lord Lichfield insisted that the portal should be suitably ornamented so as not to appear out of place!

1⅝ *Tixall Bridge (No. 106) and Milford (Sow) Aqueduct* 44½

No. 106 is a 'second generation' bridge of red brick that replaced an earlier one. These later bridges, where the use of sandstone is usually confined to the saddleback coping, are quite attractive,

* A hut for storing tools and providing shelter for employees.

but Tixall bridge is marred by an unsightly pipe. Many services are carried across the canals with no attempt whatever to integrate the pipework with the supporting structure. This situation may alter when canals are old enough to be scheduled as ancient monuments!

There is another old wharf next to Tixall bridge, near a gravel pit on the flanks of Old Hill. Two types of rock occur at Old Hill. On the higher ground are the Bunter Pebble Beds, dull red sandstones with strings or pockets of pebbles, and nearer the canal is similar material, but of very different origin. This is sand and gravel deposited by the rivers flowing from melting glaciers during the last ice age. The quarry probably worked these 'fluvo-glacial gravels', as they are called, but the pebble beds would have been an equally suitable source of building material. A pleasant modern bungalow has been built in the old quarry, set amid silver birch trees. Residential development figures prominently in the canal story of today and unfortunately the house at Old Hill is not typical. Too many architects ignore the opportunities offered by our waterways.

Not far from Tixall bridge, at Hollis Ford, is Milford aqueduct, where the canal crosses the river Sow. This four-arch bridge is loftier and generally more substantial than the one across the Trent at Haywood. It is also built of Tixall stone, but it has stone parapets with octagonal turrets at the corners. Milford aqueduct was engineered under Brindley's supervision by Thomas Dadford senior, who later became involved in the building of canals at Dudley and elsewhere in the West Midlands. The contract with Dadford was awarded on 24th October 1771. The original course of the Sow can be seen as a rushy backwater on the Tixall side of the aqueduct, providing a good example of the way rivers were diverted when these early bridges were built.

There is a contribution from the 20th century next to the aqueduct, in the form of a concrete 'pill box'. The siting of a gun emplacement here shows great foresight on the part of the Home Office during the last war. This would have been an obvious choice of route for any army of occupation who happened to be advancing from Milford to Tixall! If it survives demolition, one day it may rank among hill forts and Norman castles as a memento of our island's military history.

The canal turns abruptly to the west after the aqueduct and
continues along the southern side of the Sow valley. The obvious
route between here and the Trent & Mersey would have followed
the south bank all the way. If Brindley was responsible for choosing the north side, he must have had a very good reason for it,
particularly as two extra aqueducts were required. The Wolverhampton historian William Pitt gives us a clue to the probable
reason in his account of Staffordshire agriculture, written about
1800. In a chapter on the Anson estate he said that 'they (the
Staffs & Worcs and Trent & Mersey canals) are conducted on the
sides of the natural rivers most distant from the demesne, and so
as to be no nuisence or inconvenience to the premises'. Anson had
greater influence than Clifford, both locally and in Parliament, and
Pitt's comment implies that he may have been responsible for the
route taken by the canal. The departure at Milford from the usual
design of bridges and aqueducts may also have been to meet the
requirements of Anson.

There was evidently much discussion on the route between
Milford and Haywood before the bill for the Staffs & Worcs was
submitted to Parliament. The 1766 Act contains scant information
on the line of the rest of the canal, only mentioning the main
places along it, but three entire clauses are devoted to the portion
between Milford and the Trent & Mersey Canal, a distance of
under 2 miles. Every field is mentioned by name and the route is
described in minutest detail, even including particular trees along
the line. Although the description is impressive, the survey can
hardly be attributed to Brindley and was probably carried out to
satisfy the whim of the Honourable Thomas Clifford Esq. Long
before work started on this section it was evident that the chosen
course was impracticable and a second Act was obtained, in 1770,
authorising a line a little farther to the north. This Act states that
'the making and carrying on of the said Cut or Canal in the
particular Course thereby directed will, from the Lowness of the
said Lands and Grounds, tend greatly to the Prejudice of the said
intended Navigation, as the Safety of the said Cut or Canal will be
greatly endangered by the Floods which frequently overflow
many of the said Lands and Grounds'. We now know that the
line of the canal was simply transferred from the flood plain of the
Sow to the gravel terrace mentioned previously. The actual

crossing of the river was to be near a place called Hollis Ford, which meant diverting the road between Tixall and Milford that crossed the ford. The diversion was to be carried out at the Canal Company's expense and the fine bridge that takes the road over the Sow was part of this diversion.

The canal widens considerably on the *inside* of the bend beyond the aqueduct, though the extra width is now silted. The bend would be widened on the outside to enable boats to negotiate it more easily and this may represent second thoughts on the siting of the aqueduct. Alternatively, it may have been a layby for boats stopping overnight, as old maps show a short footpath across the field to the 'Barley Mow' at Milford. However, such pubs were normally alongside the canal and invariably there was stabling nearby for the horses of the boatmen. There is still a stile at the back of the pub, but whatever the habits of boatmen in years gone by, present-day boaters are not advised to use it, unless demand justifies the erection of a footbridge across the intervening railway. The route crosses the four tracks of the electrified main line from London to Manchester! The 'Barley Mow' is now a good modern pub with a restaurant and can be reached from Tixall or Milford bridges (Nos. 106 and 105), both about ½ mile from the pub.

Milford Common is near the 'Barley Mow' and is worth a visit if summer weekends are avoided. Ever since Lord Lichfield opened his 'pleasure gardens' to the public last century, this corner of Cannock Chase has been very popular with visitors from the Industrial Midlands. Outcrops of Bunter Sandstone give added character to the common and the Oat Hill Nature Trail on Cannock Chase is within easy walking distance.

2¼   *Milford Bridge (No. 105) (Plate 10)*   43⅞

After crossing the plain around the junction of the rivers Trent and Sow, the canal clings to the hillside a few feet above the river meadows. It continues to do so for many miles and also on the southern section in the manner so typical of the early canals. This was of course the easiest way to build an artificial waterway. Earth was scooped from the hillside to form a channel and the excavated material was banked to contain the water and support

37

the towpath. If there was any likelihood of water draining away through the underlying strata, the canal was lined with 18in. or so of clay 'puddle'. Much of the Staffs & Worcs is on marls or glacial clay and as a rule only embankments and aqueducts were puddled, but there was plenty of suitable material along the canal for sections that had to be lined. All this digging was carried out by hand, with wheelbarrows as the only mechanical aid, and the sweat and toil in creating some 2,000 miles of waterway is beyond comprehension. The workmen were dubbed 'navigators', since they were building the navigations, and this later became short-ened to 'navvies'. The navvies of the later canals went on to build railways, taking their name with them, and it has persisted to this day to include workers on any form of construction. In Brindley's day, as later, the behaviour of the navvies left much to be desired and one can sympathise with Anson for wanting to keep the Sow between himself and the canal!

Not far from the Sow aqueduct is Milford bridge, a delightful little turnover bridge that is as compact as Haywood is expansive. Here we have one of the earliest examples of a bridge that carries the towpath from one side of a canal to the other. (A *roving bridge* conveys it across a branch or arm.) No. 105 has all the usual features of Brindley's bridges, but the effect is enhanced by the sandstone parapet that rises and falls in a series of straight sections. The bridge has a towing path on one side only, terminating in a ramp of bricks laid on edge leading on to the bridge. This enabled a horse to cross the canal without the boatman having to remove the towline. The number of the bridge is significant, since it follows consecutively that of Tixall bridge. For some reason, only bridges *over* the canal were included when the list of plates was drawn up in the early 1830s. There are four major aqueducts on the Staffs & Worcs and none are numbered.

The presence of a turnover bridge here is a consequence of the technique of building contour canals that was pioneered by Brindley and persisted until the end of the century. When the canal crosses from one side of a valley to the other, as at Milford, the towing path must necessarily cross to the other side of the canal. This 'towpath rule' is occasionally broken when a land-owner objected to uncouth boatmen having easy access to his estates, but there is no instance of this on the Staffs & Worcs.

$2\frac{5}{8}$-$3\frac{3}{8}$ *Walton, Stoneford and Lodgefield Bridges* $43\frac{1}{2}$-$42\frac{3}{4}$
(Nos. 104 to 102)

Between Milford and Baswich the canal can only be reached by field paths or bridle ways. Throughout the Middle Ages the Sow valley was a low-lying area of swampy land that was flooded periodically, and there were few places where safe and permanent crossings could be made, such as at Hollis Ford. The swamps had been drained by Brindley's day, but attempts at flood control were only partially successful and improvements to the drainage are still being carried out. This meant that all bridges along the section are of the accommodation variety, merely linking fields on each side of the waterway. Accommodation bridges had to be provided and maintained by the Company and along the Staffs & Worcs about half the bridges are of this type. They are also to be found along railways, although cattle and implements crossed the lines on the level wherever possible, and they are again commonplace on the motorways.

Walton bridge (No. 104) takes its name from the neighbouring village on the main road from Stafford to Lichfield and is a later addition, but the next four bridges were built at the same time as the canal. Stoneford (No. 103) is in fact the first truly 'standard' Brindley bridge we have met on our journey along the canal. Its name no doubt refers to one of the few places around here where the Sow could be crossed. If this was the case, there is no sign of a ford now. Next to the bridge are the foundations of a remote cottage that belonged to the Canal Company. This was the home of a lengthsman whose job it was to look after the exposed section along the Sow valley. In the railway embankment and not far from the bridge is an outcrop of the Bunter Pebble Beds, the stony red sandstone that is responsible for the high ground to the south of the canal and that also underlies the whole of Cannock Chase. Both the canal and the Trent Valley Railway follow the outcrop of this rock, where it emerges from superficial deposits of gravel, clay and silt along the river Sow.

There is a small brick building on each side of the canal at Lodgefield bridge (No. 102). Until recently these housed the pumps for a brine pipeline that crossed the canal at this point.

39

Between Baswich and Haywood, the rocks underneath the Staffs & Worcs are sandstones of the lower division of the Trias formation, but most of central Staffordshire and indeed much of Cheshire, Worcestershire and Warwickshire, is covered by the colourful Keuper Marl of the upper Trias. The landscape of the marl country is usually fairly featureless and is mainly pastoral, though occasional beds of sandstone produce some relief. The marls are often suitable for brick making, and here and there are signs of marl holes and old brickworks, but their main economic value is in the vast deposits of rock salt that occur in layers throughout the formation. Besides being an indispensable household commodity, salt is the basis of the alkali industry and countless other industries are dependent upon it. Saline springs have been known around Stafford since ancient times. There was one across the Sow, not far from St Thomas's Priory, and Baswich no doubt obtained its name from another, since 'wich' is always associated with salt. However, deposits of salt were 'discovered' by accident in 1881, when Stafford Corporation were boring for a water supply on Stafford Common to the north of the town. Two main beds of salt were found and the extraction of brine started in 1893. The Corporation pumped brine to the baths in Stafford and by 1920 three firms were extracting the mineral from under the common. One of these pumped brine to a works 2 miles away at Baswich for processing. A second works was built just before the last war near Lodgefield bridge, sandwiched between the canal and railway, and this refined brine until 1971. Modern methods usually ensure that brine extraction is carefully controlled, leaving pillars of salt to support the rock above, but industry around the common had been affected by subsidence for many years. After a long legal battle, the case went against the mining company, all pumping of brine ceased in the Stafford area and the works at Baswich was dismantled.

Exploration for a very different mineral was made between the railway and canal near Lodgefield bridge. Although the area is covered by the Pebble Beds, nowhere are they very thick and below are the coal seams of the Cannock Coalfield. A borehole here reached carboniferous rocks at about 150ft, but drilling stopped before any coal seams were reached.

$3\frac{3}{4}$ *Saint Thomas Bridge (No. 101)* $42\frac{3}{8}$

St Thomas bridge is one of Brindley's that still carries traffic on the only route across the Sow between Tixall and Stafford. The lane is narrow and has several sharp bends where it crosses the main river and the branch to the old flour mill at St Thomas. The settlement at 'Centimus', as it is known locally, grew around an Augustinian priory. This was founded in 1175 by the 'Black Canons' and dedicated to St Thomas Beckett, five years after the saint's murder at Canterbury. The priory went the way of all religious houses in the reign of Henry VIII, being closed in 1538, but in the intervening years the canons left their mark on the area and made life easier for the canal builders several centuries later. The causeway that carries the lane from Baswich above the level of normal floods is probably their handiwork, and they constructed a mill at St Thomas to supply the needs of the priory. This spot, just below the junction of the rivers Penk and Sow, was an ideal one for a mill. The change in height was only a few feet, but there was a plentiful supply of water.

The priory was acquired by the Fowler family after the dissolution, and for two hundred years it was a Catholic house, like Tixall Hall. Shortly before the coming of the canal it passed into Protestant hands and the mill survived all these changes to close down earlier this century. Little remains of the old priory, but the settlement is a pleasant collection of Georgian buildings in an attractive setting.

$3\frac{7}{8}$ *Sow Navigation (Stafford Branch, $1\frac{1}{4}$ miles)* $42\frac{1}{4}$

Unlike all neighbouring county towns, Stafford had no navigable link with the sea throughout the Middle Ages and did not get one until some years after the building of the Staffs & Worcs Canal. The Sow passed by the town walls, but it is only a small river and the Trent itself was not navigable beyond Burton. With the coming of the canal, a wharf was built at Radford for the benefit of the town and the $1\frac{1}{2}$-mile branch to Stafford was not completed until 19th February 1816. Proposals for the branch were made in 1798, with aqueducts across the Sow and Penk, but this costly scheme was dropped in favour of a tramway from Radford. This evidently was not a success and in 1810 a plan emerged for making both rivers navigable, with a connecting lock at Radford. Eventually the Sow Navigation locked down to the river near St Thomas and missed the Penk altogether. It was owned by Lord Stafford, but the S&WCCo. acquired the lease in 1838 and then carried out various improvements. Coal was carried on the branch during the early years of this century and Ernie Thomas, proprietor of Calf Heath Marina until he died in 1973, took a load of swedes and mangels to the town just before the First World War. Stafford mill was a short distance upstream from the town's wharves and Ernie related how it had to be shut down before boats could turn. Trade on the Sow Navigation had fallen off to such an extent by the 1920s that the Canal Company did not renew the lease when it expired on 25th March 1927 and the branch became derelict. It is a great pity that the branch has been allowed to deteriorate. Familiar towns seem totally different when visited by boat and there is a unique fascination in mooring 'at the end of the line' in the heart of towns like Ellesmere, Coventry and Loughborough. Navigation could be restored to the Sow Arm without too much difficulty or expense and perhaps Stafford will one day be added to the list. In the meantime, it is an interesting town that well justifies the 1½-mile walk along the towing path from St Thomas.

The roving bridge at the junction of the Sow Navigation and the main line has been demolished and its site is occupied by an overflow weir. There is a short, drained pound with sandstone walls beyond the junction and next to it are the foundations of a cottage whose occupant probably collected tolls from traffic on the branch. The pound led to a small aqueduct across a drainage channel and then straight into Baswich or St Thomas lock. The drainage leat carries water from land drains along the low-lying Penk valley and takes any surplus from the canal. It starts near Deptmore lock and runs close to the Staffs & Worcs for almost 2 miles before entering the Sow near St Thomas. The channel was in existence before the end of the 18th century and may have been constructed by the Canal Company to drain the canal bank and get rid of flood water.

The brickwork of Baswich lock was intact in 1971, but has since been swept away during the recent spate of improvements

ROUND AND ABOUT STAFFORD

to drainage along the Sow valley. It was built to the same dimensions as locks on the main line and had a nominal fall of 6ft 6in., the exact amount depending on the level of the river.

The branch entered the Sow just beyond the tail of the lock and not far from the mouth of the river Penk. The remainder of the branch was along the Sow, which probably required little deepening, as the water had previously been impounded by the Augustinians for their mill at St Thomas. However, substantial realignment was necessary. The river between Baswich and Stafford meandered across the flood plain in a series of tight curves and about ½ mile of new channel was constructed. A series of swampy 'oxbow lakes' were left to the south of the new course and the towpath crossed to the north of the navigation to avoid them. The branch terminated at Green Bridge near the centre of Stafford (Plate 11), near a coal basin that was infilled during the 1930s and now serves as a car park. However, at one time the Sow may have been navigable as far as Stafford mill beyond the bridge. The wheels, foundations and machinery of this ancient mill have been preserved and the pond is incorporated in an attractive park.

| 4⅛ | *Baswick (Baswich) Bridge (No. 100)* | 42 |

Between St Thomas (No. 101) and Baswich (No. 100) bridges the canal forsakes the westerly course it has followed from Haywood and turns towards the south. The route between Baswich and the end of the canal at Stourport is always within 1 mile of a straight line between the two places, except for a slight diversion at Calf Heath. Contrary to popular belief, this directness is characteristic of the waterways with which Brindley was closely involved. The meanderings of the Oxford Canal or the Birmingham were probably due to the efforts of his assistant and brother-in-law, Samuel Simcock. Although Brindley's task was relatively easy on the Staffs and Worcs, since the canal follows river valleys most of the way, its directness is still a tribute to his ability as a surveyor.

The basin of the earlier salt works at Baswich was between the junction with the Sow Navigation and the railway viaducts. Coal was delivered at the wharf here and salt was taken away in substantial quantities. As mentioned previously, brine was not obtained at Baswich, but was pumped along a pipeline that followed the towpath of the Sow Navigation to a point where rail and canal transport were available. The site of the salt works is now occupied by a factory where concrete posts are made.

The twin viaducts at Baswich carry the Trent Valley line across the Staffs & Worcs Canal, the drainage channel and the river Penk. The line was opened for goods traffic on 15th September 1847 and the iron columns supporting the section over the Penk may date from this time. The opening of the line was in fact delayed for several months while five bridges were strengthened with additional girders and these bridges probably included the one at Baswich. The viaduct was almost entirely rebuilt this century, perhaps to carry the magnificent Stanier 'Pacifics' that were a familiar sight on this line, and the second viaduct came into being when the line was electrified in the early 1960s.

Baswich ends with a 'k' on the plate of bridge No. 100, but this was not necessarily an error on the part of the pattern maker. Priestley's map of 1830 calls the village 'Berkswick', so the final 'k' may have been a compromise! A footpath from the bridge leads to Baswich church, passing an outcrop of Bunter Pebble Beds on the way. The church was mostly rebuilt in the 18th century, but its medieval tower is a landmark for some distance along the canal.

$4\frac{1}{2}$ *Meadow Bridge (No. 99)* $41\frac{5}{8}$

Meadow accommodation bridge (No. 99) is a post-1835 replacement, built of engineering bricks. On each side of the bridge a long row of poplars has been planted to stabilise the canal bank, providing further protection against flooding. This use of trees to strengthen cuttings and embankments was common practice in Telford's day—there are some fine examples along the Llangollen Canal—and one wonders whether this simple device occurred to Brindley. Along the hillside and bordering on the canal between Baswich and Radford bridges are recent housing estates on the outskirts of Stafford. This development at Weeping Cross and Baswich has been carried out with no regard whatever for the amenity offered by the canal.

Also between these bridges the canal crosses the Hopton fault, the geological feature that separates the Pebble Beds from the

Keuper Marls in this area. The downthrow of the fault is to the west, causing the rocks of the lower Trias to occur at the surface between here and Haywood. The canal continues on the marls almost as far as Penkridge, although they are often hidden by more recent superficial deposits. This is no accident, since the Penk flows over the marls rather than the more resistant Pebble Beds, and Brindley simply followed the river. The canal crosses the fault obliquely and then turns to follow it as far as Hazlestrine.

$4\frac{5}{8}$ *Radford Wharf & Bridge (No. 98)* $41\frac{1}{2}$

The Staffs & Worcs tries hard to reach Stafford, but does not quite succeed. Radford, about $1\frac{1}{2}$ miles from the town centre, is as near as it gets and a wharf was constructed here when the canal was built, goods being carried to the town in carts. This was not very satisfactory and, as we have seen, an elaborate scheme for a branch canal was put forward. This was shelved in favour of a horse tramway built by the Stafford Railway Coal & Lime Company. Opened on 1st November 1805, this was certainly Stafford's first railway and it may well have been the canal's first tramway connection. The tramway started at a basin behind the wharf and then crossed a field to the bridge across the Penk. This very fine bridge had been rebuilt in 1804 with an additional arch across the drainage channel that runs alongside the canal, indicating that the meadows along the river were drained before the end of the 18th century. The tramway ran alongside the Lichfield road, crossed over it near the town centre, and terminated at the Railway 'Wharf', near Green Bridge. In these days railways were usually associated with canals and had not acquired a jargon of their own!

Evidently the tramway was not a success, for a branch canal was again proposed in 1810 and the Sow Navigation materialised in 1814.* After less than 9 years of operation the Stafford Railway was up for sale. Among the items auctioned on 15th July 1814 were flanged rails, sills (sleepers), trucks of between 20 and 30 cwt capacity, a weighing machine at the Stafford wharf and a mobile crane. The basin at Radford may have been used for a

---

* St Thomas or Baswich lock, connecting the Sow Navigation with the Staffs & Worcs, was not completed until February 1816.

while afterwards, since Bradshaw shows it on his map of 1830, but 50 years later it had been drained. All that now remains are a few blocks of sandstone around the site of the entrance. The line of the tramway can be traced here and there along the Lichfield road, where older houses are set back to make room for it, and the only tangible evidence of Stafford's first railway emerged when workmen found a quantity of wooden sleepers under the road in 1880.

The canal bridge at Radford (No. 98) has suffered many changes over the years (Plate 12). It has been extended twice and strengthened with numerous steel girders, but the core of the bridge is original. The familiar features can still be discerned among the ironwork and alterations, but here the sandstone is red and more weathered than before. It has the appearance of Bunter Sandstone which is generally less suitable as a building material than the Keuper. Next to the bridge is the 'Trumpet Inn', a fairly modern pub on the site of an old canal house. Boats can moor here for short periods and snacks or grills are usually available.

The wharfhouse and warehouses at Radford survived until 1972, when the old buildings were regrettably demolished to allow for expansion of the neighbouring boatyard. These included the Radford Bank stores where boatmen could obtain provisions and other necessities. There was also a warehouse with double doors at street level and access from the canal bank, so that goods could be loaded directly into carts. The interchange of goods between canals and railways was common practice during the second half of the 19th century, but Radford wharf was an early example of a combined canal-rail and canal-road transhipment point. The wharf is now used by Radford Marine who build and hire boats and provide the usual services for boaters.

3

The Climb to the Summit

RADFORD TO GAILEY

Miles from Haywood		Miles to Stourport
5¼	*Barnfields (?) Bridge (No. 97)*	40⅞

The brief encounter with Stafford is over at Radford and in an instant the canal is rural again as it approaches the climb of 7 miles to the summit level. Staffordshire is noted for its industry rather than its agriculture, but it has as high a proportion of pastureland as can be found in any English county. Although the scenery for the next few miles is not spectacular, this is a delightful length of canal, particularly in late summer when the banks are lined with the gay Jewel Weed.

It is still some distance to the next lock and on this stretch is one of the mysteries of the Staffs & Worcs. The last bridge was No. 98 and the next one is No. 96 at Hazlestrine, so what became of No. 97? It appears on Bradshaw's map of 1830, but is omitted from the 1st edition of the Ordnance Survey published six years later at about the time the bridges were numbered. The only possible site for the bridge is where a ditch in the river meadow changes direction to avoid a low ramp, with a slightly larger mound on the other side of the canal. These meagre clues are near Barnfields farm, where a power line crosses the canal, and No. 97 may have been an accommodation bridge for the farm. Why it has gone completely, even to the removal of the narrows or 'bridge hole', is a mystery, particularly as so many early bridges have survived.

Across the Penk at Rickerscote there used to be a salt spring where brine flowed naturally from the Keuper Marl. According to William Pitt, the 'spa water' from it was 'highly saline, moderately

sulpherous, and considerably chalybeate' and 'possessed of pro-
perties similar to the waters of Cheltenham and Leamington'!

5½   *Hazlestrine Bridge (No. 96)*   40⅝

If you look hard and long enough at the stunted stack of Hazlestrine brickworks, glimpsed through the trees as No. 96 is
approached, it is easy to be convinced that smoke is drifting
lazily from it. Old chimneys have a habit of doing this, though it
is many years since bricks were made here. The Keuper Marl at
Hazlestrine is right at the bottom of the series, just a few feet
above the sandstone, so that the rock sequence is similar to that in
Tixall Park. Quite early in the 19th century both building stone
and clay for brick making were extracted, and the works was still
active in the 1920s. All this quarrying has left behind a vast
excavation in the hillside to the east of the canal, though it is now
very overgrown.

Most of the output from the works went away by canal, along
the 250yd Hazlestrine Arm that leaves the main canal near No. 96.
The arm is being cleared by members of Stafford Boat Club to
provide moorings and its junction with the canal is the first place
after Tixall Broad where a full-length narrow boat can 'wind' or
turn, since the Stafford Branch is now closed. It seems that there
was no roving bridge at the junction and that horses crossed by
No. 96 to reach the arm. This remote spot, favoured by fishermen,
is only accessible by canal or along a very rough track. The lane
starts out on Keuper Marl, crosses the underlying sandstone
where the marl has been removed, and joins the main road after
crossing the Hopton fault and the Pebble Beds. Even those who
are unfamiliar with the geology of the area could not fail to notice
the change in character of the rocks, particularly after a prolonged
wet spell.

5⅞   *Deptmore Lock & Bridge (No. 95)*   40¼

The lock at Deptmore, or Deepmore, is the first of eleven that
take the canal up to the summit level. The average rise of each
lock is a little under 9ft, but there is a wide variation in height
and also in the distance between them (see Appendix III). In

Brindley's day the rise and siting of a lock was decided by the natural profile of the land through which the canal ran, in this case the Penk valley. The movement of large quantities of earth was thus avoided, but it meant that the canal was wasteful of water and difficult to maintain. A deep lock with a shallow one above it could, in principle, eventually drain the intervening pound, and with the locks the other way round the section would be 'running weir' most of the time. Conditions were never quite as bad as this in practice, but subsidiary supplies were usually necessary and part of the lengthsman's job was to keep the water somewhere near its correct level. Most pounds between here and the summit at one time had supplementary feeders and even today it is necessary for the Board's employees to check levels at frequent intervals, particularly during the 'cruising season'.

Irregular lock-rises only occur on early canals, for it was not long before the engineers realised their mistake. It may have been that their attention was drawn to it by canal committees suffering wastage of water and loss of revenue from reduced loads, and well before the end of the 18th century new locks were of constant rise. They were also grouped together in flights wherever practicable and a single supply at the summit was adequate in most cases. There are many examples of this practice, but perhaps the best are to be found on the Shropshire Union Canal, completed in 1835. On this canal are several flights, with a constant rise of about 6ft at each lock and many miles of waterway between each flight. Although it is doubtful whether the views of the boatmen were considered, they must have welcomed this development. Flights of locks are much easier and quicker to work than a string of isolated ones.

No. 95 used to be an accommodation bridge across the tail of Deptmore lock, but the lock house is now reached by a cast-iron footbridge inscribed 'S&WCCo.' This is a split bridge with a gap wide enough to pass a towline through it. Originally the line had to be unhitched at most locks until cantilever bridges were introduced on the canal, probably in the early 19th century, to avoid this inconvenience. Many locks along the Staffs & Worcs have split bridges that are identical to that at Deptmore.

As the canal approaches the lock it crosses a drainage ditch and then a small brook that later merge to form the channel running

D

alongside the canal as far as St Thomas. Next to the aqueduct over the brook is a sluice where surplus water can be diverted from the long pound. There are several sluices down the locks and along the pound between here and Tixall, but the main control of flow is carried out at Deptmore. A few years ago a landowner in the Penk valley claimed that water from the canal, possibly originating at the sewage works near Aldersley, was polluting streams running into the river. The Waterways Board was obliged to stop using all storm-water sluices between Gailey and Acton Trussell and surplus water has since had to be let through each lock. There are also a few 'emergency' weirs along the flight to cope with torrential rain, but these are not always effective, as we shall see.

Some water finds its way into the canal from an overgrown arm below Deptmore lock. This leads to an old marl hole where bricks may have been made during the building of the canal.

| $6\frac{1}{4}$ | *Roseford Bridge (No. 94)* | $39\frac{7}{8}$ |

Sometimes an accommodation bridge, usually associated with a large and prosperous farm, was completely rebuilt towards the end of the 19th century or early in the present one, and Roseford (No. 94) is such a bridge. It is built of brindled engineering bricks and there is no sign of a plate, though it is included in the numbering sequence. This was presumably a result of the great change in farming brought about by the introduction of steam traction. Brindley's bridges were not always capable of withstanding the heavy loads imposed by the massive engines with their ploughs, threshing machines and other equipment. They were, after all, designed to carry nothing heavier than a horse and cart. Only a few bridges on the Staffs & Worcs were affected, but elsewhere many that carried roads were rebuilt during the period 1880 to 1910, particularly on the Birmingham system.

| $6\frac{1}{8}$ | *Acton Bridge (No. 93)* | $39\frac{1}{4}$ |

Acton Trussell, whose name seems to typify the charm traditionally associated with the English village, straggles between bridges 93 and 92. Whatever tranquility and seclusion it may have had in the past has now been lost. Acton has fallen victim of the

tendency for people to drift away from the towns and is becoming
a dormitory of Stafford. It has also recently been exposed to the
gaze of travellers along the M6 motorway, but these are not the
first intrusions on its privacy. Acton bridge (No. 93) bears the
scars of an earlier invasion. Only the foundations of Brindley's
narrow bridge remain and the rest has been rebuilt and later
widened, doubtless for the same reason as No. 94. The canal itself
may well have been resented when the 'navvies' disturbed the
peace of Acton, but the countryside soon adapts itself to up-
heavals like these.

Acton wharf, next to bridge No. 93, was still in use at the
beginning of the century, for de Salis included it in his *Bradshaw's
Canals and Navigable Rivers* of 1904. These rural wharves only
went out of use when lorries began to appear. On the other side
of the canal and to the south of the bridge, the towing path
widens to form a track for ¼ mile. This formerly led to the 'Newhouse Inn', a pub built for the use of the boatmen. Tradition has
it that the pub closed after a boater had been killed in a brawl
there, but declining traffic doubtless hastened its closure.

7¼   *Acton Moat Bridge (No. 92)*   38⅞

Bridge No. 92 and the neighbouring house take their name from
a moat centuries older than either of them. Here Brindley had the
bright idea of including one arm of the moat in his canal, providing a ready-made channel for a few yards. There is a slight
widening of the canal at this point and an L-shaped moat on two
sides of the house. Brindley repeated this at another moated house
near bridge No. 74 and these two sections must surely be the
oldest along the Staffs & Worcs, perhaps on any Midland canal!

7¾   *Shutt Hill Bridge (No. 91), Wharf & Lock*   38¾

The lane between Acton and Penkridge passes the tiny church of
St James before it crosses the canal at bridge No. 91. The road has
a double bend here that must have been a hazard long before cars
appeared, for a skew extension was added many years ago. Early
skewed road bridges are uncommon on canals and this is the

51

nearest approach to one on the Staffs & Worcs. (Houndel bridge, No. 45, also has a skew extension.) The original bridge has a key-stone by way of ornament and is built partly of stone. Although it could well be contemporary with the canal, the bridge lacks the usual signs of Brindley's work. At this point the canal reaches the edge of Teddesley Park, the home of Sir Edward Littleton in Brindley's day, and he may have insisted on a distinctive bridge at Shutt Hill.

There are three old wharves at Teddesley and the first is next to Shutt Hill bridge. The iron post set in the corner of the wharf probably had a pulley and was to assist boats in making the sharp turn into or out of the lock. The main cargoes here would be coal and lime, both coming from the south. The basin is now over-grown, but some timber staging of the wharf has survived among the rushes. The lock itself is one of the shallowest on the Staffs & Worcs, with a rise of only 6ft. The stream from Spring Slade pool on the Teddesley estate approaches the canal in a deep cutting at this point and flows under the lock tail on its way to the Penk. The stream was diverted when the canal was built and the culvert under the canal has since been altered several times. The lock weir is immediately over the culvert and the Canal Company went to some lengths to ensure that surplus water flowed into the lower pound and did not run to waste through the culvert. The stream could have supplied the canal at the wharf below the lock, but if it ever did, all traces of a weir or sluice have disappeared.

There is a change of scene above Shutt Hill lock as the canal follows Teddesley Park for over a mile. Fields give way to woods on one side, though the river meadows of the Penk continue to flank the canal on the other. Teddesley was only a fraction of the Littleton estates, which stretched from Acton to Gailey, a distance of over 5 miles. Sir Edward was, with Anson and Clifford whom we met at Haywood, one of the promoters of the Staffs & Worcs. He also held several shares in the Company and served on the Committee for over forty years, so it is not surprising that he allowed Brindley to take the canal in a direct line through his estates, within ½ mile of the mansion. The original home of the Littletons was a couple of miles away at Pillaton and, when Sir Edward inherited the property in the middle of the 18th century, its ruinous condition caused him to enclose part of Cannock

Chase and build Teddesley Hall. The work was financed from a hoard of gold coins from the reigns of the Tudors and Stuarts, discovered at Pillaton when an old fireplace was being altered. The new hall was unpretentious by the standards of the day, but Sir Edward built imposing blocks of stables, offices and other outbuildings. Although Teddesley Hall was demolished as an army 'exercise' about 1956, the stables and servants' quarters are still used by Mr E. Buxton, who purchased Teddesley farm and part of the estate from the 5th Lord Hatherton.

Sir Edward died in May 1812 and was succeeded by his nephew, Edward J. Wallhouse, who was then 21 years old. He assumed the name of Littleton, since this was a condition of the inheritance, and immediately moved to Teddesley. When created a Peer in May 1835 he took the name of Hatherton, the home of his own family. In this way the name of an insignificant hamlet near Watling Street ever after became inseparably linked with the Staffs & Worcs Canal. The enthusiasm of the 1st Baron Hatherton for the canal even surpassed that of his great uncle and, as we shall see, many improvements at a crucial period in the life of the canal were due to him. Later Hathertons also involved themselves in the affairs of the Company and there was always a member of the Littleton family on the Committee until the nationalisation of our waterways in 1947.

The woods, that form a belt along the canal and also on the northern boundary of the park act as a screen between the canal and estate. In spite of his enthusiasm for the canal, Lord Hatherton obviously did not wish to see his investment earning interest! The woodland is called the 'Wellington Belt', after the Duke of Wellington who regularly visited Teddesley. Gentry from far and wide stayed at the hall in Sir Edward's day. In the words of William Pitt, 'His mansion was noted for the scene of old English hospitallity, where plenty of roast beef and good ale were provided for all decent visitors, without riot, profusion, or wastefulness'! The Duke and other 'decent visitors' continued to descend on Teddesley after the death of Sir Edward and the Belt was planted by his young nephew about 1815, partly to improve the shooting for his guests.

Parkgate Bridge (No. 90), Wharf & Lock
and the Teddesley Hay Feeder

In Sir Edward Littleton's day one of the entrances to Teddesley was next to the principal wharves of the estate at Parkgate. Lord Hatherton must have objected to the phaetons, curricles and carriages of his distinguished guests mingling with the coal carts; for about the time he became a peer he arranged for a new drive to be built. This crossed the canal over ½ mile away, with the wharves discreetly out of sight. The old drive became a footpath and the lodge perhaps a wharfhouse. The wharves continued to be used for many years and it even became necessary to rebuild and extend bridge No. 90. The wharf above Parkgate lock is again a hive of activity, for the Teddesley Boating Centre has recently been established here. Cruisers can be hired and there is a slipway and other boating facilities. Canal cruising is booming at present and hire centres are mushrooming at every available site along attractive canals like the Staffs & Worcs. However, there is nothing new about pleasure boating on canals, though only in recent years has it actually been encouraged. As on other canals, provision was made for pleasure cruising on the Staffs & Worcs in the Act of 1766. All owners or tenants of land adjoining the canal could use pleasure boats free of charge, provided they did not get in the way of working boats or use the locks without first obtaining the Company's permission.

Nearly all important wharves along the canal had a 'winding hole' nearby, usually on the offside, where boats could turn. There may have been one just below Parkgate lock, though it is not now evident, aside from a slight widening of the canal. If there was a winding hole here, it must have been difficult to keep clear, as a feeder joins the canal at this point. This inconspicuous and overgrown supply is in reality the tip of an iceberg, for behind the Wellington Belt is a network of feeders, culverts and channels that drain several thousand acres of farmland and were once the main source of water for the northern end of the Staffs & Worcs.

The system of feeders on the Teddesley estates was authorised in the second Staffs & Worcs Canal Act of 1770. The Company could use the brook that rises in 'Springwall Slade' (now known as Spring Slade) and several other streams rising on the enclosed common land of Teddesley Hay. These watercourses all belonged to Sir Edward Littleton, and the Company was also empowered to build reservoirs on Sir Edward's land, provided that an acre was covered with water at all times to a depth of at least 3ft to preserve the fish. Initially the Company only constructed one reservoir on Teddesley Hay, and this was Pottall Pool. The reservoir is now drained to the level of the outlet sluice, but to this day it contains a fair quantity of water, presumably in accordance with the clause in the 1770 Act to safeguard Sir Edward's fish. The Act also enabled the Company to build leats and feeders through the Littleton estates.

Although Sir Edward Littleton acquired vast tracts of marsh and waterlogged land when he enclosed parts of Teddesley Hay in the middle of the 18th century, he realised that adequate drainage would convert it into a prosperous and productive estate. The wetness of the land had long been appreciated, for early maps that show little else give prominence to numerous parallel streams running from the Hay to the Penk. Sir Edward built Teddesley Hall on one of the few sound areas where Keuper Sandstone occurs near the surface and embarked on a drainage programme that was to last for 80 years or more. However, long before Sir Edward died in 1812, there was an elaborate system of drainage channels, feeders and reservoirs that not only made the land more fertile, but also provided the Canal Company with water at a time when it desperately needed extra supplies.

The plateau of Pebble Beds on Cannock Chase, the main source of all this water, conveniently enabled an almost level feeder to be built to get rid of it. The Teddesley Hay feeder ran along the 360ft contour, parallel to the entire flight of locks between Shutt Hill bridge. The iron post set in the corner of the wharf collected many small streams and a feed from Pottall Pool on the way, and ended at Calf Heath reservoir, falling about 50ft in 8 miles. Calf Heath reservoir itself was built at about the same time as the canal, feeding it at Gailey wharf. It is interesting to note that all original bridges on the Teddesley feeder and supply from Pottall have brick dripstones that are reminiscent of the arches of Brindley's bridges. In addition, there was a subsidiary supply taken from a point lower down the Spring Slade brook. This followed the 315ft contour to Lodgerail pool, an artificial lake in front of the hall, supplied the mill at Woolgarston and then fed the canal at Longford. There were various other interconnecting leats and channels and the whole system is shown on the 2in. Ordnance Survey field maps of 1817. (See also figure A2, Appendix III.)

Sir Edward did much towards getting water away from the estate, but his method of actually draining the land was inadequate. His land drains were neither deep enough, nor were they of suitable construction, and many acres were still waterlogged when young Edward Wallhouse succeeded him in 1812. Although Edward continued the work started by his great-uncle, it was not until Bright joined his staff as bailiff that any real progress was made. Bright was an expert on drainage and by 1850 the system at Teddesley had become a wonder of the age and a model for other landowners. Yet another use was made of the water, perhaps not entirely due to Bright, but certainly much improved by him. A reservoir high up on the estate was connected by an underground 15in. diameter culvert to a mill $\frac{1}{2}$ mile away, at Teddesley farm. The mill had a wrought-iron overshot wheel, 38ft in diameter and also underground, and the tail race emerged from a 500yd tunnel to supply Lodgerail pool, another mill and then the canal. It is fair to say that not a drop of water on the estate was wasted.

The feeder at Parkgate was a late addition to the network. Originally the overflow from Lodgerail pool flowed across swampy ground and into the canal above Parkgate lock. The able Bright succeeded where earlier bailiffs had failed by the simple expedient of diverting the overflow so that it joined the canal *below* the lock. This was carried out in preparation for the new drive and on 23rd April 1835 Edward wrote in his diary that, 'The whole of the ground . . . was a complete shaking bog, on many acres of which it was impossible to stand, till I drained it this spring.'

In spite of all this water pouring into the canal from the Teddesley estates, the demands imposed by increasing traffic continued to exceed supply. A plan put forward by the Canal Company in 1825 for a second reservoir at Pottall was thought to be too expensive and was abandoned, but on 28th September 1836

Lord Hatherton gave the Company permission to build a reservoir at Spring Slade, at the start of the Teddesley feeder. At the same time additional reservoirs at Gailey were considered, but it was several years before they materialised.

The Canal Company only leased the Teddesley feeder and when the lease expired in the 1940s, traffic had declined to such an extent that the Company decided not to continue the arrangement. Much of the feeder still serves its original purpose of draining the land and some water still finds its way into the canal. Short sections are choked with rushes and the central part has been filled in and the land cultivated. The entire line of the feeder is on private land with few public rights of way and it can only be seen from the numerous roads that cross its course. Spring Slade pool is now only used for fishing and Pottall went out of use many years ago. According to the report by the Royal Commission on canals of 1905, 'Pottall Reservoir is now practically empty and rendered entirely useless for canal purposes owing to the pumping operations of the South Staffordshire Waterworks Company at Huntington, near Cannock.' The pool is near the A34, $1\frac{1}{2}$ miles to the north of the pumping station and various brick-lined culverts Shutt Hill and the summit at Gailey. It started at Spring Slade, and the 30 to 40ft high dam, all built towards the end of the 18th century, and the later main sluice can still be seen. The pool itself is still 'practically empty' and is gradually diminishing as spoil from a nearby gravel pit is being dumped into it. The Canal Proprietors were not the only ones to suffer because of pumping operations at Huntington. The supply of drinking water for Teddesley came from a reservoir near Pottall and this too was drained. In consequence, the SSWCo., or their successors, have to supply water to all houses on the estate free of charge for ever more.

8$\frac{3}{4}$ *'Fancy' (Teddesley) Bridge (No. 89)*   37$\frac{3}{8}$

After so many Brindley bridges, some modified and some not, No. 89 comes as a complete surprise. Boatmen often had their own names for places on the 'cut' and they called it the 'Fancy bridge', but they cannot be blamed for this one. It is Fancy bridge to the the locals for miles around and has been for generations. The name certainly suits it better than the prosaic 'New Bridge' of the

Ordnance Survey or 'Teddesley' of de Salis. A little renovation would not come amiss and the brick infilling of the parapet does nothing to enhance its appearance, but what a fine bridge it must have been when built. It is faced with Keuper stone and has abutments and octagonal columns, with fragments of an iron railing amongst the ivy. Fancy bridge was intended to be distinctive and there certainly is no other bridge like it on the Staffs & Worcs.

The age of Fancy bridge is significant. A month before Edward Littleton became the 1st Baron Hatherton on 8th May 1835, the masons began to build the abutments for the bridge that was to carry the new drive to Teddesley Hall. Edward recorded that he contracted to pay £200 to his stone mason for building the bridge, and it was ready at the end of 1836. Lord Hatherton wrote in his diary for Christmas Day, 'We now have intense frost and snow, real Xmas weather. We all went to Church by the new Penkridge Road, through the beech wood, over the new bridge across the canal, and open today for the first time.' Now Fancy bridge is included in the number sequence, though it does not appear ever to have had a plate, and the plates were probably added to other bridges during the second half of 1835. They could not have been erected much later, for the Grand Junction Railway was being built near Penkridge during October of the same year and its bridge across the canal at Slade Heath, a few miles to the south, is not included in the number sequence. (See also the Cross bridge at Hatherton Junction.)

The parapet of Fancy bridge was filled with brickwork by the Army during the Second World War to provide cover for gunners. It was appreciated that the pill box at Milford could not hold the aqueduct against an invading army indefinitely, and Fancy bridge provided a second line of defence! Fortunately, Eric de Maré photographed the bridge before it was altered and an illustration of it is included in his *Canals of England*.

The third wharf at Teddesley is a little way beyond Fancy bridge and next to it was a small basin, just big enough to take one narrow boat. Much of Teddesley Park is on the Keuper Marl, but the canal has been gradually approaching the outcrop of the Lower Keuper Sandstone, eventually crossing it at Wood Bank on the fringe of the park. There were several small quarries in this Penkridge stone, as it is known locally, and those near the canal account for the presence of the wharf. The weathered stone edging of the wharf and basin has been there a very long time and the quarries may have been worked while the canal was being built. They were still in use when the new drive was opened, for a track from it leads past the wharf to the quarries. A stream enters the canal via the basin, after following an artificial course under the track. Since the final section of the 'lower' feeder to Woolgarston mill was drained, water from Spring Slade and Lodgerail pools has flowed into the canal at this point. Originally this particular supply only drained a particularly wet part of the estate known as the 'Osier Beds'.

From Wood Bank the canal follows the Keuper Sandstone as far as Aldersley, though much of it is covered by more recent glacial material, and the Penk wends its way across the marls to the west. The ground now begins to rise slightly and the locks get closer together as the softer marls are left behind.

9   *Longford Bridge (No. 88)* $37\frac{1}{8}$

There are two bridges at Wood Bank, with 200yd and 200 years separating them. The first carries the M6 motorway and is just as typical of the 20th century as Longford bridge is of the 18th. Although both carry roads across the canal, their style and method of construction could not be more different. Brindley's bridge of dressed stone and hand-made bricks cost in the region of £50, a sum that today would barely cover the cost of one of the massive reinforced beams of the concrete M6 bridge. Fine structure though it is, the new bridge will not look as attractive as Brindley's after it has been there for 200 years, if it lasts that long. Brick and stone mellow with age, but concrete becomes stained and jaded soon after it is exposed to our English climate.

Longford bridge carried the lane to Wood Bank until the motorway was built about 1964. This lane was severed by the M6 and is now a backwater, though hardly a quiet one. Today Wood Bank is reached by a magnificent concrete bridge near Longford lock. The canal is on a fairly high embankment here, over the valley of the Woolgarston mill stream, and the bridge crosses the embankment and canal in one sweep. Most pounds along the climb to the summit had individual supplies in addition to the main feed from Calf Heath reservoir. These were to compensate for the irregular rises of the locks and several of the intermediate supplies came from the Teddesley Hay feeder. The auxiliary supply for the pound below Longford lock left the mill stream higher up the valley and entered the canal next to a clump of trees a few yards before the present Wood Bank bridge. It is many years since the feeder was last used and motorway construction swept away all trace of it. All water from the northern end of the Teddesley Hay feeder now runs into the stream and it also collects the overflow from Spring Slade and Pottall reservoirs. Two mills were driven by the stream and the lower one at Woolgarston, known as the 'bone mill' was 300yd from the canal. Hazel mill, higher up the valley, was an iron forge early in the 18th century and later it was used to grind corn.

9¼   *Longford Lock & Broom Bridge (No. 87)*   36⅞

Some distance from Longford bridge lies Longford lock, deeper than average with a rise of 10ft. Bridge No. 87 across the lock tail is obviously a later addition, since it is called 'Broom bridge' and is built around the massive stone blocks of the lock approach. Now an accommodation bridge, it used to carry the track leading to Wolgarston bone mill. When the canal was constructed, bridges were built over lock tails wherever possible, utilising the fall of the lock to avoid the cost and effort of providing long ramps. We have seen examples of this at Tixall, Shutt Hill and Parkgate, but here is an instance of a later bridge that is similarly sited. The flood-weir for the next pound is immediately above Longford lock and the channel from it drains into the stream from Wolgarston and Hazel mills.

10   *Penkridge Wharf, Lock & Bridge (No. 86)*   36⅛

Longford lock still stands amid fields, but the town of Penkridge is just around the next bend, where a recent housing estate backs on to the canal. Like Acton Trussell, Penkridge has seen many changes over the years, only here the effects are more pronounced. It was once a quiet market town straddling the turnpike road between Wolverhampton and Stafford, but when the Staffs &

Worcs came, it spread eastwards to meet it. Although Penkridge was an important centre throughout the canal era, the next major change was not until the late 1930s, when a dual carriageway was constructed along much of the old turnpike, now the A449 trunk road. For the next 30 years heavy lorries thundered down the main street on their way between industrial towns of the Midlands, but now the M6 motorway acts as a bypass and Penkridge is relatively quiet again. It has good communications with neighbouring towns, through the electrified main line and motorway, and is becoming a 'dormitory' town, though some light industry has moved here. This trend can be seen from the canal as it passes by the fringe of Penkridge. Housing estates start near Longford lock and continue until well beyond Filance bridge (No. 84).

In recent years there has been another significant development at Penkridge; it has become an important cruising and boatbuilding centre. Although the principal maintenance depot for the canal was at Stourport until nationalisation, there was a small yard at Penkridge wharf. One of the few employees of the old Company who was still working for the Waterways Board in 1972, Charlie Merrick, was in fact an apprentice carpenter there in the 1920s and later he became a bricklayer at Penkridge yard. The section between Gailey and Haywood is now the responsibility of Fradley depot on the Trent & Mersey Canal and late in 1968 the wharf at Penkridge was taken over by the Bijou Line Cruiser Company. This firm has since expanded rapidly. The wharf has been extended and piled to provide extra space for mooring and the neighbouring winding hole cleared out to enable full-length narrow boats to turn there again. Bijou Line is one of the few hire companies that offer the useful facility of a one-way cruise. By prior arrangement, hirers can start or end their cruise at Penkridge or the other centres owned by the company at Gargrave on the Leeds & Liverpool Canal and Lapworth on the Stratford Canal. More recently a second firm, Canal & Rivercraft Ltd, has been established at Penkridge wharf, who construct and fit-out boats for private customers and hire firms. The old house and other buildings at the wharf have been renovated and are well adapted to their new rôle, and it is a pity that some of the wharf buildings at Radford could not have received similar treatment.

A curious object was dredged from the winding hole by the Waterways Board—the trunk of an elm tree, split down the middle and planed to an octagonal section. The centre is bored out to form a pipe about 1ft in diameter and one end is closed by a leather flap-valve. It was probably the bottom 15ft or so of a pump cylinder from a pit shaft, dating from the early or middle 19th century, but how it came to be in the canal at Penkridge is a mystery. Next to Penkridge lock is the skeleton of an ice breaker that used to work on the northern section.

The supplementary feed to the pound above Penkridge lock entered the canal at the wharf, although the leat behind the buildings has now disappeared. The feeder was only a short one from the stream that runs under the wharf and canal to join the Penk on the other side of the town. The headwaters of this stream are near the Teddesley Hay leat, near its junction with the drainage channel from Littleton colliery. In addition to letting the Company have water from his estates, Lord Hatherton also arranged for water from his mine at Huntington to join the main feeder system. Today this only follows the leat for a few yards, before being diverted into the stream.

Penkridge bridge (No. 86) is yet another variant of Brindley's standard pattern. Here the semi-circular arch, which would not be out of place across the chancel of a Norman church, only spans the canal. The appearance of the arch is completely spoilt by a pipe and recent footbridge, but there are better examples a little farther on at Otherton and Rodbaston. The towing path has a miniature tunnel all to itself that appears to be of later date. No. 86 is the first of several original bridges across lock tails of the Staffs & Worcs that do not include the towing path. This may have been an economy measure, for it is both easier and cheaper to build a bridge if the towing path is omitted. The combination of a lock with a narrow bridge across the tail is a common feature of Brindley's canals. It must have been assumed that boatmen could easily unhitch their horses and lead them over the road while their boats were locking up or down. This system may have worked well enough while traffic was fairly light, but it was soon changed. Separate arches were sometimes added on the earlier canals, as probably happened at Penkridge, and later canals had a towpath under all bridges, except where split bridges were provided.

No. 86 has also been extended to the north, allowing the B5102 road to be widened. This happened to most bridges carrying major roads and here, as elsewhere, the extension encroaches on the lock. The balance beams of the bottom gates had to be shortened, making them difficult to open, and arches were let into the bridge parapet to give clearance to the shortened beams. Modern technology has come to the rescue and now there are cranked beams of steel, but the gates are still difficult to work!

Penkridge lock, with a rise of 9ft, has cast-iron quoins for the gates, inscribed 'P 1933'. The wooden quoins on most locks along the Staffs & Worcs were changed during the period 1925 to 1938 and the iron ones usually have the initial letter of the lock, in this case 'P' for Penkridge, and the date of replacement. Some weirs were raised about this time, reputedly to reduce dredging costs, and the lock improvements may have been part of the same scheme. The levels quoted in this guide are taken from the Company's section of the canal, dated 1908, and present levels are sometimes slightly different. If this has occurred, the towing path has often been raised a few inches under bridges.

Until recently there was an old wooden notice next to the lock, erected by the Canal Company and carrying a barely legible notice warning would-be trespassers. This was an unusual relic, for the majority of notices along the Staffs & Worcs were of enamelled steel sheet, with black lettering on a white background. Signs of this type are usually associated with railways rather than canals, where cast iron was normally used for the purpose, but it must be remembered that the canal was active and independent right up to nationalisation in 1947. The enamel signs were about the only concession made by the Company towards the 20th century. The observant might still find an occasional notice, but most have been removed by vandals or souvenir hunters and a few forlorn wooden 'crosses' near locks and bridges are all that is left.

Also near the lock is the 'Boat Inn', another pub that was built because of the canal and was used by the boatmen. There are several rings for casual mooring above the lock and the licensee will provide snacks for present-day travellers along the canal.

There are other pubs in Penkridge and one of them, an old coaching inn ½ mile away in the main street, commemorates the Littleton family. The 'Littleton Arms' retains several features of its days as a staging post on the coach route between Birmingham and Liverpool or Manchester. The Littletons are also remembered, perhaps more conventionally, in the fine medieval church at Penkridge. Their memorials are excellent examples of carved alabaster, a form of gypsum that came from Tutbury in Staffordshire. Large quantities of the mineral have been mined and quarried from the Keuper Marls there since the 12th century. Alabaster was widely used for ornaments and memorials, particularly during the 18th and 19th centuries, and much of it was carried by canal to other parts of Britain or for shipment abroad.

10⅛   *Princefield Bridge (No. 85)*   36

Penkridge wharf extends as far as Princefield bridge (No. 85). There was a mid-19th-century Company cottage here until 1972 and the 1880 Ordnance Survey shows a weighing machine between the cottage and the canal. The bridge is an original one and it carries Francis Green Lane, at one time the main drive between the Littleton's hall at Pillaton and Penkridge. Pillaton Old Hall, a mile to the east of the canal and on the other side of the M6, was on the verge of collapse in Sir Edward Littleton's day, but it has outlived the mansion he built in Teddesley Park. The Tudor brick hall, with the earlier stone chapel of St Modwena attached to it, is a sinister overgrown place, partly inhabited and partly ruined. It is little wonder that Sir Edward chose to move his household to Teddesley.

10⅛-10¼   *Filance Lock & Bridge (No. 84)*   36-35⅞
            Lyne Hill Bridge (No. 83)

Filance lock, a deep one, did not have a keeper's house and it probably came under the control of the keeper at Penkridge. No two locks are identical on the Staffs & Worcs and the appeal of Filance is its size and simplicity, with massive wing-walls at the tail leading straight to the bottom gates, unobscured by a foot-bridge.

There is a storm-water weir on the way to Filance bridge (No.

84). The sills of storm-water weirs are slightly higher than on lock weirs and they act as 'safety valves' if the level of the canal should rise suddenly. Next to Filance bridge is the 'Cross Keys', a well-known canalside pub (Plate 13). The stretch between here and Filance lock was a popular mooring place in the canal's heyday and the appearance of the pub and Brindley's bridge in these times is recorded by de Maré in *The Canals of England*. Penkridge now sprawls as far as Filance, but the 'Cross Keys' is still very much a canalside hostellry. Although a sign proclaims that 'All Boating Enthusiasts are Welcome', those with other canal interests are not excluded!

At last Penkridge is left behind by the time Lyne Hill bridge (No. 83) is reached. This is quite an interesting bridge, for a remote and narrow one of the accommodation variety that leads nowhere in particular. The arch has an unusually shallow curve, the sides are straight and partly of sandstone and the wing walls are of stone. This must be an early bridge, but in no way does it conform to Brindley's pattern. The towing path under the arch is edged with 'diamond' blue bricks and may have been raised slightly at some time.

11   *Otherton Lock & Bridge (No. 82)*   35⅛

A little imagination is required to appreciate the picturesqueness that Otherton once had. The lock house has been demolished and only the garden wall remains, the texture of the massive sandstone blocks in the bridge is lost under a coat of white paint and the bridge plate has gone. Even so, it has not been possible to disguise the classic lines of the lock tail at Otherton. The lock itself is another deep one and it has an iron bar running along the towpath side. These bars were fitted along many of the locks to prevent towlines from wearing away the brickwork because the abrasive action of grit-laden towlines was considerable. Most locks retain their original sandstone edging on the offside, whereas the side adjoining the towpath has usually been rebuilt.

The water from the lock weir disappears under the site of the house and then, instead of joining the canal again below the lock, runs to waste along a small stream. This is surprising, when the Company went to great lengths to conserve every drop of water, but a close look in the undergrowth reveals that originally this was part of the feeder system. The diverted stream is only a little lower than the canal and the two run side by side for some distance. Near the lock tail are two other channels, one from the lock weir and one leading back to the canal, with the remains of a sluice at the junction. Water could be diverted into the canal from the stream or weir and it could also run to waste, depending on the level of the canal. The Teddesley Hay feeder crosses the stream near its source and water from the feeder still runs into it.

$11\frac{1}{8}$-$11\frac{1}{4}$ *Otherton Lane Bridge (No. 81)* 35-$34\frac{7}{8}$
            & Otherton (Littleton Colliery) Basin

The M6 motorway approaches the canal at Otherton and then follows it as far as Rodbaston. In the shadow of the motorway is Otherton Lane bridge (No. 81), with some early work of red sandstone and recent parapets. The railway bridge ahead is also recent by canal standards. It was built about 1900 when the earlier tramway from Cannock & Huntington colliery was rebuilt and extended to join the main line at Penkridge.

It is hard to visualise the hive of activity that could be seen at Littleton colliery basin little more than 20 years ago. Boats carried coal from here to Stourport Power Station until mid 1949 and this was one of the last sources of commercial traffic on the canal. When the station opened in 1926 all coal consumed there went by canal, but a mere 20,000 tons, 5% of the total, travelled by water in 1949, and 13,000 tons started its journey at Otherton.

The original basin at Otherton was 8oft wide and 1ooft long and there was provision for two boats to be loaded from tubs or trucks at wharves along each side. When the present railway was built in 1900/2, the basin was lengthened to 330ft and a raised pier constructed down the middle, so that trucks could unload directly into boats underneath it (Plate 14). These improvements increased the length of wharfage to about 1,000ft and up to 12 boats could be loaded simultaneously. This vast basin was filled in when the M6 was built, but some of its coal sidings on the other side of the motorway are still in use. The site of the entrance can just about be discerned, opposite a concrete wharf on the main canal.

The railway line is absolutely straight from Otherton basin to Littleton colliery, a distance of 2⅜ miles. It also has a fairly uniform slope of 1:45, except where the gradient eases towards the canal and steepens slightly near the colliery. Although the line is now standard gauge, the earthworks may have been intended for a tramway where tubs from the pithead could travel down the incline direct to Otherton basin. Whatever the original plan, the tramway never carried coal and the 1883 Ordnance Survey map does not show any track within 1,000ft of the colliery.

The story of the railway and colliery is an interesting one. Besides being closely allied to the fortunes of the Staffs & Worcs in the present century, the events at Huntington were typical of the difficulties met by mine owners as they had to dig deeper and farther afield to find workable seams. The tramway and first basin at Otherton were built while two shafts were being sunk by the Cannock and Huntington Colliery Company about 1878. These shafts were on the Teddesley estate and the mineral rights were then owned by the 2nd Lord Hatherton, Edward Richard, who inherited the property in April 1863. The first 360ft of both shafts passed through the Bunter Pebble Beds and considerable quantities of water were encountered. Until recently the bulk of the domestic water supplies for the Midlands came from these strata and the South Staffordshire Waterworks Company still has a pumping station at Huntington. The water was an embarrassment to the mining company, but they managed to keep it at bay by lining the shaft. Then, when they had penetrated 60ft into the Coal Measures and thought that the danger had passed, water broke in and rapidly filled both shafts. The company were unable to drain the shafts and the mine was abandoned before any coal had been raised. Work on the tramway ceased and Otherton basin became derelict without ever being used.

Meanwhile the Cannock coal industry went from strength to strength and in April 1888 the 3rd Lord Hatherton, Edward George Percy, inherited a vast fortune in coal and two flooded shafts. Frustrated by lost Royalties, Lord Hatherton employed S. & J. Bailey, Mining Engineers of Birmingham, ten years later to pump the shafts dry and increase their depth to 1,620ft. In 1899 the Littleton Colliery Company was formed, headed by Charles Holcroft of Kingswinford. The railway was built to standard gauge using the existing earthworks and was at the same time extended to join the L&NWR main line at Littleton Colliery Sidings, near Penkridge. The two winding shafts, a third shaft to drain the mine and the railway were completed early in 1902 and production started soon afterwards. A quarter of a million pounds had been spent in developing Littleton colliery, but almost 100ft of coal had been proved and Lord Hatherton's confidence in the mine was soon justified. Over 1,000 men were employed there by 1908 and this number was still increasing in the 1920s when most pits in the Black Country were closing down. Coal has always been the main cargo carried by Midland waterways and in the early days the Staffs & Worcs Company relied heavily on the Black Country canals for trade. Much of the coal carried by the Staffs & Worcs during the present century came from the Cannock Coalfield and Littleton was one of the main suppliers. For many years the mine was by far the largest in South Staffordshire and is one of the mere half-dozen that are still in use. The mine did not have a particularly good record of safety in the early days and it was sometimes known as the 'Slaughter Pit'. When jobs were hard to obtain during the years of depression, it is said that men would wait outside the gates to fill a vacancy created by a fatality underground!

$11\frac{3}{4}$ *Rodbaston Lock & Bridge (No. 80)* $34\frac{3}{8}$

Rodbaston bridge (No. 80, Plate 15) is another fine example of the type already met at Otherton and Penkridge, but again the lock house has been demolished. It was still there during the building of the motorway and the Ministry of Transport went to great trouble and no little expense to build an accommodation bridge over the road for the benefit of the lock keeper. Unfortunately, the lock keeper could not live with his noisy neighbour, after the previous seclusion of Rodbaston. Within a very short time of the opening of the motorway about 1966, he left Rodbaston and the house was pulled down. However, a local farmer and fishermen find the bridge useful and it provides a safe point of access to the canal.

The lock weir at Rodbaston is smaller than others along this section and sooner or later the canal was sure to object to this

violation of engineering principles. After a long period of torrential rain, the low embankment between Rodbaston and Boggs
locks was breached during the night of Saturday, 26th May 1969.
The land between the canal and motorway was flooded and, to
make matters worse, the culvert under the bank was blocked by
debris. This normally carries surplus water from Gailey 'New'
reservoirs and a supply from the lower one flowed into the canal
for the first time for many years. The Annual Rally of the Staffs
& Worcs Canal Society was being held at Penkridge at the time
and most of the boats involved were marooned by the breach.
However, the Waterways Board achieved the remarkable feat of
repairing the bank and reopening the canal by the following
Tuesday. The storm-water weir that should have taken the surplus
is actually below the lock, near the site of another supply from the
Teddesley Hay feeder. This source of water was still in use in the
early days of nationalisation and control was effected by means of
a weir and couple of sluices a short distance upstream.

Rodbaston, or Redbaston, as it used to be, is the first of four
locks that are quite close together, compared with others on the
Staffs & Worcs. The Canal Company even regarded the group as
a flight, although there is ¼ mile between each lock. They only
built keeper's houses by the top and bottom locks and the 1933/6
iron quoins are inscribed G4 (Rodbaston) to G1 (Gailey). Rodbaston lock has a rise of 9ft 6in. and the remainder have equal
rises of 8ft 0in.

12⅛-12⅜   *Boggs & Brick-kiln Locks*   34-33¾

Boggs and Brick-kiln locks are an impressive pair and full of
interest. Both have the familiar 'in and out' stone quoins of original locks on the canal (Plate 16) and yet both have undergone
substantial changes. Bradshaw's map of 1830 (Plate 81) shows the
four locks of the flight as having quite different rises, varying
between 6ft 6in. and 9ft 6in. No steps appear to have been taken
to compensate for the irregular lock heights by means of separate
supplies for each pound and the Company must have relied on
lock keepers letting water down the flight to keep traffic moving.
If the information given by Bradshaw is correct, this system was
tolerated for the best part of a century and the locks must then

have been altered. To attain the present heights, Brick-kiln would have been raised by 18in. and Boggs lowered by the same amount, giving them rises of 8ft, as at Gailey. There are no obvious signs of this work being carried out, except that enormous weirs and bypass channels were added to both locks about the middle of the 19th century. The channel at Brick-kiln runs parallel to the canal and behind a wooded island for 200yd, in order to slow down the flow and reduce silting of the canal. The lie of the land prevented this from being done at Boggs and here the channel widens out before joining the canal. In this way substantial quantities of water run unimpeded from the summit level and Calf Heath reservoir down to Rodbaston lock and this probably accounted for the breach of 1969.

The name of Boggs lock may refer to the area of peaty land nearby that was a swamp until it was drained. Bricks were obviously made near the next lock at some time, perhaps when the canal was being built.

The improvements to these locks were probably carried out when Gailey reservoirs were constructed. There are two reservoirs, the upper and lower, and they were 'New' because the earlier one at Calf Heath had been there for almost a hundred years when they were built. The supply from the lower pool entered the canal near the tail of Boggs lock. The feeder from it is now severed by the M6 motorway, but it had fallen into disuse long before the road was built. The upper reservoir connected with the Teddesley Hay feeder and received its supply from the lower one, partly by gravity and partly by means of a steam pump. The levels differed by about 3ft and the engine house and sluices can still be seen on the bank between the two reservoirs (Plate 17), though for many years the engine has been replaced by an electric pump. The reservoirs no longer supply the canal, but both are still owned by the Waterways Board. The lower one is used by a yachting club and the other is at present tenanted only by wildlife.

12⅝   *Gailey Wharf, Lock & Bridge (No. 79)*   33½

There has been a wharf at Gailey since the opening of the Staffs & Worcs. There are two reasons for its importance in the early days of the canal era. The first is that at Gailey the canal is crossed by

Watling Street, Britain's finest Roman road that sweeps across the country from Canterbury and London to Uriconium and then swings south towards Hereford. It was an important thorough-fare until Telford engineered his Holyhead Road in the 1820s, but it again came into its own, as the A5, when Telford's road through the Black Country became congested. Gailey was therefore an important wharf for the transit of goods for many years. The second reason for Gailey's prominence is perhaps not uncon-nected with the first. It was the site chosen by Brindley for his summit lock and it was here that one of the main water supplies joined the canal. The earliest reservoir is at Calf Heath, and is about the same age as the canal. The feeder from it runs along-side the A5 for 600yd and disappears under a house to join the canal at Gailey wharf. Although it is not normally used now-adays, the feeder is kept clear and could supply the canal if re-quired. The Teddesley Hay feeder, with all its ramifications, ran into Calf Heath reservoir and a later leat brought water from the Hatherton Branch.

The most striking feature at Gailey is the 'round house' (Plate 18), the only house of this type along the canal that is still in-habited. It is not known why these tower-like houses were built in this way, but the reason usually given is that they enabled toll clerks to have a clear view of the canal in each direction. This is certainly not true of the one at Gothersley, for this was simply a wharfhouse, and so also was the round house at Gailey in all probability, as the toll office was at the other end of the lock. There are numerous round houses along the Thames & Severn Canal of the late 1780s, a canal in which the S&WCCo. showed considerable interest. The Company contributed to the cost of surveying the Thames & Severn and generally did all it could to promote the undertaking. Perhaps the Committee simply liked the appearance of the round houses and wanted a few on their own canal! The round houses at Gailey and Gothersley were built about 1804/5. There are various other cottages and warehouses at Gailey and wharves line both sides of the canal.

There was a pub, the 'Plough', and stables at Gailey, but these were swept away when the A5 was widened. Brindley's bridge also suffered when this happened and only a few traces of his work remain on No. 79. As at Penkridge, there is a later arch for the towing path and the bridge was also extended to the north, the bottom gates now having cranked beams.

The hire fleet of Gailey Canal Cruisers, established by Ernie Thomas in the early 1960s, was based at the wharf here and appropriately the firm's slogan is 'Go Gailey'. In 1967 he moved his fleet to Hatherton Junction, but the wharf and gardens still bear signs of Ernie's handiwork, though they are not as immaculate as they used to be. The wharf, which has an old crane, is set at an angle to the main canal so that boats can turn, and part of it is built over the end of the $8\frac{1}{4}$-mile feeder from Calf Heath reservoir and Spring Slade pool.

4

The Summit Level

GAILEY TO COMPTON

At Gailey the Staffs & Worcs ends its climb of 100ft from the
Trent valley. The next lock is 10 miles away where the long
descent to the Severn starts at Compton. The summit pound
crosses sandstones of the Lower Keuper series, but rarely do
these rocks appear at the surface. They have on several occasions
been planed by glaciers moving over them, only to be covered by
sand and gravel as the glaciers retreated. These events of long ago
gave Brindley an ideal route for his canal across the main watershed of England. Aside from one minor detour, he was able to
steer a straight and level course towards Compton at about 340ft
above sea level and with few cuttings or embankments.

$13\frac{1}{4}$ *Gravelly Way Bridge (No. 78)* $32\frac{7}{8}$

The first settlement along the canal after Gailey is Gravelly Way.
Its name, in common with Calf, Slade and Coven Heaths, is a
reminder of the effect the last ice age had on the landscape, though
the pebbly heathlands have been under cultivation for many years.
There are remains of a wharf near Gravelly Way farm and the
building may once have served as a wharfhouse.

Immediately after Gravelly Way bridge (No. 78) the canal
plunges without warning into the industrial region of Four
Ashes (Plate 19). This is mainly a one-sided affair, for opposite
the odorous works of the Midlands-Yorkshire Tar Distillery the
canal is flanked by Calf Heath Wood. The distillery was formerly

a branch of the MTD whose main plant was at Oldbury on the Birmingham Canal, prior to its demolition in 1973. This was the destination of the 'gas' and 'tar' boats of Thomas Clayton (Oldbury) Ltd that delivered liquid cargoes there from gas works all over the Midlands until 1965. The S&WCCo. naturally hoped for similar traffic when part of the works was 'evacuated' to Four Ashes during the Second World War. Although the distillery is ideally situated for canal transport, the expected trade did not materialise and all materials and refined products travel by road or rail.

13⅞   *Calf Heath Bridge (No. 77)*   32¼

Calf Heath bridge (No. 77) is at Four Ashes, but it is not called by that name for the simple reason that Four Ashes did not exist when the canal was built. The community here originated around the canal wharf and has since spread towards the railway station and main A449 road. The wharf served local farms and perhaps small forges along the Penk in the early days and continued to be used when most rural wharves had fallen into decay. The reason is that cargoes for the 'Black Works' were delivered here earlier this century. The winding hole near bridge No. 77 was excavated at about this time, though as often as not boats had to back to Hatherton Junction before they could turn. A small warehouse and weighing office still stand behind the wharf and across the road is a letter box where mail has been posted for almost a century. Calf Heath bridge has been widened and its 'hump' removed for the benefit of traffic from the works and gravel pits around Four Ashes, but has managed to keep part of its original arch.

A few yards from No. 77 at the entrance to the 'Black Works' is a clue to the mysterious process that went on there. An iron container with a plaque proclaims 'Pan process for making lamp black brought to England by Auguste Wegelin of Cologne 1911 and used at Four Ashes to 1957'. One would hardly expect to find a carbon-black works here in the midst of rural Staffordshire and it is even more surprising to discover one that is obviously proud of its contribution to industrial history. The whole process depended on a plentiful supply of turpentine and this was delivered by boats belonging to Thomas Clayton. These boats were as black as the carbon they were helping to produce and were a far cry from the brightly painted craft usually associated with the narrow canals, including those of Clayton in later years.

Before he started as an apprentice carpenter with the Canal Company at Penkridge yard, Charlie Merrick went to school in Four Ashes. This was not long after the First World War and as he journeyed to and from school, Charlie watched the chimneys of the 'Black Works' grow higher and higher as the works were being built. He was probably witnessing an early attempt to move industry away from the Black Country, at a time when mining in the South Staffordshire Coalfield was declining rapidly. The works are still there and the experiment may perhaps be regarded as successful, but many years elapsed before other firms moved to Four Ashes. Although the industrial estate may not have developed as quickly as was intended, Four Ashes has recently become world famous for its deposits of gravel. This is not so much due to the quality or quantity of the sand and gravel here as the story of the ice age that unfolded as they were worked.

The story starts a little over 80,000 years ago, when retreating ice carved an uneven surface on the Keuper Sandstone to form the floor of the present quarries. Rivers from a remote glacier to the north then brought down sand and gravel to cover the eroded surface to a depth of about 10ft. While this was happening, the climate changed several times from intense cold to fairly warm and the landscape varied from tundra to steppe. The clue to these events lies in layers of peaty loam that occur at intervals throughout the gravels and sometimes contain fragments of beatles and plants. The ice returned for the last time about 20,000 years ago, carrying clay boulders from as far afield as West Scotland and the Lake District, to form the present land surface. Present working of the gravels is mainly restricted to deposits on the east of the canal, but there are old pits on both sides where these features can sometimes be seen. The peaty layers are fairly local, but otherwise the pits give us an idea of what underlies most of the summit level of the Staffs & Worcs.

$14\frac{3}{8}$ *Long Molls Bridge (No. 76)* $31\frac{3}{4}$

The Staffs & Worcs turns sharply to the east at Calf Heath bridge, along the only major deviation from a straight line drawn between Baswich and Stourport. The canal continues its easterly course until Saredon brook is crossed near Hatherton Junction and then returns to the original line at Slade Heath. Saredon valley is not deep and could have been crossed on an embankment without too much trouble. The detour may have been to save building a long bank, but it is interesting to speculate that Brindley chose this devious route to avoid a vast lake that occupied the floor of the valley above Deepmore mill. Bradshaw clearly shows a lake at this point on his map of 1830, but contemporary cartographers were not so emphatic about it. Inaccuracies occur elsewhere on Bradshaw's map, but if the lake existed, the canal followed the shoreline for well over a mile and crossed a backwater on a short embankment.

Near Long Molls bridge (No. 76) the canal runs along the fringe of Calf Heath. This is now mainly under cultivation, but the long straight roads and pebbly soil are typical of heathlands. By way of contrast the lane over No. 76 twists and turns over Saredon valley, crossing the brook by an old iron bridge near the headwaters of 'Bradshaw's Lake'. Long Moll would be delighted to know that her name is immortalised by one of the best examples of Brindley's bridges on the Staffs & Worcs. She must surely have been a legendary character when the bridge was built two centuries ago and her secret will perhaps be revealed one day.

14⅞   *Hatherton Junction (Plate 20)*   31

Haywood Junction may have decayed in recent years, but the same cannot be said of Hatherton. A little over seven years ago Ernie Thomas brought his hire-fleet here from Gailey to create Calf Heath Marina and today Hatherton Junction is thriving as never before. Before the 'Thomas Takeover' there was nothing here except a couple of bridges, the canal manager's house, Calf Heath locks and the toll clerk's cottage. Now there are wharves, boats, a general store that supplies the needs of both locals and boaters, a licensed restaurant and boatyard, all set amidst rose gardens.

Few were better qualified than Ernie Thomas to operate a cruising centre and boatyard. His father started work on the 'cut' in 1868 when Churchbridge locks at the other end of the Hatherton branch were brand new and the Staffs & Worcs itself was less than a century old. Ernie joined him on the canals in 1910 and thereafter worked with 'day boats', aside from serving in the army during the First World War. 'Day boats' or 'Joeys' were by far the commonest type of canal craft, particularly in the Midlands, and were used over fairly short distances. If they had a cabin, it was a small affair compared with the living quarters on the long-distance 'monkey boats'. Not so very long ago the firm of E. Thomas (Walsall) Ltd had about 400 of these boats at work on the BCN and neighbouring canals, with 17 tugs and 30 mules to haul them. As with most carriers on the BCN, the firm's main traffic was in coal and at times the fleet carried as much as 10,000 tons a week. Collieries with canal connections closed one by one—among the last to go were Sandwell, Hampstead, Holly Bank, Grove and those around Anglesey basin—and gradually the boats were withdrawn. However, the name of the firm can still be seen on the stern of a few boats around the BCN. In 1972 refuse from Pearce & Cutler on Oozell's Street Loop and Raleigh Industries on the Engine branch was still carried to a tip at Moxley, near Darlaston.

In spite of his successes as a businessman and services to the community as a councillor for Walsall, Ernie Thomas was always a boatman at heart. It comes as no surprise to find that he retired to a spot passed many times with his mule and day boat in years gone by—if running a hire-fleet and marina can be regarded as retirement. When he left Walsall he brought with him a number of his employees, men like Fred Moore who have also spent a lifetime on the 'cut'. Calf Heath Marina is geared to the second Canal Era and is founded on experience gained in the first, with Ernie Thomas providing the link between them until he died in 1973.

The Staffs & Worcs is joined by its most recent branch at Hatherton Junction. The Hatherton branch was built between 1839 and 1840, at a time when mining in the South Staffordshire coalfield was spreading north towards Cannock. The 'Cross Bridge' carrying the towing path to the branch can best be described as more functional than decorative when compared with its counterpart at Haywood, but it is nevertheless of interest. It has no number, lying between bridges 75 and 76, which immediately tells us that the numbering of bridges on the main canal took place before 1839.

Strictly speaking, Hatherton is no longer a junction, for the branch has not been navigable for almost 20 years. The canal is now closed and sections have been sold to riparian owners, but it is a main source of water for the Staffs & Worcs and is used as a drainage channel. The branch climbs 44ft in 3⅜ miles and all the eight locks except one had an equal rise of about 6ft—very much less than on the main line. The section between the junction and the pound above Calf Heath locks is now private property, formerly owned by Ernie Thomas, who lived in the canal manager's house.

Both locks at Calf Heath are in working order and the lower one is used to teach novice boaters the rudiments of lock operation. Below the lock is one of the many attractive features to be found around Hatherton. Before running into the canal, surplus water from the pound above the lock flows over a battlemented weir and then cascades through a water garden. The cottage next to the bottom lock, now a store, was once the home of the toll clerk. In the early days of this century when traffic was at its peak, Bill Farr collected tolls on loads entering and leaving the Hatherton Branch. Bill had an attractive daughter whose boyfriend from Wolverhampton used to bring him a bottle of 'Scotch' when visiting Hatherton. One day when she was filling a vase of roses with water from the canal in preparation for such a visit, the girl fell into the pound between the locks and was drowned. Bill idolised his daughter and he never fully recovered from the shock.

Although the shallowness of locks on the Hatherton branch simplified water control, it had a curious side effect of great inconvenience to the boatmen. Bottom gates of locks have a 'footboard' to enable boatmen to cross the lock when operating gates and paddles. On this branch the footboards are much narrower than on the rest of the Staffs & Worcs and Ernie related how this was done for the benefit of the 'Glosters'. These were highly individual boaters from Gloucestershire, Young, Rice, Walker, Dudfield and others, who were more akin to farmers than men who earned their living on the canals. The Glosters carried hay for the pit ponies at Littleton and mines around the top end of the Hatherton branch, returning with loads of coal. The high light loads on the outward journey cleared the deep locks along the main line easily enough, but fouled the footboards along the Hatherton when passing through the open bottom gates. Narrowing the boards enabled the Glosters to increase their hay loads, but working the locks was then a hazardous operation. All this happened a long time ago, but to this day the footboards of Calf Heath locks are narrow.

A side wall has been partly removed from the upper lock of the Calf Heath pair to form an ingenious dry dock and slipway for the boatyard. Although the locks are no longer owned by the Waterways Board, a measuring weir has been installed above the second lock to monitor the supply to the main line. The Thomas territory terminated near the head of this lock, where an old overflow channel leaves the canal. This had a small bridge under the lane to Calf Heath and then joined Saredon brook.

Where it survives, the towing path of the Hatherton branch is often overgrown and much of it is now private property, but the many interesting features of the branch can usually be reached from road bridges without too much difficulty. The rest of the branch is described in full in Chapter 7.

15⅜   *Deepmore Bridge (No. 75) & Wharf*   30¾

The canal crosses a tree-lined embankment after leaving Hatherton Junction and there is a small aqueduct over Saredon brook. This is the bank that separated the backwater from the main expanse of 'Bradshaw's Lake' and the land to the east was notoriously wet when Ernie purchased it. As there was little else that could be done with it, he created a pool here and landscaped the banks and island. The canal turns sharply to the west at the end of the embankment and follows the former 'shoreline', now marked by the leat to Deepmore mill, for about ¾ mile. Deepmore bridge (No. 75) and wharf are about half way along this section. The bridge has a nameplate and was obviously there before 1835, though not long before, judging by its style. If the lake existed, the bridge must have been built after it was drained, or the track between here and the mill would otherwise have been submerged. Deepmore corn mill must have been of some importance, for it had its own wharf next to No. 75 and a winding hole a little way along the canal. It is many years since the wharf was last used, but de Salis mentions it and presumably it was still operative in 1904. After Deepmore bridge the canal continues to follow the 'shore-line' until the mill leat is augmented near No. 74 by the stream from Shareshill. This stream is the boundary between Saredon and Shareshill parishes and on the bridge is a boundary stone inscribed with 'S.P.' on each side. The leat itself may once have supplied the canal, for permission to use water from Saredon brook was granted in the 1770 Act. The leat then contours past some old clay pits and ends at quite a small pond behind the mill.

Did 'Bradshaw's Lake' exist? From evidence on the ground and such information as can be gleaned from old maps, the answer is 'No'. The boundary on Bradshaw's map follows Saredon brook and the long leat to Deepmore mill, and to this day much of the enclosed area is waterlogged after a prolonged wet spell. Brad-shaw, or whoever carried out the survey for him, may have visited the area after a particularly wet winter. On the other hand, he *could* have been right!

16   *Moat House Bridge (No. 74)*   30⅛

Known locally as the 'Moat 'Us', No. 74 carries an unsurfaced byway that has changed little since the canal came. This same lane crosses Long Molls bridge (No. 76), but the County Council lost interest in it at Deepmore mill. The bridge has been rebuilt and red bricks of the earlier one are just visible above the waterline.

The story here is much the same as at Acton Moat (No. 92). Half the moat lies amidst trees in the field to the north of the canal and still has sufficient water to support a wide variety of pond life. As at Acton, one side of the remainder is now canal. Owing to a slight difference in alignment, there is an imperceptible widening of the 'moat' section at the end of the shallow cutting that follows the bridge. Nothing remains of the 'Moat House', but bits of brick, tile and sandstone occur in the black earth bounded by the moat and are best seen when the field is newly ploughed. Other items in the soil include slag and dolerite—hardly what one would expect to find on the site of a medieval moated manor in the midst of rural Staffordshire.

Laches bridge (No. 73) is much later than the canal and is probably about the same age as No. 74, since their styles are similar. The towing path between here and Moat House is in a very bad condition and in places has disappeared altogether. Compared with many 'Cruiseways', the Staffs & Worcs has a good towing path at present for most of the way, though the less considerate cruiser owners are doing what they can to remove it. Rarely is the path a public right of way and it is the responsibility of the Waterways Board only to maintain the banks. At present it has neither the funds nor the staff to do so adequately. Local Authorities are slow to include towing paths with other paths under their control, partly because of liability should an accident occur, but schemes of this nature are likely in future. Far more people use the towing paths than cruise the canals and one hopes that before long these receive the same care and attention as is given to municipal parks.

Towing paths were originally provided for the mules and horses, of course, and their deterioration was one of the factors that brought horse-drawn traffic to an end. From the 1920s onwards motors gradually supplanted horse boats on many canals, but on the Staffs & Worcs they continued until nationalisation. Bank erosion was not the only inconvenience caused by the motors, for they also carried headlamps. Horse boats did not normally have lights at night, as the sudden glare of an approaching boat at a lock or bridge hole could easily cause a horse to end up in the 'cut'. A winding canal is more difficult to navigate in the dark than a straight one and the sharp bends between Slade Heath and Four Ashes were particularly troublesome for boats going 'down' the cut to Haywood. Boatmen travelling 'up' had the benefit of the lights of Wolverhampton and the glare of Black Country furnaces, whereas Stafford was black as pitch. This made a noticeable difference even as far out as Gailey. It was to assist horse boats in night navigation that lock approaches and bridge holes were outlined in white.

With the passing of horse boats went a technique that was a pleasure to watch. This was 'baccering' and 'driving'. When boats travelling in opposite directions met, someone had to be on the towpath to pass one rope over the other. Only one person was needed and he led or 'drove' the horse all the while. Horses going in the opposite direction went on their own, or 'baccered'. The method of working a particular canal was agreed mutually and on the Staffs & Worcs horses heading for Haywood baccered and those in the opposite direction were driven. 'Baccering' is said to have originated from the habit boatmen had of diving into the cabin to fill their pipes, leaving horse and boat to look after themselves. Horses and mules were judged by their ability to baccer and Ernie Thomas once had one trained to perfection. Long before an approaching boat came into view, this mule's ears would shoot forward, giving Ernie ample time to nip ashore at the next bridge if need be.

The canal makes another sharp turn at the end of Laches Wood, this time to the south to rejoin the line it followed from Baswich to Four Ashes. Calf Heath bridge is just under a mile away, but the 'Deepmore detour' has added a further 2 miles to the journey. The railway from Manchester and Liverpool to Birmingham approaches the canal here and for no obvious reason there is a recent-looking concrete wharf just around the corner. The reason in fact disappeared in 1969, when the steam-driven pump of the South Staffordshire Waterworks Co. was dismantled and the engine house demolished. Electric pumps were then installed, but coal had not been delivered at the wharf for several years, probably since the closure of Littleton colliery and Hawkins's basins.

There were two basic requirements for pumping stations built towards the end of the last century—rocks containing an inexhaustible supply of water and easy transport of coal. The former are abundant along the Staffs & Worcs and many earlier stations of the SSWCo. are sited along the canal. The water in the Bunter Pebble Beds at Littleton colliery has always been a nuisance, but at Slade Heath it supplies Midland towns at a rate of 2 million gallons or more a day. Although the Lower Keuper Sandstone has very much less water and underlies the greater part of the summit level, this formation is absent around Slade and Coven Heaths. After a few feet of glacial 'drift', the boreholes pass through the older Upper Mottled Sandstone for 150ft before penetrating about 300ft of Pebble Beds, and both strata contain considerable quantities of water. The siting of this pumping station was obviously the result of a careful survey. Boreholes a little to the north or south along the canal would have been much deeper to achieve the same yield. Similar reasoning accounts for the siting of most pumping stations along the canal.

There is another borehole near Aspley farm, in the field opposite Laches Wood. A trial boring for coal was made here in 1900 and four seams were found at depths of between 1,800 and 2,000ft. It is doubtful if a mine was ever envisaged here and the trial may have been to see if there was sufficient coal to justify extending Holly Bank colliery in this direction. Later the whole area was perforated with borings as a preliminary to the sinking of Hilton Main shaft in December 1919. Although there is coal at depth along much of the Staffs & Worcs, there were plenty of more accessible seams a few miles to the east and nowhere does the canal bear the scars of mining activity.

| 17⅛ | *Slade Heath Bridge (No. 72)* | 29 |

The railway crosses the canal just before Slade Heath bridge (No. 72). This was the Grand Junction Railway that opened to passengers on 4th July 1837, making it one of the earliest main lines in the country. If the bridge is original, as it certainly appears to be, it is a tribute to the early railway engineers. The line is now heavily used by express electric passenger and freight trains. The bridge helps us to date the number plates on the canal bridges. The Act for the railway was passed in 1834 and the bridge is not included in the sequence, so the plates were fitted between the building of the 'Fancy' (No. 89) and the railway bridge, in 1835 or 1836.* Subsequently the Grand Junction became part of the L&NWR and then the L&MSR with the grouping of 1924. There is quite a sharp bend where the railway crosses the canal and the corners of the bridge are protected by much-grooved rollers on the towpath side.

Slade Heath bridge is another that has seen many changes. Original work is now confined to the lower courses of the southern half. It has been extended to the north using blue bricks

* It may have been the policy of the Staffs & Worcs Company to exclude railway bridges from the system of numbering. If this is the case, the dating of bridge plates is between 1835 and the building of Cross bridge at the Hatherton Junction about 1839.

and the final stage was the rebuilding of the older arch in brindled brick. The reason why an apparently minor road bridge has received so much attention is that until the Stafford to Wolverhampton road was realigned it crossed the canal by No. 72, again at Cross Green (No. 71) and finally at Coven Heath (bridge No. 70). The A449 trunk road of the 1930s avoids bridges 71 and 72 altogether, leaving Slade Heath on an 'abandoned loop'. This is an early example of a feature of the countryside that has become commonplace in recent years.

$17\frac{5}{8}$ *Cross Green Bridge (No. 71) & Wharf* $28\frac{1}{2}$

Few boatmen on the Midland canals did not know of Cross Green. Nearly every pub along the Staffs & Worcs had stabling where the boaters could leave their mules overnight, but the 'Anchor' at Cross Green had a long row of stables, so popular was it as a stopping place. Locals used canalside pubs, of course, but they were quiet, dreary places until the boating families arrived, often quite late at night. The horses were given hay in the stables while the canal folk enjoyed themselves in the 'public'. In the days of horse boats, the men played bar quoits interminably. It was many years before darts appeared in the public bars.

The 'Anchor' of today bears little resemblance to the pub that was here at the turn of the century, but it is still popular with users of the canal. Boats can moor here for short periods and snacks or meals can be obtained.

Cross Green bridge (No. 71) has suffered much the same treatment as No. 72 and for the same reasons, but with an important difference. When the builder extended the 1769 bridge he took the trouble to include a sandstone block inscribed '1822'. It is a pity that others did not follow his example when modifying works along the canal. The stage-coach era was at its peak in the 1820s and it could be that the turnpike road and bridges 71 and 72 were modernised to improve the service between Birmingham and Liverpool or Manchester.

Old wharves crowd one after the other along this section of canal. There may have been one at Slade Heath and they were certainly at Cross Green and the next two bridges. The Staffs & Worcs is usually regarded as a link in the chain of waterways between Birmingham or the Black Country and the coast, but with so many rural wharves it is clear that a considerable trade originated or terminated on the canal. There is no obvious association between these wharves and any village, estate or farm, but all were on the turnpike road. As at Gailey, their main function was presumably for the interchange of goods between road and canal. The cottage near No. 71 looks as though it started life as a wharfhouse and the winding hole between bridges 71 and 72 is one of several cleared out recently to enable the excursion boats from Calf Heath to turn. The presence of a winding hole near a wharf could be significant, for it would only be needed if boats habitually ended their journey at the wharf rather than called there to deliver a part load.

18⅛   *Brinsford (Stafford Road) Bridge (No. 70) & Wharf*   28

No. 70 is usually known as Stafford Road bridge, though de Salis prefers 'Coven Heath Bridge and Second Wharf', and its correct name is Brinsford. The old turnpike road from Stafford to Wolverhampton crossed the canal for the third time here, but No. 70 is the only crossing of the present A449. The bridge was completely rebuilt with the typical brick walls and concrete decking of the late 1930s when the road was widened and realigned. The style is not the only difference between this and earlier bridges. When the Staffs & Worcs was built, any necessary deviations were made by the road rather than the canal, but now the canal has to negotiate No. 70 as best it can. As the canal resumes its southerly course after the S-bend, the towing path crosses one of the main storm-water weirs of the summit level.

18½   *Coven Heath Bridge (No. 69) & Wharf*   27⅝

The first signs that the canal is approaching Wolverhampton are at Coven Heath, for there is a small sewage works owned by the town's Corporation next to bridge No. 69. About a million gallons of treated effluent enter the canal every day from this works. Although the waterway was sometimes known as the Wolverhampton Canal and the Company's Head Office was in the town, a difference in level of about 150ft prevented the canal from actually passing through the town centre. Coven Heath bridge has a curious mixture of materials and styles. The south wall has original stonework supporting a parapet of engineering bricks, but only half the original arch exists in the north wall.

'Coven Heath Second Wharf' was one of those along the Stafford turnpike and the first, next to bridge No. 69, may have served Pendeford Old Mill a few hundred yards to the west of the canal. The mill had been derelict long enough by 1880 to become 'Old Mill Farm', but it must have been in use when the canal was built. About ½ mile south of Coven Heath bridge there is a weir that allowed surplus water from the canal to drain into the mill pond. The weir is next to the Pendeford brook and a little farther on is the site of a feeder from the brook. The Canal Company was empowered by the Act of 1766 to take water from the brook, and it may have been one of the main sources of water for the southern section while the northern was being built.

Pendeford Old Mill achieved fame just over a century before the canal was built, during the flight of the young King Charles II. The Royalist army was soundly beaten at the Battle of Worcester on Wednesday, 3rd September 1651 and the king, then only 21 years old, spent the night in hiding at Boscobel house, the home of William Penderel. William was the eldest of five brothers and another, Richard, took Charles during the following night to Madeley in an unsuccessful attempt at crossing the river Severn. The pair returned to Boscobel early on Saturday to meet Colonel Careless who was also in hiding there. Two days earlier Careless had led the last abortive charge over the cobbles in Worcester. Several groups of Roundhead soldiers were searching Brewood Forest and the woods around Boscobel and Charles and Careless spent most of Saturday hiding in the celebrated oak tree near the house. Of all the incidents of the king's adventurous flight into exile, this above all is remembered by breweries and schoolboys alike!

Charles set out for Moseley Hall during the night of Sunday, 7th September, accompanied by the Penderel brothers and a servant of Charles Gifford of Chillington called Yates. One of the brothers, Humphrey, lived at Pendeford Old Mill and Charles travelled on the aged horse from the mill, the rest walking beside him armed with bill-hooks and pistols. Richard, William, Humphrey and the horse stopped at the mill and the others continued to Moseley Hall. Had the Staffs & Worcs been there at the time, the fugitive would have crossed it by bridge No. 69!

After a day or two at Moseley, the king went to Colonel Lane's house at Bentley and then to Bristol disguised as the servant of Lane's daughter, Jane. The pair arrived in Bristol on 12th September, just over a week since the battle, but Charles was unable to board a boat. The king had over a month of stirring adventures and narrow escapes before he eventually arrived at Shoreham in Sussex and set sail for France on Wednesday, 15th October 1651.

The story does not end there. When the king was restored to the throne of England nine years later he remembered the help he had had from the Penderels while 'on the run'. The family was granted a perpetual pension and descendants still benefit from it. The five brothers had nothing to do with Pendrell Hall at Codsall Wood, for this was built in the middle of the 19th century, but it was named in honour of them by the Giffords who owned the house. Moseley Old Hall, a couple of miles to the east of Coven Heath, is now owned by the National Trust and Boscobel, 6 miles to the west, is in the care of the Ministry of Works. Both have an assortment of 'priest's holes' and other secret rooms and are well worth a visit.

19⅜ *Forster Bridge (No. 68) & Wharf* 26¾

Nearly every wharf we have encountered in our journey along the Staffs & Worcs thrived during the canal era and went out of use with the arrival of the motor lorry, if not before. The wharf near Forster bridge (No. 68) is an exception. It did not appear until about 1927 when many of the others had gone and the traffic to it was horse-drawn long after motor boats had become well established. The reason for this unexpected development is the rubbish tip behind the wharf where noxious waste material from Courtaulds (Wolverhampton) Ltd was dumped. The horse-drawn boats to this wharf were among the last commercial traffic on the canal and the load they carried was certainly the least salubrious. The works was at Dunstall, a little over 2 miles nearer Wolverhampton, and the waste was carried in containers.

There used to be a stone next to the towing path where the

canal narrows near the wharf, and it was sufficiently prominent to be marked on the Ordnance Survey map of 1884. It was probably swept away when the wharf was built and may have been one of the mile stones along the canal. The Act of 1766 required that stones should be erected every mile, so that there could be no dispute about the toll to be paid. In the early days the rate per mile for a particular load was simply multiplied by the number of stones passed by the boat. A similar stone is shown near Compton, 3 miles away, but neither are an integral number of miles from Stourport or Haywood. In those days 'one hundred weight' was taken as 120lb., so perhaps the stones were slightly less than 1 statute mile apart to compensate for this!

A few yards before Forster bridge, the canal enters what can only be described as a spectacular cutting, called 'Pendeford Rockin' by the boatmen. It has not the depth of Telford's cuttings at Smethwick and Woodseaves, excavated 60 years later, for here the canal is little more than 10ft below the level of the surrounding land, but it is hewn from solid Keuper Sandstone for a distance of 600yd. The sandstone has kept discreetly out of sight since Teddesley, but at the 'Rockin' it has thrown off its mantle of clay, boulders and gravel, causing great inconvenience to Brindley and his navvies. Although the rock is soft and easily worked, the barest minimum was removed and the canal is not much wider than a boat. A clause in the 1766 Act required the Company 'to cut proper spaces at convenient Distances from each other in such parts of the Cut as shall not be of sufficient breadth for Two Boats to pass'. Whether or not this anticipated the 'Rockin' is a matter of conjecture, but there are three passing places in the cutting, one on the towpath side and two on the other.

No. 68 was an accommodation bridge on the footpath between Marsh Lane and Wobaston until the new road was built a few years before the last war. The present brick and concrete structure is similar to Brinsford bridge (No. 70) and may have been built at the same time. Below it the foundations of the old one can still be seen, anchored to the sandstone sides of the cutting and built of the familiar low-grade pebbly bricks. The new road connects factories near the canal, including Marston Excelsior, with the former aircraft factory of Boulton & Paul Ltd. The latter moved there during the last war from Norwich, which was thought to be too near the east coast for an aircraft factory. A site next to the Shropshire Union Canal at Pendeford was chosen, since fuel for the boilers could be delivered by canal and there was an airfield between the two canals. The firm's main contribution to the war effort was a revolutionary gun turret that gave aircraft complete protection, where previously guns had only fired along the line of flight. The Defiant fighter was built at the works and had the new gun turret, but it was cumbersome and easily out-manoeuvred. Not many Defiants were built, but the gun turrets were fitted to hundreds of bombers.

$19\frac{5}{8}$ *Marsh Lane Bridge (No. 67)* $26\frac{1}{2}$

Part of Marsh Lane bridge (No. 67) is original and the fairly early extension on the south side is of the 'keystone' variety. Beyond it, between the Staffs & Worcs and Shropshire Union Canals, is an old airfield known locally as 'Wolverhampton Airport'. The air-field only ever had a grass runway and was established in the early 1930s when 'flying machines' were novel and popular. Air displays were frequently held at the airfield and about 1938 Amy Johnson flew from here. It saw great activity during the war years after it had been extended as far as the Boulton & Paul factory, but an attempt to create an airport here after the war was not successful and the field was mainly used by flying clubs. Now most of the buildings are empty and neglected and there are plans to build houses on the airfield.

$20\frac{1}{2}$ *Autherley Junction* $25\frac{5}{8}$

Junctions with other canals were the lifeblood of the Staffs & Worcs for very little of the traffic it carried originated on the main line of the canal. Connections with waterways from the industrial region to the east were welcomed, but the junction at Autherley was one the Company did not want. Thomas Telford and the BCN were behind it. In 1824 the Birmingham Committee asked Telford to survey their canal and suggest ways of improving it. Much of the Birmingham Canal was realigned as a result and he probably recommended a new route to Merseyside, as bottle necks on the Birmingham would otherwise have simply been transferred to the antiquated Staffs & Worcs. The proposed canal, the

Birmingham & Liverpool Junction, received full support from the Birmingham Company and Telford was appointed as engineer. The shareholders included representatives from nearly every canal company in the Midlands, including Edward Littleton and Sir John Wrottesley from the Staffs & Worcs. Work started in 1826 and the canal opened nine years later, a few weeks after the ailing Telford died. The B&LJ was not the last canal to be built, but it is one of the finest from the engineering point of view and is perhaps Telford's greatest work, just as the Staffs & Worcs is Brindley's. The brief life of the B&LJ Company expired in 1845 when it merged with the Ellesmere & Chester to become the Shropshire Union, or 'Shroppie', as it is usually known.

The lack of a direct connection between the Birmingham Canal and the Shropshire Union saved the day for the S&WCCo. Traffic from the BCN had to traverse 1,000yd of the Staffs & Worcs before it reached Autherley and carriers paid dearly for the privilege. Through traffic between Autherley and Haywood dwindled after the opening of the Shropshire Union, but the drop in income was to some extent countered by the compensation tolls. Originally this was to have been 2s a ton, but proposals were made to bypass the 1,000yd section with the Tettenhall & Autherley Canal & Aqueduct and the toll was eventually reduced to 2d a ton.

The S&WCCo. were also difficult over water supplies to the Shropshire Union, whose summit is 6in. lower than the earlier canal, but again they were forced to reduce their charges from time to time. The stop lock at the junction passes a mere 2,000 gallons or so and any other water needed by the Shropshire Union was carefully measured at the sluice next to the lock and was paid for. The roving bridge across the junction has a dual purpose, for it is also an accommodation bridge, No. 1 of the Shropshire Union (Plate 21). The canal bridge had over 60 years of development behind it when the Shropshire Union was built and in every respect Telford's bridges are better designed than the old bridges on the Staffs & Worcs, though this does not make them any more pleasing. Telford worked from carefully drawn plans, whereas Brindley had at best a rough sketch. The work of an outstanding civil engineer is unmistakable in any age, whether on canals or motorways, and can be identified by the way in which it blends into the landscape. The Shropshire Union is as fine an example of 'environmental planning' as one could hope to find anywhere, though Telford would not have called it that. The bridges in particular are less rustic than on the Staffs & Worcs and their curve of stonework follows the line of the parapet instead of the arch.

No account of Autherley Junction or 'Cut End', as it was to the boatmen, would be complete without a mention of Sam Lomas who occupied the toll office here. His working life was spent on the canals and, unlike many old hands who found themselves in the employ of the Waterways Board, he was just as enthusiastic about pleasure cruising as he had been about commercial carrying. There was little point in passing through 'Cut End' during office hours when in a hurry. Sam used to emerge from his office as soon as a boat entered the stop lock. On would go the kettle, with little provocation Sam would produce the biggest cup imaginable and with no prompting whatever he would entertain with tales from his inexhaustible stock of canal stories. One of his favourites told how he reported at the Middlewich Wharf Office on 24th July 1916 to start work with the Shropshire Union Company the day before his fourteenth birthday. The boss said, 'I can't start you till tomorrow because you're not 14 till then, Sammy, so sit on the step outside and watch the boats go by.' Sam would add, 'And that's what I've been doing ever since!' After nationalisation he graduated from toll clerk to 'Traffic Representative in the North Western Division', but 'Ambassador' would have been more appropriate.

In January 1959 Sam received the B.E.M. for 'meritorious service' and the medal was certainly well deserved. He was liked by everyone and in his way did much to promote interest in our canals during the years of uncertainty immediately after nationali-sation. Sam made several appearances on television and on one occasion when he was being interviewed at Stourport, MacDonald Hastings asked him what the back end of a canal boat was called. Sam replied 'the starn'. MacDonald then asked him what the other end was called and back came the reply, 'the fur end'! Sam never really retired and his presence at Autherley has been missed since he died in May 1970. Autherley Junction is now the head-quarters of Water Travel, with all the usual cruising facilities.

Cruisers may be hired or repaired, there is a general store and boat club and small boats can be hired for a few hours or longer periods.

One of the main feeders joins the canal between the junction and Oxley Moor bridge (No. 65) and a few years ago this was a source of silting, pollution and controversy. The Barnhurst Sewage Works of Wolverhampton Corporation occupies the land between the Staffs & Worcs and the Shropshire Union and both canals receive purified effluent from the works. The Staffs & Worcs's share, averaging about 5 million gallons a day, enters the canal at a basin near the junction. This basin was built in 1888 when the works were completely rebuilt and improved 18 years after they opened. In effect the works then ceased to be a farm, for the volume of sewage was becoming too great for its treatment to be satisfactorily combined with farming. However, it continued to be known as 'Barnhurst Sewage Farm' for many years. Boats brought lime to the basin for use in the settling tanks and coal for the boilers of steam pumps was delivered there. The boats departed with pressed sludge 'cake' for agricultural use to be delivered at farm wharves like the ones we have seen on our journey down the Staffs & Worcs. The wharf and the network of narrow-gauge railways connecting it with the works were used until 1913, when the sludge pressing plant was abandoned. Storm water was diverted to the basin in 1923 and four years later it received treated sewage from the newly-installed purification plant.

For many years the works adequately coped with 'traditional' sewage, but the domestic detergents that appeared in the 1950s passed straight through the system and into the canal. The basin soon became the source of a particularly unpleasant form of pollution and as often happens, the remedy appeared long after the cause. Every lock on the Staffs & Worcs and the Shropshire Union became a sea of greasy foam every time paddles were operated and boats disappeared from view to emerge enveloped in the stuff. The composition of detergents has since been modified and improved methods for treating them have been introduced. The amount of detergent entering the canal is now negligible, though the quantity treated has more than doubled since the problem first arose. The other inconvenience suffered by canal users was silting of the channel near the outfall. Some silting still occurs, but it is dredged periodically, the cost being met by Wolverhampton Corporation.

New and improved plant has again been installed at Barnhurst and in a few years the average daily outfall will be increased to about 10 million gallons. The manager of the works, Mr Peter Barnes, claims that the effluent will then be as pure as any in Europe. Aside from the legal and moral implications of pollution, Mr Barnes has a personal reason for ensuring that this claim is fulfilled. In addition to managing a modern sewage works, he is keenly interested in waterways and is a member of the Staffs & Worcs Canal Society!

The headquarters of Wolverhampton Canoe Club, next to Barnhurst basin and opposite the boatyard of Gregory's Canal Cruisers is unfortunately a continual target for vandalism. This is a great pity, for canoe clubs on canals deserve every encouragement. Many young people get their first introduction to waterways through canoeing and will always have an interest in them, even if they do not later indulge in other forms of recreation on the canals. There are few towns along the Staffs & Worcs and vandalism is less of a problem than on many neighbouring waterways, but it is serious enough on the outskirts of Wolverhampton. There is no simple solution to the problem, but it is surely the duty of those interested in canals to do what they can to educate the young to value their heritage and take a pride in their surroundings.

$20\frac{5}{8}$ *Oxley Moor Bridge (No. 65*)* $25\frac{1}{2}$

Although the original bridge at Oxley Moor survived until recently, it was totally inadequate for the increasing volume of traffic that crossed it twice a day from 1945 onwards. 'Overspill' estates appeared at Aldersley in the 1930s, but immediately after the war, houses spread like a bush fire towards Barnhurst and Bilbrook, and the flames are still spreading. Bridge No. 65 is on the way to factories to the north and east of Wolverhampton and its rebuilding in 1968 was long overdue. The new bridge is of clean, open design that would lose nothing by the replacement of the original cast nameplate.

* The number on the recent plate is incorrect. No. 66 was to the north and was presumably demolished at the time the junction was built.

Beyond the bridge are the inlet, outfall and pumphouse belonging to the Goodyear Tyre Company. Water was pumped from here to the works at Oxley. The settling tanks of the first sewage farm at Barnhurst were on the west of the canal and from here most of the sewage was channelled to fields between Dam Mill and Pendeford for natural purification. New holding tanks have been built near the original works and the outfall enters the canal at this point. Ahead are two aqueducts where sewage from Wolverhampton crosses the canal. The second, a many-arched masterpiece in blue brick (Plate 22) and one of the oldest parts of the Barnhurst complex, would be an impressive bridge were it not dwarfed by two lofty railway viaducts. Wolverhampton Corporation, justly proud of the public service they intended to provide a century ago, wrote a short essay about it on a sandstone block. It is a pity that the stone was chosen for ease of carving rather than resistance to the sulphurous Midland atmosphere, and its message is now barely legible. The inscription reads:

WOLVERHAMPTON MAIN DRAINAGE
THIS STONE WAS LAID BY
ALDERMAN HAWKSFORD
JULY 3RD 1868
ALDERMAN J. LANGMAN, MAYOR
A. MORGAN, ENGINEER
G. FORD, CONTRACTOR.

The laying of the stone was accompanied by an elaborate ceremony and two years later the aqueduct collapsed while it was being tested. However, it was soon repaired and has been in use ever since. The Council's pride was somewhat misplaced, for it took several outbreaks of cholera and many years of debate before funds were made available for the work. Even then it was not until well into the present century that the filth and stench of poorer parts of Wolverhampton disappeared for good.

The three-arch viaducts at Oxley (Plate 22), similar in many respects, represent very different periods in the history of railways. The first was on the Shrewsbury & Birmingham Railway, opened on 12th November 1849. In spite of its name, the railway only ran from Wellington to Wolverhampton. The line into

Shrewsbury was owned jointly with the Shropshire Union Company and beyond Wolverhampton the S&B had running powers over the Stour Valley line of the L&NWR. The line ended at Wolverhampton High Level station and there was a branch to Victoria basin on the Birmingham Canal. The S&B first attempted to exercise its running powers in November 1851, but found the way blocked at Wolverhampton by a powerful L&NWR engine surrounded by officials, the Mayor and most of the town's police force, with the army standing by! Round one was lost, the battle moved to the courts and the first through train to Birmingham ran on 4th February 1854. This pettiness was typical of early railway companies and was not unknown on the canals. On 1st September 1854 the S&B became part of the GWR empire and joined the company's line to London at the Low Level station. This is now a parcel depot and after an absence of over a hundred years, Shrewsbury trains have returned to Wolverhampton High Level. The viaduct at Oxley was on the Paddington to Birkenhead main line of the GWR, but the curves, embankments and bridges here prevented the heavy 'King' class locomotives from going beyond Wolverhampton.

The second viaduct at Oxley is on the Wolverhampton & Bridgnorth Railway. It was built by the GWR, a company that should have known better, when the railway age was nearly at an end. Work on the railway started in 1913, was suspended during the First World War and was resumed in 1919. The first train ran on 1st January 1925, but not to Bridgnorth. The section beyond Wombourn was never built and the line joined the earlier Kingswinford Branch at Baggeridge Junction, running parallel to the central section of the Staffs & Worcs. Even while the railway was being built, buses were running through the area to be served by it and passenger traffic only lasted for seven years. The line was used by goods traffic as a western bypass of the Black Country until it was closed on 1st March 1965.* The railway came too late for it to be a serious competitor of the Staffs & Worcs. The monograph *By Rail to Wombourn* by J. Ned Williams is an excellent account of this extraordinary enterprise.

The viaduct remains as a monument to the Wolverhampton &

* The track between Tettenhall and Wombourn is now a public footpath.

Bridgnorth, either because it would be too costly to demolish or because its neighbour would be weakened if it were removed. The main difference between the two bridges is that the piers of the later one each have a couple of oval apertures to reduce the load on the foundations. However, the main significance of the second aqueduct at Oxley as far as the Staffs & Worcs is concerned is that here the canal crosses the 'official' watershed of England. North of the arches is the catchment area of the Trent and that of the Severn is to the south. The impression created by the high viaducts and embankments of the triangular railway junction at Oxley is that the canal 'crosses the line' in a deep cutting. There is a cutting here, but its true depth is quite insignificant, as is apparent where the 'High-Speed Gas' pipeline crosses the canal. Nature again came to Brindley's aid at Aldersley. Towards the end of the glacial period great quantities of melt water and rock material carved the Aldersley Gap. This is a steep-sided valley with a flat bottom about 100yd wide and standing at a height of just under 350ft above sea level. The Aldersley Gap enabled Brindley to avoid the high ground of Wolverhampton and Tettenhall and continue his summit through the watershed to Compton.

21   *Aldersley Junction & Bridge (No. 64)*   25⅛

For many years Aldersley was by far the busiest and most important junction on the Staffs & Worcs. While the navvies were still at work, Mathew Boulton, Samuel Galton and other Midland industrialists were busy launching a canal to link Birmingham with Aldersley. Traffic on this canal, the forerunner of the powerful Birmingham Canal Navigations, entered the Staffs & Worcs for the first time on 21st September 1772, six days before the untimely death of James Brindley when he was 56 years old. He must have been delighted to see the Birmingham making progress, for this is exactly what he had envisaged over a decade earlier—a 'trunk' system linking the main rivers with 'branches' radiating to the coalfields and centres of industry. Taking the analogy a stage further, he may even have had visions of a profusion of 'twigs' penetrating individual collieries and works! Aldersley Junction made the fortunes of both the companies involved, particularly in the early days, and without it neither would have prospered.

Aldersley was one place where the mighty BCN could not call the tune, though it tried hard enough from time to time. The Staffs & Worcs is the senior canal, if only by a couple of years, and consequently had the right to all lockage water from the Birmingham Canal. Aldersley is at the foot of Wolverhampton locks, the 'Twenty One' (Plate 24), and it would have been difficult to arrange matters otherwise. Even so, the BCN made an unsuccessful attempt to obtain powers to pump water from the bottom lock back to the summit level. This flight of locks takes the Birmingham Canal steeply up the side of the Aldersley Gap and on to the Black Country plateau, a total height of 130ft.

Looking at the grass-covered mounds and carelessly demolished buildings around the junction, it is hard to visualise the scene at Aldersley right up to nationalisation. Facing the Staffs & Worcs were the Company's toll office and various houses, and the toll house of the BCN was just across the junction, at the bottom of the 'Twenty One'. Families on moored boats added to this isolated community and a steady stream of boats passed through the junction, mostly between the BCN and Shropshire Union towards the end. A forlorn oil lamp bracket survived on the bridge below the bottom lock for some time after the houses had been pulled down and the boats withdrawn, but this too has gone.

What a contrast to Autherley, where the S&WCCo.'s only acknowledgement of the existence of the junction was the roving bridge, and this was only for the Company's convenience.

Of all the buildings at Aldersley, the roving bridge alone remains intact (Plate 23). This part of the Staffs & Worcs was opened on 28th May 1772, only four months before the Birmingham, and bridge No. 64 can only be a matter of months younger than some of the original bridges on the canal. Yet what a contrast there is between the style of this bridge and, say, Marsh Lane (No. 67). It is tempting to regard the Staffs & Worcs bridges as being designed by Brindley and to attribute No. 64 to Robert Whitworth or Samuel Simcock, his engineering assistants who superintended the building of the Birmingham Canal. For all that it is a pleasant bridge of red brick with a wide arch springing from towpath level. There is also an arch on the offside that looks

G   97

as if it were put there when the bridge was built. If so, it seems that the houses and the habit of using this side of the canal for mooring both originated when the junction was made.

The account of Autherley and Aldersley would not be complete without a mention of the confusion over the names of these junctions that existed before the Ordnance Survey put matters right a few years ago. The trouble started with the Act of 1768 for the Birmingham Canal that authorised a line to join the Staffs & Worcs at 'Autherley otherwise Aldersley'. In 1830, Bradshaw evidently subscribed to this view, for he has 'Autherley and Aldersley' and the Birmingham & Liverpool Junction simply ends at 'Stop Lock'. When the Shropshire Union opened in 1834, an attempt to transfer Autherley ½ mile to the north succeeded for a while and was acceptable to the Ordnance Survey in 1882. However, by 1920 the Survey had had second thoughts. The junctions became Autherley No. 1 and No. 2 and Aldersley moved to the junction on the Wolverhampton & Bridgnorth Railway, which was then being built!

Bearing in mind how near Aldersley Junction is to Wolverhampton, it is a singularly remote spot, with only a footpath linking it with a lane that, until recently, went nowhere in particular. With no mains services or access for vehicles, it was inevitable that Aldersley Junction should die when commercial traffic went from the canal. Fortunately, the architecture if not the atmosphere of Aldersley has been preserved by Eric de Maré in his *Canals of England*.

21⅜   *Dunstall Water Bridge (No. 63)*   24¾

No. 63 is a curious bridge, being half accommodation, half aqueduct, and one of the rare occasions where a stream passes *over* a canal. The Smestow brook rises to the east of Wolverhampton, heads north as if bent on joining the Trent, and then turns west to follow the 'Twenty One' down to Aldersley. From No. 63 it follows the canal most of the way to Stourton, where it joins the river Stour and so to the Severn. The brook approaches the canal at a higher level and one would have expected the Canal Company to have used it as a water supply, but they were prevented from doing so by mill owners along the river. The Smestow sets out at a disadvantage. It starts amidst industry and flows through or near several factories, including Wolverhampton Gas Works, so it is highly polluted by the time it reaches the aqueduct. Not only are its waters void of life; vegetation shrinks from the water's edge, leaving a no-man's land of blackened earth.

Although the area is Dunstall, the plate on No. 63 is inscribed 'Tunstall Water Bridge'. It is tempting to blame the error on an apprentice pattern maker, but 'Tunstall' appears on the 1st edition Ordnance Survey of 1834. Dunstall Hall, whose lands lay to the east, was about 600yd away on the far side of what is now Wolverhampton Race Course. Horse racing came to the town as early as 1825 and Lord Hatherton often attended meetings at the course in what is now West Park, perhaps combining visits with meetings of the Canal Committee, held at the Head Office at 87 Darlington Street or an inn in the town. The course was moved to Dunstall Park in late Victorian or Edwardian times.

The Smestow only rises a few miles away, but by the time it had reached Dunstall its waters had gathered sufficient momentum to drive a corn mill that stood between the hall and bridge No. 63. The footpath over the accommodation section in fact connected Aldersley with the mill and hall and went across the middle of the race course. Because of the danger to pedestrians, or because it afforded a free view of the racing, the footpath was closed at the bridge.

The arch of Dunstall Water bridge is of brick and the water section is reinforced by iron plates whose strengthening ribs appear in the bed of the stream. The original bridge must have been built at the same time as the canal, though it has been repaired from time to time and refaced. The course of the Smestow used to be about 200yd to the north and when the canal was built, all the water was diverted into the existing mill leat and over bridge No. 63. The brick culvert that joins the canal near the remnants of Dunstall Mill wharf replaced the earlier channel of the Smestow. The 1766 Act enabled the Company to use streams within 500yd of the canal for supplying it with water, but if in doing so they deprived any mills or forges, the owners were entitled to compensation. After Dunstall Mill, the waters of the Smestow went on to drive over thirty mills before entering the Severn. Corn, wire and slitting mills, forges and even carpet works relied on the Smestow and Stour for power. The Canal Company very wisely took the Smestow over the Staffs & Worcs on an aqueduct and went elsewhere for supplies of water.

At the end of the 19th century the canal still passed through farmland between Aldersley and Newbridge, though Tettenhall was beginning to spread along Aldersley Lane. Hordern Road was built at about the turn of the century to link this development with the centre of Wolverhampton and an entirely new bridge was built across the canal. Hordern Road bridge is therefore not No. 62, as is usually stated in books about the Staffs & Worcs, because the numbering of bridges took place many decades earlier. For a bridge built so recently, it was constructed with singular lack of foresight. The bridge was narrow and after it the road immediately had a sharp double bend to avoid the last of the cottages in Aldersley Lane, for in those days an Englishman's terraced cottage was still his castle. Some years later the Wombourn Railway crossed the bend and Hordern Road bridge became a serious hazard, particularly after the introduction of the bus service between Wolverhampton and Codsall. After endless queues of cars, angry scenes and several accidents, Hordern Road bridge was rebuilt a few years ago.

The railway bridge probably dates from 1927, when Courtaulds opened their rayon factory on part of Dunstall Park race course. All Courtaulds factories had their own railways and this one passed over the Staffs & Worcs and connected with the Wombourn line. Most of the ingredients used to make artificial silk or 'Rayon' are not readily stored in bulk and a continuous supply is essential. At Dunstall Park the raw materials were delivered by rail and canal. The siding was mostly worked by a couple of green saddle-tank engines with 0–4–0 wheel arrangement. The senior engine, 'Rosabel', arrived soon after the works opened and was joined by her sister 'Annabel' in 1936. For many years these engines busily shunted trucks or tankers containing coal, wood pulp and such unwholesome substances as sulphuric acid and caustic soda. Some of the ingredients were also carried by canal and delivered to the wharf next to the railway bridge. These came in the 'acid' boats of Cowburn and Cowpar from their chemical works at Trafford Park, Manchester. The boats worked in pairs and, unlike the majority of boats working the Staffs & Worcs, their livery was immaculate. Motor and 'butty' were usually named after birds, like 'Swan' and 'Flamingo', for example. The only other gaily-painted boats to use the canal regularly within living memory were occasional 'Joshers' of Fellows, Morton & Clayton. Waste material from the works was taken to the wharf in containers for shipment in horse-drawn boats to the tip at Pendeford and coal was delivered to the Victoria basin on the south side of Hordern Road bridge.

The Cowburn & Cowpar boats left the Staffs & Worcs long ago, but the waste traffic continued until the 1950s. 'Rosabel' was replaced by an outsider called 'Dafydd' when she was scrapped in 1956 and 'Annabel' carried on until the siding went out of use in 1962, three years before the Wombourn line itself closed down. Improved man-made fibres have supplanted Rayon, the works closed in 1970, and no longer do the tall stacks pollute the air with acrid fumes.

The building of Hordern Road immediately created additional access to the Staffs & Worcs in a part of Wolverhampton that was developing rapidly. Even at this late stage in the life of the canal, two wharves were built near the bridge. That on the offside was one of Walker's wharves that dealt with domestic coal and opposite is the Victoria basin of Double Pennant Cruisers. The name of this basin suggests that it and presumably the adjoining road were built during or shortly after the reign of Queen Victoria, which ended in 1901. (Neither the road nor the basin are shown on the 1888 edition of the 6in Ordnance Survey map.) The basin started life as a boatyard and was later taken over by Courtaulds for use as a coal wharf and was equipped with a weighbridge. After Courtaulds ceased to obtain coal by canal Victoria basin was used by Johnny Tool as a depot for domestic coal and in 1958/9 the basin reverted to a boatyard when it was acquired by Double Pennant. The firm's main activity is the hiring of cruisers and the provision of all the associated facilities, but boats are also built for sale and there are two slipways.

Between Hordern Road and Newbridge on the offside of the canal are several decrepit boathouses. Pleasure boating on the

Staffs & Worcs is as old as the canal itself and it was particularly popular in the early years of the present century. The owners of these boathouses were possibly exercising their right under the 1766 Act to navigate freely along the summit level. Although riparian owners were denied this right as a result of the 1968 Transport Act, they are entitled to compensation for the loss and in effect can still enjoy free boating.

22   *Tettenhall New & Old Bridges*   24⅛
              (Nos. 62 & 61, Plate 25) & Wharves

The paths of Thomas Telford and the Staffs & Worcs crossed at Autherley and here they do so again. In the early days the turnpike between Wolverhampton and Shrewsbury went over the canal by bridge No. 61 and then wound steeply up the steep escarpment of Upper Mottled Sandstone to the Upper Green at Tettenhall. Now Telford had other interests beside canals. In the first 20 years of the 19th century over a thousand bridges and almost as many miles of road were built under his direction. His finest road is the one between London and Holyhead that follows Watling Street as far as Weedon and then heads for Birmingham and Wolverhampton. When Telford carried out the survey between 1815 and 1817 he decided to include most of the Wolverhampton–Shrewsbury turnpike. He also intended that no gradients should be greater than 1 in 20, immediately ruling out the Tettenhall section. Instead he built a new bridge across the Staffs & Worcs with approaches on high embankments and leading to the impressive sandstone cutting of Tettenhall Rock. The bridge was rebuilt in 1939, but 'Newbridge', as the area is known, refers to its predecessor of 150 years ago. Looking towards the Rock from Newbridge, one can understand why the poet Robert Southey gave Telford the nickname 'Colossus of Roads'.

Telford's New Bridge was much narrower than the present No. 62, but it can be safely assumed that his design was more pleasing. Its inclusion in the number sequence provides another clue towards the dating of the bridge plates, if any is needed. The road was open throughout early in 1826, with the opening of the Menai suspension bridge, but the Midland section was probably in use a few years earlier. It is interesting to note that canal companies like the BCN were not the only ones to attempt to put their houses in order when railways appeared on the horizon. The turnpike trusts also embarked on a frenzy of improvements. As usually happens when bridges are rebuilt, Wolverhampton Corporation did not bother to replace the nameplate. Instead they mounted a plaque in the wall, facing the road of course, simply stating, 'This bridge was widened and reconstructed in 1939.'

Newbridge boasts two coal wharves, perhaps because it is only a couple of miles from the centre of Wolverhampton, and both have always been in constant use. The second and earlier one near Tettenhall Old bridge is now the boat-building yard of Leisure Craft Marine. The first, Walker's, is next to bridge No. 62 and it has had a most unusual career for a canal wharf. A fleet of rowing boats was established here during the last century and is at present operated by Water Travel.* These boats have always been very popular. For many years, works clubs and other societies have included a row on the Staffs & Worcs in their social programme and on summer evenings the canal between Compton and Autherley is often thronged with rowers. Another popular excursion started from Tettenhall—a horse-drawn 'Joey' boat used for Sunday School 'treats' and other excursions. The favoured itinerary was along the Staffs & Worcs to Autherley and then along the Shropshire Union through Chillington Park and as far as Brewood or Wheaton Aston. The Staffs & Worcs was thus a pioneer in the use of canals for pleasure and trip boats still ply from Newbridge, Oxley Moor bridge and Autherley, though they are no longer horse-drawn.

Today Newbridge is a convenient casual mooring for pleasure boaters. Shops are near at hand and access is easier from the Old bridge than from the New. Not far to the west of the canal and nestling under Tettenhall Rock is the 'Mitre', a popular pub in pleasant surroundings on the Lower Green. There used to be a canalside pub between the two bridges, but there was no stabling and it was not a regular stopping place for the boatmen. It was pulled down, probably when No. 62 was rebuilt and widened, and replaced by the 'Newbridge', whose sign commemorates Telford's work at Tettenhall.

The elevated ridge at Tettenhall has always made it a desirable

* The rowing boats are now based at Autherley.

place to live and many leading industrialists had their homes there. Even in the early years of the 19th century there was 'a good resident Gentry', according to William Pitt. The ridge between Stockwell End and Wightwick is still crowned with Victorian and Edwardian mansions, though nowadays they are mostly flats, clubs or hotels. It is perhaps no coincidence that in 1878 one of the first trams of the Midlands clanked its way from Wolverhampton to a terminus at the top of Tettenhall Rock. Among the 'resident Gentry' were the Wrottesley family whose estates lay a few miles to the west of Tettenhall. Sir Richard Wrottesley, Dean of Worcester, was one of the original subscribers to the Staffs & Worcs and the family continued to take an interest in the canal, though not so actively as the Littletons and Hathertons. Lord Wrottesley is the patron of St Michael's church at Tettenhall and his family are buried there. This fine old church, under the lee of the Rock, was destroyed by fire during the small hours of Friday, 3rd February 1950. Smoke was billowing from the vestry when the alarm was raised at 12.59 a.m. and by 1.45 a.m. three hoses were bringing water from the Staffs & Worcs near Newbridge. The fire was under control within an hour of being reported, but by then the building was a gutted shell. The 15th-century tower survived and the rest of the church has since been rebuilt.

A. Jeremiah Butler (Plate 26) and his son Leslie, General Managers of the canal during the years immediately prior to nationalisation, also lived at Tettenhall. 'A.J.' was said to have been an office boy on the Aire & Calder Canal before he joined the staff of the Staffs & Worcs, and his son succeeded him in 1937. The Butlers were responsible for many improvements, including the iron quoins and sills on most locks along the canal. These are still perfectly sound and the fitting of new gates on the Staffs & Worcs is very much easier than on the majority of waterways, thanks to the foresight of the Butlers. Les Butler in particular knew every inch of the canal and was respected by those who worked under him, but the Transport Commission sent him to Liverpool when they gained control of the waterways in 1948. Butler's deputy, Edward H. Arnold, is another of the Company's employees who is still with the Waterways Board. He joined the Company in 1937 and is now the Board's Development Officer.

Tettenhall is noted for its pears, known as 'Tettenhall Dicks'.

These have been grown in the parish since time immemorial and are a small hard fruit that will not keep unless gathered well before it is ripe and is only palatable if stewed. It is not surprising that Tettenhall Dicks are highly localised and it is a wonder that anyone should bother to grow them! However, early in the 19th century local markets were full of Tettenhall pears about Michaelmas and they were 'exported' by canal to places as far afield as Lancashire.

The Aldersley Gap continues to Tettenhall and here the Smestow brook, Staffs & Worcs Canal, Wombourn Railway and Henwood Lane all crowd together through the narrow valley. Although there was barely room for it, the GWR managed to squeeze one of the main stations of the Wombourn line into the valley at Newbridge, with access from the old road. There are two platforms, though the 'up' (eastern) one was never used, a booking office, goods shed and station buildings, all now used as industrial premises. Not far from the station a fine girder bridge carried the line across the Staffs & Worcs and coffer dams were placed in the canal in July 1914 when the bridge was erected. Officially it is a 'Warren Truss', but any local will tell you it is the 'Meccano Bridge'.

The canal narrows slightly at the aqueduct over the Graiseley brook. Before the canal came, this brook entered the Smestow a little to the north and Brindley appears to have built the present culvert and then diverted the stream, as he did with the Smestow itself at Dunstall. In each case the original line is to the north of the present one and it seems likely that work on the canal proceeded northwards from Compton. The storm-water weir near the Graiseley brook was rebuilt and enlarged in 1971 to act as a 'safety valve' for the increased outfall from Barnhurst sewage works.

Although the canal crossed the watershed a couple of miles away, the boundary between the two catchment areas is only a few hundred yards to the west. Like the Smestow, the Penk could not make up its mind whether to head for the Severn or Trent. It rises near Tettenhall waterworks, flows southwards for a while, swings to the north near Wrottesley Park and then approaches the canal at Pendeford. However, from Compton onwards all streams head purposefully for the Severn and so does the Staffs & Worcs. This is the end of the summit level and is also the half-way point of the canal.

5

Down the Smestow

COMPTON TO STOURTON

Miles
from
Haywood

Miles
to
Stourport

The Smestow brook has been ravaged by man, but the scars of industry along the valley through which it flows have long since healed. Although Compton is an equal distance from the Trent and Severn, brooks flowing southwards have three times the fall of those draining to the north, providing an abundance of water power that was utilised to the full. Before it became cheaper to use steam engines to drive machinery, mills and forges occurred every mile or so along the Smestow and Stour and their tributaries. There are none of the materials usually associated with 'heavy' industries along the valley, but iron was brought here in great quantities for processing, particularly after the Staffs & Worcs and its branches had been built.

The countryside too is different along the southern section of the canal, though the change occurs gradually at first. As with much of the scenery along the Staffs & Worcs, the last ice age was responsible for the contrasting landscapes traversed by the two halves of the canal. The course of the Trent was little influenced by the glaciers and the river is relatively mature, but the Severn is a mere juvenile by comparison. The ancestor of this river flowed northwards towards the Dee, but its way became blocked by ice and glacial debris. A vast lake formed around what is now Shrewsbury and eventually overflowed southwards at Ironbridge. The new Severn rapidly cut a deep channel for itself through the Coal Measures and Triassic rocks of eastern Shropshire. Existing streams, meandering quietly to the sea, suddenly found the

106

ground cut from under them and a fairly flat area was transformed into one of steep valleys and swift-flowing streams.

Although these events were to the advantage of the ironmasters, they did not produce good 'canal country', but Brindley took each obstacle in his stride and carried the canal along narrow valleys that had even been avoided by road builders. As a result, the southern section of the Staffs & Worcs is as beautiful as any canal in the country and is at the same time a great engineering achievement of its day.

22⅞   *Compton Bridges (Nos 60 & 59),*   23¼
Lock & Wharves

It was at Compton that work started on the canal very soon after the Staffordshire & Worcestershire Canal Act had been passed on 14th May 1766. Cutting of the first stage was carried out southwards and in November 1770 the canal was reported open as far as Stourport. Works on this section, particularly around the locks, differ in detail from the slightly later northern part of the canal and may be more representative of the efforts of Brindley. Although most of the detailed construction was carried out by his assistants Hugh Henshall, Samuel Simcock and Thomas Dadford senior, Brindley undoubtedly kept a close watch on progress in the early stages.

There is reason to believe that the first lock to be built by Brindley is at Compton, setting the standard for all narrow locks on Midland canals. There was no doubt in Priestley's mind about this, for he mentioned it in his *Navigable Rivers and Canals* of 1831, when there may have been people around who could remember the canal being built. There is another tradition that Brindley stayed with relatives at Kinver while surveying this end of the canal and during his visits he experimented with a model of a lock. In support of this tale, a family of Brindleys lived at Union Hall, now Brindley House, Kinver, and there is crumbling brickwork along a brook near a place called Compton! Brindley is the subject of much folklore, possibly originated over a beer by 'navvies' after a day of canal cutting. Some ring true and others are entirely myth, but it is fairly certain that Brindley did in fact build his first lock at Compton. What is not clear is where the water came from to supply the partly completed canal. The Company probably used the Penford (Pendeford?) Mill feeder mentioned in the 1766 Act, and may have come to some temporary arrangement with mill owners along the Smestow.

The lock at Compton makes a disappointing start to the descent to the Severn, considering its significance in the development of the narrow canal. At the other end of the 10-mile summit we have the round house, boatyard and other buildings at Gailey wharf, but now there is not even a lock house at Compton. The lock still has wooden quoins, but the sandstone coping on the towpath side was replaced in A. J. Butler's day by 'diamond' blue bricks. This was done at many locks along the canal, for this side became worn by towlines to the point where it was dangerous. As we have seen on the northern section, the wear was sometimes reduced by attaching an iron bar to the masonry and similar devices can often be seen on the ends of bridge parapets. There are also two deeply grooved iron bollards to assist in the working of the lock.

Bridge No. 60 has the usual sandstone quoins and drip course of original bridges, but there is no towing path and the curve of the arch is slightly shallower than on similar works on the northern section. It is interesting to note that the lengths of segments in the drip course are very irregular, but there are usually about six pieces, with twelve on bridges that span both canal and towing path. During the last war a massive block of concrete and brickwork appeared on the bridge, part of some local defence strategy. There is no evidence to suggest it was in any way connected with the defences at Milford and Teddesley. The fall of 9ft 4in. at Compton is close to the average fall on the descent to the Severn and is a foot higher than on the northern section. Oddly enough the locks are more uniform on the earlier part of the canal, with little variation in height until the valley begins to flatten out towards Stourton, where the fall of each lock is reduced to 7ft.

The attractive circular weir at Compton is typical of the southern Staffs & Worcs, but the lock weirs are by no means identical. Some are only half a circle and others rectangular, oval or completely irregular. Did Brindley do this for his own amusement, if indeed he was responsible for them at all, or was he carrying out experiments in hydraulic engineering? The fact that these unusual weirs are only south of Compton perhaps indicates that different engineers were responsible for the two halves of the canal. The sill of Compton weir has segments of dressed stone, but the engineering bricks of the outer wall were certainly laid a long while after the canal was built. The reason given for these unusual weirs is that they saved space and this may be true in some cases, for they are usually on the same side as the towpath, but identical weirs occur where there is plenty of land available. A weir has to be a narrow rectangle to give maximum sill length in minimum area and a circular weir has the opposite effect. Although the old weir at Compton is still used, most of the surplus water now passes over a new weir of conventional pattern, installed to cope with the outfall from Barnhurst. Across the Smestow from the weir is the site of Compton flour mill, the second along the brook.

Although Newbridge and Compton are the same distance from the centre of Wolverhampton, Compton seems to have been preferred for the shipment or delivery of goods, for it has more wharves and warehouses. This could be indicative of heavier traffic towards Stourport and Bristol than along the northern section, for southbound boats starting at Compton would save a mile of canal and one lock. It was also a main stopping place for through traffic, with plenty of stabling and three pubs near the canal. Now there are two; the 'Odd Fellows' Hall' near the canal was rebuilt in 1938 and 'The Swan' was a farmhouse that probably became an inn after the canal was built. Both now provide snacks and neither are strictly canalside pubs. The third, the 'Boat Inn', was a little way along the road to Wolverhampton.

Bridge No. 59* has been carrying traffic travelling between Wolverhampton and Bridgnorth for over two centuries and, with No. 60, must surely be the oldest on the canal. The part carrying traffic in the opposite direction is not quite as old, but is still of great age. This northern half has a keystone and springers of sandstone and a pronounced flare down to the waterline. The arch of the other side is original, though the wall above it has been replaced. Both No. 59 and No. 60 are called 'Compton Bridge' on

* No. 59 was rebuilt in 1974.

their plates. This duplication of names also occurs at Wightwick and Hinksford on the southern section of the canal.

It is not so many years since coal came by boat to Walker's wharf on one side of the bridge and to Low's on the other, and one of them is still used as a fuel depot. When one remembers that 25 tons or so of coal had to be shovelled out of the boats by hand, it is remarkable that the numerous wharves around Wolverhampton survived as long as they did. The boat in which the Company inspected the canal, the *Lady Hatherton*, was moored in the dock to the south of No. 59. All around Compton and extending as far as Wightwick are several sandpits that worked the Upper Mottled Sandstone of the Bunter series. This colourful stone is too soft for use as building material, but the rounded grains make it eminently suitable for use as moulding sand. There are many places where Bunter Sandstone occurs in the west Midlands and the concentration of quarries at Compton is due entirely to the presence of the canal. It was a simple matter to load the sand into boats and take it direct to foundries in the Black Country. These wharves were still in use during the 1930s and the winding hole for the sand and coal boats was between Compton and Wightwick Mill lock.

There is a relic of another water restriction imposed by the Act of 1766 a short distance beyond the last wharf at Compton. The Canal Company were only permitted to keep sufficient water to operate the locks and any surplus was not to flow over the lock weirs. A weir with a slightly lower sill was to be installed below each lock so that surplus water flowed into the pool of the next mill down the Smestow or Stour. These weirs, or their remains, can still be seen along the southern part of the canal and one was a little way beyond Compton.

At 5.30 a.m. on Saturday, 9th September 1972, the canal was breached near the weir. After a long dry spell, torrential rain in the Wolverhampton area caused the Smestow brook to overflow its banks and enter the canal below Compton lock. Water surged down the canal until it was checked by Wightwick Mill lock and then burst through the bank to return to the Smestow. The towpath was swept away, a large hole was scoured in the canal bed and the boat *Rum Tub* was left high and dry at Compton bridge (Plates 27 and 28). Almost 1,000 tons of clay were required to fill the hole and navigation was restored about three weeks afterwards.

$23\frac{1}{2}$-$23\frac{7}{8}$ *Wightwick Bridges (No. 58.to No. 56)* $22\frac{5}{8}$-$22\frac{1}{4}$
& Locks

The pattern at Wightwick is much the same as at Compton, except that there are two locks here. Wightwick Mill lock comes first, with its circular weir, and nearby are another wharf and sandpit. There is no right of access through the mill yard to the A454 road that runs parallel to the canal between Compton and Wightwick, but there is a public footpath at the next lock. Like Compton, both locks have brick and stone bridges (No. 58 and No. 57) spanning the tails, with the towing path keeping to the outside. It is surprising, and fortunate for us, that the Company did not 'modernise' their canal by rebuilding these bridges. As it is they add much to the charm of the waterway.

The large winding hole above Wightwick lock was a particularly important one in the days of working boats. It was dredged to full depth to enable loaded boats to turn, whereas many were only deep enough to 'wind' empty boats. The weir leading from the winding hole is unusual for the southern Staffs & Worcs in that it is conventional. A few weirs at locks have straight sills and these are nearly all on the offside, those with closed sills being mainly on the same side as the towpath.

Bert Hardman, retired lengthsman, lived at the lock cottage here for 40 years. Bert lived at Rocky lock for a couple of years when he joined the Staffs & Worcs in 1929 and moved to Wightwick in 1932 after a brief spell at Bumble Hole. Like Charlie Merrick of Standeford, Bert served under both 'A.J.' and Les Butler and assisted in carrying out many of the lock improvements between Stourport and Penkridge. He could turn his hand to most jobs, from driving the steam dredger to hedge layering. One of the more unusual tasks given Bert was an order from Les Butler in person on 30th May 1940. In the event of an air raid, this instructed him to go to Dunstall Water bridge where he would be assisted by Charlie, Bert Hughes and three others in placing stop planks in position. The party were then to assist a gang doing the same thing at Marsh Lane bridge. Bombing around Wolverhampton was not too serious, but the potential target of the Boulton & Paul aircraft works made this precaution necessary.

Below Wightwick lock is the wharf of one of the last sandpits of the 'gap'. The quarry is now overgrown and wooded, but Bert Hardman well remembers it being in use. Wightwick bridge (No. 56) was rebuilt a few years ago and its plate, fixed to a side wall by the contractors, is not at all out of place on the new structure. The main wharf at Wightwick, to the south of No. 56, has seen many changes. At one time it served an adjoining sandpit and lime was also distributed for use on farms in the neighbourhood. Limestone from mines at Dudley or Walsall was carried down the 'Twenty One' to Aldersley and then to Wightwick to be burnt in a row of kilns at the wharf. More recently coal was delivered there and now it is shared by a garden centre and Walker's Mermaid Hire Cruisers. Mr Walker's ancestors were boatmen. They came from the Tewkesbury area and belonged to the distinguished band of 'Glosters' who carried hay to collieries around Cannock. The Walker family settled at Compton about 1874 and opened a depot for domestic coal. Three other coal wharves followed, including the one at Wightwick in the early 1920s.

Wightwick was another stopping place favoured by boatmen, with the usual stabling and the 'Mermaid' inn near at hand. The old pub had a drastic 'facelift' recently and the decor is now distinctly nautical, though with the car rather than canal trade in mind. There used to be a smithy next to the inn and there was another near bridge No. 56 which was used by the boatmen. A few hundred yards up Wightwick Bank is the Manor, home of the Mander family and now owned by the National Trust. It has a four-poster bed in which Charles II is said to have rested after his defeat at Worcester. Wightwick is at the end of the gap followed by the canal from Aldersley and two old windmills, now converted into houses, stand guard over the entrance to the valley. The last of the long line of mansions of the 'resident gentry', Wightwick Hall, is also nearby. The Wombourn Railway and the canal parted company at Compton and at Wightwick the Staffs & Worcs, Smestow and Bridgnorth road go their several ways.

24¼-24¾   *Castle Croft and Mops Farm Bridges*   21⅞-21⅜
(Nos. 55 & 54)

Bridges 55 and 54 were both rebuilt in late Victorian or Edwardian times. As was noted at Acton and Roseford, several bridges were strengthened when farming entered the 'steam' era and here we have further examples of this. Castle Croft (No. 55), though only linking a track with fields, was rebuilt completely by the grandfather of George Wood, who lives at Greensforge lock. To avoid closing the canal, the new bridge was built around the arch of the old one and the earlier brickwork was then removed. The redbrick foundations of the original bridge can be seen to this day. 'Stoppages' for maintenance meant lost revenue and the Company tried to confine them to public holidays or to carry out work without closing the canal. In later years prolonged stoppages were even more serious, for traffic temporarily transferred to rail or road often never returned and was lost to the canal for ever.

Bridge No. 54 has only been extended and its name, Mops Farm, no doubt referred to the original farm here. The magnificent Georgian farmhouse is now called Pool Hall, after the neighbouring canal reservoir. The Pool is the seventh reservoir on the canal and is one of a pair at Dimmingsdale. Its sinuous waters are used by Wombourn Sailing Club and casual fishing is allowed, permits being obtainable from Pool Hall. The presence of Dimmingsdale reservoirs, three locks down from the summit level, requires some explanation. Although lock heights are fairly uniform along this section, eight locks from Awbridge onwards have falls of about 10ft, slightly greater than average. Furthermore, there is said to have been a three-lock staircase at the Bratch when the canal was built. A boat going uphill would then have required three times as much water as one going down and the reservoirs provided the extra water. Both were for storage and were filled when water was plentiful. Pool Hall has a weir and sluice of dressed sandstone and an earlier culvert that is no longer used. At present the reservoirs are connected to the canal and act as large side ponds, though they could still be used to supply the canal in times of drought.

$25\frac{3}{8}$-$25\frac{5}{8}$ *Dimmingsdale Bridges (Nos. 53 & 52)* $20\frac{3}{4}$-$20\frac{1}{2}$
& Lock

Dimmingsdale bridge (No. 53) was originally built of Keuper
Sandstone, presumably because abundant deposits of this stone
occur locally. It contains fragments of Brindley's work and has
been greatly altered and extended. Although Dimmingsdale was
evidently of some importance in the early days of the canal, as
there is a substantial wharf and basin here, a wharfhouse and
other buildings are lacking and the nearest pubs are about $\frac{1}{2}$ mile
away—the 'Holly Bush' to the west at Ebstree and the 'Greyhound' at Lower Penn in the opposite direction.

Dimmingsdale wharf is an enigma. The basin is edged with
dressed stone blocks, but there are few clues as to its purpose. It
appears to have been constructed at the same time as the canal and
it was certainly in use for many years, as the Company's Table of
Distances mentions a wharf and warehouse at Dimmingsdale.
The hamlet of Lower Penn is quite near, but would hardly have
required such a substantial basin. Lower Keuper Sandstone
forms the ridge of the Orton Hills a mile or so to the east and was
extensively quarried for building purposes. This stone may have
been shipped from the wharf, perhaps even while the canal was
being built, but there are equally suitable points for loading
farther south. It could have been for the distribution of coal and
lime to surrounding farms, except that it is far more elaborate
than other rural wharves along the canal.

The most likely explanation for the existence of Dimmingsdale
wharf, and one deserving of further study, is that it was on the
route between Black Country furnaces and Trescott forge on the
river Smestow. Iron would have travelled this way to be processed
at the forge and may then have been shipped from the wharf after
the opening of the canal. It may also have been a loading point for
coal from mines in the Black Country before the junction with the
Birmingham Canal was made in 1772, or even afterwards to avoid
extra tolls, many locks and several miles of canal. In support of
this theory, 'Coalway Road' on the outskirts of Wolverhampton
is along a line between pits around Goldthorn Hill or Ettingshall

114

and the Staffs & Worcs at Dimmingsdale. The basin has recently been cleared out and is now used for private moorings.

Today Dimmingsdale is dominated by one of the pumping stations belonging to Wolverhampton Corporation, a clean-lined building in the 'Odeon' style favoured in the early 1930s. Its site was partly dictated by the line of the canal, since the pumps were originally driven by steam engines and the boreholes had to be sunk to a depth of over 1,000ft in order to reach the most productive reserves of water. Coal was taken to the boilers from a wharf on the canal along a short narrow-gauge railway whose tracks are still embedded in the concrete. The excavation for the wharf was carried out by the Canal Company's steam dredger, driven by Bert Hardman, when the station was built about 1932. The land between the station and canal is now covered by well-kept lawns.

Opposite the waterworks is the inlet of Dimmingsdale reservoir, the eighth and last along the Staffs & Worcs. The water passes through settling pits to remove silt before it enters the canal or reservoir. (Like the Pool (No. 7), this is a storage reservoir and water can pass either way.)

Dimmingsdale lock was often known as 'Old Bob's', after a lengthsman who lived at the lock cottage here and provided stabling for the boatmen's horses. Not all stabling along the Staffs & Worcs was attached to a pub, but there was usually one nearby. Old Bob's was an exception, but it was a popular stopping place for all that. Perhaps there was a well-worn track, long since disappeared, across the fields to the 'Holly Bush'! The stables were next to the lock, on the opposite side to the cottage, and the money he received for looking after the mules supplemented Old Bob's wages.

Control of the extra water required by Bratch locks was carried out near Dimmingsdale lock. There is no weir at the lock, but a channel nearer the waterworks carries the statutory amount of surplus water from the 1½-mile pound. Part runs into a brook running alongside the canal and the rest is returned to the canal below the lock. The arrangement for apportioning the water is similar to that at Otherton lock.* The brook itself prefers to remain anonymous and rises near Penn Fields, Wolverhampton, joining the Smestow south of Wombourn. Before doing so, at one

* An enlarged bypass weir was installed in 1974.

115

time it supplied power to the Heath mill. On the opposite side of the canal and behind the site of the stables is the dam of Dimmingsdale reservoir. This is only a little higher than the lock, which has a fall of 11ft, and the sluice in it controlled the flow of water into the pound below. Operation of the sluice and checking the levels in the canal and reservoir were among the duties of Bert Hardman. The point where the feeder enters the canal was opened out to form a winding hole. This was used by coal boats returning from the pumping station. The reservoir itself is in very pleasant surroundings, slipping away from the canal behind a hill near the pumping station to reappear near the lock (Plate 29). Now the haunt of waterfowl and fishermen, there are plans afoot to create a navigable link with the canal and to build a marina here.

The towpath has been on the west of the canal for the last 23 miles, since it changed sides at Milford bridge (No. 105), but it crosses the canal at bridge No. 52 in apparent violation of the 'towpath rule'. Now between Wightwick and Botterham the Smestow has cut a steep-sided valley in the glacial sands and gravels that cover the Upper Mottled Sandstone, particularly around Trysull. This is difficult 'canal country' and, though Brindley followed the Smestow closely the rest of the way, he left the river at Wightwick and chose a more direct route through Wombourn. At Dimmingsdale the stream from Penn approaches the canal from the east and the towpath promptly changes sides.

25¾-26   *Ebstree Bridges (Nos. 51 & 50) & Lock*   20⅜-20⅛

The lock at Ebstree, or Ellestree as Bradshaw has it, does not appear to have had a cottage and presumably 'Old Bob' and other keepers at Dimmingsdale lock looked after it. The weir is an interesting variation on the circular theme, the sill having the shape of a horseshoe. Ebstree accommodation bridge (No. 50) was a good example of the 'second generation' of bridges, being built in the late 18th or early 19th centuries. The evidence for this was the use of sandstone for the parapet and keystone, coupled with walls of red brick, features met with elsewhere. The extensive switching station of the CEGB, built a few years ago at Lower Penn, completely overshadowed Ebstree bridge and severed the

track leading to it. With little regard for any historical or architectural importance the bridge may have had, it was demolished
in October 1973 on the grounds that it was no longer required.

The Supergrid is now such a familiar feature of the canal scene
that it is rarely noticed when it crosses a waterway, but no one
could be oblivious of the phalanx of giants striding from all
points of the compass towards Penn Grid Station. Normally these
towers do little to improve the landscape, but the image of one,
backed by billowing clouds and reflected in the still water of the
canal, can be quite attractive.

$26\frac{3}{8}$ *Aw Bridge* (No. 49 & Lock)* $19\frac{3}{4}$

The prettiest length of the Staffs & Worcs is between Wombourn
and Wolverley and the canal builders must have sensed this, for
the most attractive bridges and locks are to be found along here.
Every bridge is different and most have worn steps, grooved
corners and contrasting light and dark that emphasises the texture
of brick and stone. Aw bridge (No. 49) sets the scene by being
one of the finest lock bridges (Plates 30 & 31). The saddleback
coping is supported on nine brick pillars, a simple but highly
effective ornament. A low wall separates the towpath from the
waterway and snakes towards the shadows of the bridge hole, and
silhouetted against the lock are ornate spandrels of a split bridge.
Two centuries of weather and traffic have added the finishing
touches and whatever feeling is engendered by the bridge, it is
certainly not one of awe. Although it has not a single feature we
expect to find in Brindley's bridges, it may be the same date as the
canal. If this is so, then why is the bridge so different from all the
others? This may be because for the first time Brindley tried out
his 'lock and bridge' combination at a public road. This was used
many times on the northern section and also on the way to
Stourport, but between here and Compton all roads cross the
canal at some distance from locks. In a small way, Aw bridge
was perhaps an innovation, and as such deserved special treatment.

However the bridge got its name, until a few years ago it was
most appropriate. A few hundred yards to the west and too close
for comfort stood Seisdon Union Workhouse, a long, narrow

* Also 'Awbridge' or 'Awebridge'.

building of several stories with iron-framed windows, tall chimneys and a steeply pitching roof. It lay derelict for many years before it was demolished and mysterious blue lights were claimed to appear at the windows from time to time. Photographic evidence was produced, but no satisfactory explanation was forthcoming. Trysull Workhouse was certainly an awesome relic of the Victorian Welfare State. The last inhabitant of the workhouse may have been the Phantom Rider, who occasionally gallops across the fields when the moon is full. No one ever sees the mysterious horseman, but he leaves hoofmarks and a trail of destruction after his ride at dead of night.

There is a farmhouse next to the lock at Aw bridge, but no lock cottage and it may be that the farmer also had the job of looking after the lock. A circular weir on the opposite side of the canal completes the scene at this delightful spot. Below the lock the canal continues to follow the brook, though the Smestow is getting near again. It almost joins forces with the canal, but has second thoughts and swings away to the west.

$27\frac{1}{4}$ *Bratch Bridges (Nos. 48 & 47) & Three Locks* $18\frac{7}{8}$

So far Brindley's 'short cut' has been over fairly level ground, with the canal only descending about 30ft since it left the Smestow at Wightwick. At the Bratch it approaches the Smestow valley again and suddenly falls through the same height by three deep locks (Plate 32). This flight is one of the major engineering works on the canal and must have been a serious bottle neck, for it has been almost entirely reconstructed. It is said to have been built as a three-lock staircase and fragments of the earlier locks can be seen at the head of the middle and lower locks of today. Staircases are particularly extravagant of water, for as many lockfuls as there are locks are required for boats going uphill. Boats cannot pass on a staircase, so they also slow down traffic. Staircases are widely used on earlier canals where a sudden fall of land was encountered, but several canal companies later replaced them with conventional locks. The Trent & Mersey did away with theirs at Meaford and Lawford early in the 19th century, and staircase locks at the Delph on the Dudley Canal were removed by the BCNCo. in 1858.

The usual procedure was to build a new flight alongside the old, as was done at Meaford and the Delph. However, at the Bratch this was either not possible or too expensive and the staircase was apparently converted into three normal locks separated by two minute pounds. The quart that otherwise would have to go into a pint pot is diverted through culverts into two vast side ponds. The upper one is almost 300yd long and passes through a bridge under the Trysull road. Although Bratch locks can be baffling when met for the first time, they are worked in exactly the same way as a flight of three separate locks. The only difference is that the intervening pounds are a few feet long instead of a hundred yards or more. The important point to remember is that the top gates of the middle and bottom locks must only be opened when a boat is actually entering or leaving the lock and must then be closed again.

Only one lockful of water passes down the canal for each boat using the modified flight, whereas about 70,000 gallons of extra water would have been needed to operate the staircase for a boat going uphill. If these elaborate alterations were in fact carried out, they very soon paid for themselves by the substantial saving in water.

A large weir with a straight sill was built when the locks were modified and some of the sandstone blocks may have come from the earlier flight. Bratch locks were extensively repaired in A. J. Butler's day, when diamond-patterned bricks were used to edge the chambers, towing path and steps. These repairs were presumably carried out about 1927, since this date is cast in the iron quoins of the top lock.

Upper Bratch bridge (No. 48, Plate 32) was there in the 'staircase' days and its sandstone quoins were retained when the present parapet and walls of blue brick were added. The toll house, perhaps the most striking feature of Bratch locks, is a tower-like octagonal building with a central (and purely ornamental) stone chimney and iron-framed windows which give a clear view up and down the canal. No. 48 is a turnover bridge, as was evident from the grooves in the saddleback coping stones, worn by the tow ropes of boats working uphill. (These grooves were mostly filled with mortar to improve the appearance of the bridge when the locks were repainted in 1972!) The towpath changes sides here because the brook that has followed the canal from Dimmingsdale passes under the canal near the tail of the bottom lock. Aside from a short section at Swindon, the towing path stays to the west of the canal, between it and the Stour, all the way to Kidderminster. Below bridge No. 48 is the upper of the 'extra' gates, which open into a recess cut in the original masonry. The culvert to the upper side pond is at the back of the recess and is effectively sealed when the gate is open. If this happens when the lock is emptied, a lockful of water cascades down the towing path! Next to the ground paddles are iron slides, as there are on the next lock down, and these enable the culverts to be sealed when work on the lock is being carried out.

From what remains of the earlier flight, it looks as though the gates are in their original positions and it is difficult to see how the lower locks were extended to make room for the extra top gates and short pounds. The bottom lock has an overflow weir as a safeguard against misuse of the lower side paddles and this could be a relic of the staircase. A weir of this type is a usual feature of early staircase locks where there is no side pond, as at Botterham on this canal and 'The Lift' on the Caldon. Below the bottom lock are fragments of an iron split bridge and next to it is Bratch bridge (No. 47, Plate 33). This has been extended to the south, almost doubling its width, but it is still narrow and a serious hazard to traffic along the Trysull road. The pronounced batter of the original sandstone blocks is prominent in the later walls and there is an extraordinary collection of walls and steps, and also an arch to enable boatmen to leave or rejoin their boats. No such provision was made at many locks on the canal, or for boats to pass without the towline having to be unhitched, yet here nothing was spared to make life easier for the boatmen. The stonework is certainly of great age and seems to be contemporary with the canal, so why were such facilities not provided at every lock?

We are back on water-bearing rocks at Wombourn and there is a particularly fine waterworks at the Bratch. If the architect intended to make the works look like something else, he certainly succeeded, but it is not clear whether he drew his inspiration from a Highland castle or a Loire chateau! The first borehole here was sunk 150ft into the Upper Bunter Sandstone and a later hole of 640ft penetrated the underlying Pebble Beds where water occurs.

in greater quantity. Though both boreholes are shallow by modern standards, they supplied over 2 million gallons a day to Bilston in the Black Country and to villages around Wombourn until they were taken over by the South Staffordshire Waterworks Company. The Bratch is not an ideal site for a borehole—a well of the same depth a mile or so to the west would probably have had a greater yield—but the pumping engine depended on a continual supply of coal to fire its boilers. For this reason, the Bratch station and many others were built alongside the canal and here the wharf was just below bridge No. 47.

A few hundred yards from the Bratch is the farthest point reached by the Wolverhampton & Bridgnorth Railway. The remainder was never built and the line continued southwards to Himley and Baggeridge Junction. The track is now lifted throughout, but Wombourn station still stands and, like Tettenhall, is part of a small factory.

For just over a mile the Staffs & Worcs skirts round Wombourn, the largest village on the canal, though with a population of over 12,000 its 'village' status is becoming questionable. It is separated from the Black Country by the Sedgley ridge and is an expanding dormitory on the doorstep of the industrial Midlands without being part of it. Before the coming of the canal, Wombourn was a mere handful of houses around the village green and ancient church, or scattered along the banks of a small brook. This stream, the 'Wom Burn', in fact gave the village its name. The suburban sprawl of recent years has changed the character of Wombourn, but it still has something of a village atmosphere and the green is now the local cricket field. The change started with the opening of the canal. Small communities settled its banks at places with delightful names like Giggetty, Houndel, Bumble Hole and Bratch, all immortalised in cast iron on canal bridges (Plate 80). Agriculture gradually gave way to other industries, of the 'cottage' rather than the 'heavy' variety, though it did boast a small ironworks in 1866. The newcomers were chiefly nailers who worked for Midland manufacturers, using the canal for importing iron strip and sending away the finished articles.

The canal, mineral wealth and water power were responsible for the early growth of Wombourn, but quite different factors led to its recent expansion. Throughout the 19th century two families of leading industrialists lived in the area, the Shaw-Helliers of The Wodehouse and the Dudleys of Himley. Both owned large estates around the town of Dudley and elsewhere and both had interests in a number of industries, canals and other enterprises in the Black Country. Following their example, families of lesser standing moved to Wombourn and as the century progressed it became fashionable to live here, away from the smoke and grime of the industrial regions. As happened at Old Swinford and similar places, these families salved their consciences, if not their souls, by rebuilding much of the parish church at Wombourn in 1867. The railway reached Wombourn too late to have much effect on the village and it was the bus from Wolverhampton and more recently the private car that accelerated its expansion. Estates of council houses appeared between the old village and the canal in the late 1920s and houses of all types have since appeared in large numbers. Light industry has also returned and is mainly along the canal, as it had been a century earlier. Although the face of Wombourn has been transformed over the years, the Staffs & Worcs forms an unchanging link with its past, since the section through the parish is much as Brindley left it 200 years ago.

27⅝-27¾   *Bumble Hole Bridge (No. 46) & Lock*   18½-18⅜
and Houndel Bridge (No. 45)

Nearly every lock along this section is a perfect example of early canal engineering and Bumble Hole is no exception. Bridge No. 46 has the usual features of the original ones, yet it is totally different (Plate 34). What a pleasing picture the sloping parapet makes, following the shallow-pitched roof of the lock cottage beyond. The cottage itself is one of the best examples remaining on the canal, with its deep-set eaves and rounded iron-framed windows. Another oddity is a bricked-up arch on the offside, perhaps at one time a rack for stop planks. This was usual practice on some canals, but something of a rarity on the Staffs & Worcs. Bumble Hole is an unusual name and yet it also occurs a few miles away, on the Dudley Canal at Netherton. The unlikely explanation for the name is that it represents the noise made by a drop hammer at a forge. This may be plausible for the Netherton one, but there was never a forge at this Bumble Hole. Perhaps nailers from Netherton who moved to Wombourn brought the name with them!

The 'soft' sands of the Upper Mottled Sandstone that we met at Wightwick are to be seen all around Bumble Hole. Now the warm red cliffs of old quarries only add charm to the canal, but not so long ago the sand was being dispatched in boatloads for making moulds for castings and iron 'pigs'. The canal is lined with old wharves in the northern part of Wombourn parish, where the sand set out on its journey to Black Country foundries. There were wharves above and below the lock, with another near Houndel bridge (No. 45). The embankment of an old tramway from a quarry to the west of the canal can still be seen crossing swampy fields. It reaches the canal near the tail of Bumble Hole lock and the track then turns abruptly along a wharf. Some of the sleepers and rails are still embedded in the towing path.

Ounsdale was another busy spot in the days of canal carrying, as is apparent from the steps leading directly from the canal to the 'Round Oak'. The pub was a popular one and there was stabling at the back. No snacks are available here now, but light refreshments and ordered meals can be had at the 'Mount Pleasant', about 300yd along the road to Wombourn village. This area was called 'Oundsdale' when nameplates were attached to the bridges, so there was no excuse for calling No. 45 'Houndel'. Like Bumble Hole, this bridge has a bricked-up arch on the offside. By the access to the towing path on each side of the bridge are two of the posts that once had black and white enamelled signs issuing a warning to trespassers. Beyond the bridge is one of the compensation weirs that diverted surplus water to Penn brook and the pond of Heath forge. There are also one or two factories at Ounsdale, outliers of the Wombourn Industrial Estate, built to provide jobs for people that have moved to Wombourn since the 1930s. Houndel bridge (Plate 35) has had a skew extension added.

28-28⅜   *Giggetty and Wombourne Bridges*   18⅛-17¾
                        (Nos. 44 & 43)

The canal dropped without warning into a steep-sided valley at the Bratch and below Houndel bridge the waterway leaves it just as abruptly. The lower land around the canal is the meeting place of the Penn and Wom brooks and not far to the south the Wom joins the Smestow—at the village of the same name. In this hollow the Bunter sandstones again disappear below fairly level glacial or river deposits of sand and gravel. The descent of the canal is arrested briefly and the next locks are a mile away at Botterham. This sand was also quarried and there are more wharves here where it was loaded into boats, but its use was very different from that dispatched from Bumble Hole. There the grains are rounded, but here the action of ice and water has produced the 'sharp' sand used by the building trade. The canal crosses the Wom brook just past the winding hole for these wharves and nearby the brook itself crosses Giggetty lane by a ford. The first of the wharves is near Giggetty bridge (No. 44) in the midst of a housing estate and at one time there were several old cottages near here that may have been occupied by nailers.

Although most of the wharves were connected with sandpits, the one along the towing path about 300yd beyond Giggetty bridge was different. This was Heath Forge wharf which was sufficiently important to be listed in the Canal Company's official Table of Distances. There are some old cottages near the wharf and the track from them leads to Heath mill. The forge may have been here when the canal was built and was certainly very much in use during the first half of the 19th century, but by 1880 it had been converted into a corn mill. This fate befell several forges along the Smestow and Stour. Some disappeared completely and a few changed to other processes and still survive. There was a vast Y-shaped pond at Heath, with one arm fed by a long leat that left the Smestow at Trysull and the other by Penn brook directly, collecting surplus water from the canal on the way. The Wom brook avoided the pool and joined the Smestow lower down. Although the Wom is quite small, it powered a number of mills farther upstream. One of these, the Wodehouse mill about $1\frac{1}{2}$ miles from Giggetty still grinds meal for cattle food.

The last of this group of wharves is near Wombourne bridge (No. 43). This bridge has been rebuilt to carry traffic along the main road between Dudley and Bridgnorth (B4176), and again the nameplate has been retained. The pub here, 'The Waggon & Horses', replaced an earlier inn on the same site in 1939 and has for many years been known as 'The Brickbridge'. The area too is

called by that name, which is surprising, for nearly all bridges on
the Staffs & Worcs are built of brick. Perhaps this is the reason
why the Canal Company called it 'Wombourne Common Bridge
& Wharf'. Similar indecision surrounds the enigmatic 'e' of
Wombourn(e). The Parish Council, Post Office and Canal Company favour one, the Church and Great Western Railway are
undecided, the Ordnance Survey manages quite well without and
and residents please themselves!

Before it finally leaves Wombourn, the canal passes the industrial estate. A commendably enlightened bit of planning has
discreetly set the estate apart from the residential areas of the
village, separated from them by the Himley road and the canal.

$28\frac{7}{8}$ *Botterham Bridge (No. 42) & Two Locks* $17\frac{1}{4}$

At Botterham the canal rejoins the Smestow, after its 5-mile short
cut from Wightwick, and promptly plunges into the valley before
resuming its more leisurely descent to the Severn. The staircase-
pair or 'riser' here (Plate 36) has a fall of over 20ft and this fine
double lock may well be of historical importance. It is a very
early example of a staircase and the original flight at the Bratch
was perhaps identical in construction.

As at the Bratch, the bottom lock has a large overflow weir,
though whether it is original or was added later in the light of
experience is not clear. It may be a comfort to novice boatmen of
today to learn that from time to time their experienced pre-
decessors must have attempted to fill a lock that was already full!
The paddle gear of the top lock is 'second hand' from the BCN
and is more robust than that used by the old Company, being
entirely of iron. It was the practice of the S&WCCo. to fit two
separate paddles to the top gates, wound from the footboard.
Now they have mostly been replaced by a single and safer paddle
operated from the bank, or have been removed altogether.

The lock cottage at Botterham has recently been restored and
modernised and the bay window overlooking the canal has been
removed. The purist might object to this treatment, but the
alternative would certainly have been demolition. As we have
seen in our journey from Haywood, many lock cottages along the
Staffs & Worcs have been demolished, often with indecent haste

and assisted by vandals. It is a pity that a use could not have been found for more of them, if only as weekend cottages. There was also stabling here and behind the house are a couple of stalls.

There is a circular weir above the lock and below it is another distinctive bridge, this time with a 'cranked' parapet. This bridge carries the straight, rough lane that leads from the Himley road to the lock. Any sand or gravel that may have been here has long since been swept away by the Smestow and we are now back on the Upper Mottled Sandstone of the Bunter Series. This sandstone outcrops along the land and around the locks. The Smestow twists and turns in a series of tight meanders in the floor of the valley and below the lock surplus water flows into one of the river's excursions towards the canal. The elaborate weir and spillway carried compensation water for the pool of Swindon forge. Nearby are a small warehouse and wharf and a cottage that used to be the 'Boat Inn'. It is many years since a pint was pulled here, or poured from a jug, to be precise, but until the early years of this century Botterham was quite a busy place. The reason, in addition to trade from the canal, may have been the mill at Smestow about $\frac{1}{4}$ mile upstream. Next to the cottage a new pipe crosses the canal, large but inelegant when compared with the crossing of the Elan Valley pipeline near Wolverley. This pipe links the storage reservoir at Hampton Loade with the new and totally enclosed reservoir astride Sedgley Beacon hill.

29$\frac{1}{4}$-29$\frac{1}{2}$ *Marsh Bridge (No. 41) & Lock*   16$\frac{7}{8}$-16$\frac{5}{8}$
and Swindon Bridge (No. 40), Lock & Wharf

Swindon is dominated by its old ironworks (Plate 37), once the source of much trade on the canal and the pride of the Baldwin family and now in a state of suspended animation with an uncertain future. Early iron making and forging was a cottage industry, situated where water power and wood for charcoal were abundant. With iron not too far away, the Smestow and Stour valleys were ideal for the industry. The introduction of coke for smelting caused the industry to become concentrated in the Black Country, where coal was abundant and iron ore fairly plentiful, but the hilly terrain and lack of canal or river transport meant the change took place more slowly than elsewhere. Consequently, works along the Stour and Smestow, with the Severn not far away, managed to survive until the Staffs & Worcs arrived to give them a new lease of life. The introduction of the puddling process for making wrought iron by Henry Cort in 1784 gave the forges another fillip and the iron industry actually expanded during the first half of the 19th century. Many puddling furnaces were built along the banks of the rivers and cast 'pigs' for them were brought by canal from Dudley, Netherton and Cradley. By 1852 there were 63 puddling furnaces along the Stour and Smestow, almost 5% of the total for South Staffordshire and Worcestershire, including the Black Country, and by 1873 the number had increased to 77.

There is said to have been a forge at Swindon in the 17th century and the compensation weir at Botterham indicates that there was probably a mill or forge here when the canal was built. Only its pond is shown on the Ordnance map of 1834 and the 1852 list of furnaces included in Beete Juke's account of the South Staffordshire Coalfield does not mention Swindon. However, by 1873 there were 12 puddling furnaces and a couple of mills or forges here, owned by E. P. & W. Baldwin Ltd. After what seems to have been an uncertain start, Swindon rapidly increased in importance as far as the canal was concerned. The official Table of Distances listed it as 'Swindon Forge Bridge, Wharf, Lock and Ironwork'. The introduction of the Bessemer process for making steel in the 1860s, followed by the Siemen's open-hearth furnace, greatly reduced the demand for wrought iron towards the end of the century and many of these outlying ironworks closed down. Some of them, including Swindon, changed over to the rolling of steel strip and bar and the canal was again partly responsible for the continued existence of the works here, though the Company's amalgamation with Richard Thomas to become part of the RTB group was another factor. Steel for Swindon came in Bantock's boats from the railway interchange basin at Stourbridge, a traffic that continued until after the last war and coal was brought from Ashwood basin and the Cannock Coalfield.

The two world wars helped to prolong the life of Swindon works. Here was an established industry, well away from the main targets of enemy air attacks and linked by canal with the rest of the Midlands. The works more than doubled its size sometime between 1900 and 1920, probably during the First World War, and the chimney near the canal was built in 1943 when modernisation was carried out during the last war. While Whittington, the Hyde and Greensforge became mere hamlets and Gothersley little more than a name on the map, Swindon grew into a prosperous three-pub village, an outlier of the industrial Black Country.

Although it is many years since the forge was powered by water, the mill pond still exists next to Marsh lock and has been used as a dump for effluent from the present works. The gaunt skeletons of trees and bushes and its lifeless waters bear witness of industrial pollution at its very worst, a warning of man's environmental suicide if allowed to continue unchecked. The weir at Marsh lock is unusual for two reasons. It is oval in section, the only one of this type on the canal, and it is half way along the lock on the offside.

Either as a contribution to the war effort or simply because of the substantial traffic to Swindon works, the Canal Company improved Marsh and Swindon locks and also the waterway in between. They even violated the 'towpath rule' for the first and only time on the Staffs & Worcs. As Brindley built it, the canal had the towing path between it and the Smestow, but some time between 1900 and 1920 Marsh bridge (No. 41) was converted to a turnover bridge and the path changed sides for about 300yd. This was to enable boats to load at the extended wharf without hindrance from horse-drawn traffic. The original red-brick walls of No. 41 are set square to the canal, but the walls of blue brick and decking of the roving bridge are skewed. The 'new' towpath is edged with diamond-pattern bricks and it returns to the correct side at Swindon bridge (No. 40). Alterations to Swindon lock were carried out at the same time and the top gate was rehung on the opposite side.

After the withdrawal of boat traffic to Swindon, all materials to and from the works travelled by road. Bridge No. 40 was weakened by loads it was never intended to carry, even though it had been rebuilt and repaired from time to time. Reinforcing girders have now reduced the headroom to 6ft 6in. and No. 40 is now the lowest bridge on the canal, a distinction that once belonged to Flatheridge (No. 36), according to the boatmen.

The nearest pub to bridge No. 40 is the 'Green Man' next to the works; at the opposite end of the village are the 'Old Bush' and 'Greyhound', and all three supply sandwiches. Although they were built long before the end of the 19th century, their trade was mainly from the works rather than the canal and the 'Green Man' was in fact owned by the Baldwin family. The iniquitous 'truck' system was perhaps in operation there until its use became unlawful. There are some old stables not far from the canal, but these probably housed horses for the day boats of later years. The long-distance hauliers preferred to stop at Botterham or Greensforge.

29¾-30⅛   *Hinksford Lock & Bridges*   16¾-16
              (Nos. 39 & 38)

Hinksford lock stands quite alone and there is no sign of it ever having had a cottage. A public footpath from the Swindon road crosses the canal by Hinksford bridge (No. 39) and used to continue across the fields to a corn mill. The Company thought it worth their while to place one of their enamel notices near the bridge, even though the mill went out of use early this century. Hinksford lock was one of the last to have its wooden quoins replaced by iron ones, this being carried out under Les Butler in 1938. The weir on the offside is made up of a series of irregular segments, and Hinksford lock has a fall of only 7ft, the first of the shallow locks as the Smestow valley begins to flatten slightly.

Bridge No. 39 has no towing path and was built at the same time as the canal. Immediately below it and carved into a sandstone bank is the winding hole for boats from Swindon or Hinksford and beyond is an old sandpit. The rock beds here are near the bottom of the Upper Mottled Sandstone and for several miles the canal follows their junction with the underlying Bunter Pebble Beds. We met these pebbly sandstones around Baswich and the course of the canal has since been on more recent rocks. The top of the Pebble Beds is usually the best place to start sinking boreholes for water supplies and sure enough there is a pumping station at Hinksford. This station, built in 1900, is the first of several along the next few miles that are owned by the South Staffordshire Waterworks Company but it is the only one that ever had coal delivered by canal. The station's vertical marine engines were unexceptional and were removed in 1948.

Just before the coal wharf of the pumping station is a cottage on the offside that may be on an earlier wharf, though the Table of Distances does not mention one here. Lengthsmen's cottages are usually on the same side of the canal as the towing path and this building may have been a wharf house where a check was made on the loading of sand from neighbouring pits. A gas pipe passes under the canal near the cottage and next to it is the weir and channel that carried compensation water for the benefit of Green's forge about ¾ mile down the Smestow.

Bridge No. 38 is also called 'Hinksford', another example of the duplication of names we met at Wightwick and Compton. At one time the cartway to Hinksford corn mill passed over it, but now it leads to the neat and well-kept Mobile Homes Park of Seisdon RDC. For many years a canalside pub, the 'Old Bush', stood between the bridge and waterworks, but it was pulled down in the late 1930s and replaced by the present and highly popular house about 200yd away. The new 'Old Bush' provides snacks and a wide range of grills and its style, both inside and out, is intended to be Spanish. Although it perhaps lacks the charming atmosphere and veneer of nicotine of older canal pubs, the beer is 'home brewed' by way of compensation!

30⅞   *Greensforge Lock, Bridge (No. 37) & Wharf*   15¼

The Table of Distances, on which tolls were based, mentions a wharf and basin at Greensforge. The wharf that used to serve Mr Green's forge is still there, but there is no sign of a basin and this is in fact ½ mile to the south at Ashwood. Most of the traffic from it was southbound and perhaps by calling it 'Greensforge Basin' the Company were able to extract tolls for an extra ½ mile of canal. Green's forge was converted into a large corn mill at some time during the 19th century, possibly when the neighbouring ironworks at Gothersley closed down. The mill itself went out of nse towards the end of the century, but the imposing buildings are intact and are now a farm.

There is another circular weir at Greensforge, on the offside, and a cantilever split-bridge over the tail of the lock. Greensforge

bridge (No. 37) has been radically altered and extended in much
the same way as No. 47 at the foot of Bratch locks. The huge
stone blocks of the earlier bridge are clearly visible in the walls
and give the impression that originally the bridge did not have a
towing path. The openings, steps and stone walling that make
Aw, Bratch, Greensforge and other bridges so attractive seem to
have been moulded around and cut into the earlier sandstone
quoins. There is evidence at Greensforge and elsewhere that lock
bridges along the canal were built without a towing path and that
those on a public road, where horses crossing frequently would
be a nuisance, were subsequently modified. If this did in fact
happen, the alterations must have been carried out in the early
days of the canal, perhaps before the end of the 18th century.

Men who were employed by the old Company and who still
work on the canal barely number half a dozen. George Wood
(Plate 38), who lives at the lock cottage here, is a member of this
élite band. Like the boatmen, those who maintained the canals
were born, lived and died on the cut, as often as not. George's
father worked on the Staffs & Worcs, as did his grandfather, his
mother was born in the cottage at Greensforge and his wife,
Margaret, was toll clerk at Stewponey during the years before
nationalisation. When George's grandfather rebuilt Castle Croft
bridge (No. 55), he set out from Greensforge to walk 6½ miles to
do the job and he frequently walked the 15 miles to the Company's
depot at Stourport. George himself was a lengthsman and one of
his duties was to keep the grass scythed and the hedges trimmed
along a 3-mile section. Hedges were brushed every year and
layered periodically, and the rest of the time was spent with the
dredger or ice breaking. There were two steam dredgers in operation, one based at Gailey and working on the northern section,
and one dealt with the southern part of the canal. It is often said
that the Company were not above cutting dredging costs by
adding a course of bricks to the weirs. According to George this
was done, though for a slightly different reason. It was to keep
traffic moving on a shallow pound while the dredger was working
somewhere else and boards were often placed across weirs for the
same purpose.

Greensforge was another place where boatmen stayed overnight. The stables behind the 'Navigation Inn' are at present used

as a bottle store. A stone over the door of the inn is inscribed '1744' and '1767', but it has only recently been placed there and the authenticity of the dates is by no means certain. However, it may be that the pub was built in the earlier year for the benefit of workers at Mr Green's forge and was later enlarged to accommodate thirsty 'navvies' while they were cutting the canal through Greensforge. The pub was completely renovated a few years ago and a large car park built on the opposite side of the road. This highway divides a few yards beyond the 'Navigation' and the left fork cuts through the ramparts of a Roman fort. A recent aerial survey has revealed that this is part of an extensive Roman settlement.

$31\frac{3}{8}$-$31\frac{3}{4}$ Ashwood (Greensforge) Basin, Flatheridge Bridge $14\frac{3}{4}$-$14\frac{3}{8}$ (No. 36) and Rocky (Hockley) Lock

Not far from Greensforge is the inconspicuous entrance to Ashwood or Greensforge basin, a narrow gap through which a significant proportion of the canal's traffic passed for over a century. Ashwood basin was one of several improvements to the Dudley estates made between 1825 and 1840. In 1774 the estates were inherited by John, 2nd Lord Viscount Dudley & Ward, who brought fame and fortune to the family and rapidly became one of the country's leading industrialists. However, the Staffs & Worcs had been in use for a number of years by this time and the Dudleys only played a minor part in the story of the canal. Instead they concentrated on creating links between their estates and the Staffs & Worcs and over a period of 50 years built or promoted many miles of canal, road and railway. Towards the end of this period the 4th Lord Dudley, William John, decided to build a railway from Shutt End on his Kingswinford estates to the canal at Ashwood, partly to avoid having to pay tolls to the Stourbridge Company and partly to tap areas of the coalfield not already served by canal.

The Kingswinford Railway was financed by Lord Dudley and John Foster of Stourbridge, at whose foundry the first locomotive to work the line, the *Agenoria* (Plate 39), was built. Work started in 1827 and there was an incline down from the collieries, a few miles of level track and a second incline down to the canal

at Ashwood basin. The *Agenoria* ran along the level section and
the inaugural trip took place amidst much pomp and ceremony on
2nd June 1829. The *Agenoria* handled all the traffic along the line
for many years and this unusual locomotive, with tall chimney and
beam engine, has survived and is at present in exile in the Railway
Museum at York. The line itself was improved by the removal of
the inclines and about 1840 became part of the Pensnett Railway
that extended to all corners of the Dudley estates. There was a
substantial increase in coal traffic from Ashwood basin when
Baggeridge colliery opened early this century and from 1926
onwards, Stourport Power Station was one of the main customers.
Several carriers loaded at the basin and the Earl of Dudley had his
own fleet to carry coal to the wharf at Kidderminster (Plate 40).
Boats to 'Stourport Light', as the power station was called, were
withdrawn about the middle of 1949, several years after the
Kingswinford Railway had closed, and these were among the
last boats to load at the basin. It lay derelict for a few years
before being restored to become Ashwood Marina (Plate 41).
There are now permanent moorings at Ashwood, many of them
residential, and there are also repair facilities and other boating
services.

An account of the opening of Ashwood basin in 1829 gives its
length as 750yd, but it is now slightly over 600yd and does not
appear to have been shortened at any time. A natural valley was
used for the basin and the sides were cut back to make room for
numerous sidings and loading devices, and a weighbridge was
provided at each end. For some reason, possibly dictated by the
direction of the valley, there is an oblique junction between the
basin and the main canal. It could be that Lord Dudley expected
most of the traffic from Ashwood to travel southwards. It certainly did in later years, but the sharp turn means that northbound
boats have to reverse out of the basin. A handsome viaduct spans
the entire valley and basin in an eleven-arch sweep of brick and
stone. There are five openings that once crossed sidings and
access roads and a skewed central arch over the canal. A bank of
limekilns has been replaced by the buildings of Ashwood Marina
and the sidings and weighing machines disappeared long ago.
Access to Ashwood basin from the main canal was over
Flatheridge roving bridge (No. 36, Plate 42), but the path is now

closed. Judging by the style of Flatheridge bridge, it was built at the same time as the basin.

A few hundred yards from Flatheridge bridge and in a hollow to the east of the canal is Ashwood pumping station of the South Staffordshire Waterworks Company. The station was opened in 1893 and the pumps were driven by steam engines until 1959/60. These were of most unusual design and it is a pity that one could not have been preserved. They were horizontal compound engines of non-rotating type, built by Hathorn Davey of Leeds. The design was quite different from that of a conventional beam engine and there was no flywheel. At the end of each stroke the motion was arrested by a steam brake or 'cushion'. Two of these engines were installed when the station was built and a third was added later. The boreholes at this station pass through 100ft of low-yield Upper Mottled Sandstone before reaching the prolific Pebble Beds, and the line of the canal may have influenced the siting of the station. It would have been an easy matter to build a basin here leading to the boilers, but this does not appear to have been done. Coal was carried by carts from Ashwood basin when the railway was in use and was later brought by lorry direct from the colliery.

Hockley lock, or Rocky, as it is usually known, is set amidst fields and nestles against a low cliff towards the base of the Upper Mottled Sandstone. Like most remote locks along the Staffs & Worcs, it lost its cottage a few years ago. This was the home of Bert Hardman in 1929 and before that George Wood spent part of his childhood there. George well remembers watching the 'Glosters' who had such difficulty with their high hay loads on the Hatherton branch. Here Flatheridge bridge was the problem and they used to run water through Rocky lock to drop the level in the pound above, giving themselves a few inches more of clearance. The Glosters increased the stability of their boats with apples as ballast, and after selling the hay at collieries for the pit ponies they sent the apples to Black Country markets and returned with loads of 'big' coal. Unlike other boatmen, the Glosters scorned the canalside stables and preferred to stable their pairs of donkeys— they did not use mules or horses—in the boats during overnight stops. The last of these highly individual 'Number Ones', Jacob Rice, passed down the canal for the last time about 1930.

There is another circular weir at Rocky and cut into the cliff near the head of the lock is a small cave. There are a number of these along the Staffs & Worcs and they are said to have been used as shelters or temporary homes by the 'navvies' who built the canal. The fall of Rocky lock is only 7ft, as the Smestow valley continues to level out towards the Stour.

32-32⅜   *Gothersley Lock & Bridge (No. 35)*   14⅛-13¾
                    and Round House Wharf (Plates 43-44)

Gothersley lock follows hard on the heels of Rocky and appears to have shared its lock keeper. Gothersley has a fall of 7ft, very much less than the next two locks along the canal, but the Company did not need to provide an additional supply on the intervening pound. Lockage and surplus water from the Stourbridge Canal adequately compensated for the irregular changes in level. A winding lane now crosses the tail of the lock by bridge No. 35, but in years gone by it was a track leading to Gothersley ironworks. This same track crossed the adjoining brook by a substantial two-arch bridge, evidently intended to withstand heavy loads. A tramway or cart-track may have lead to a wharf above Gothersley lock for northbound traffic, perhaps boats heading for Green's forge, but the main wharf for the ironworks was to the south.

The still waters and silvan charm of Gothersley make it hard to visualise the scene of activity here in the early days of the waterway. Gothersley was a works of some importance, with mills, forges and possibly puddling furnaces, linked by a tramway with a wharf alongside the canal. The clerk in charge of the wharf lived in the round house, built about 1805, and its presence indicates that there must have been substantial traffic to and from the wharf. The ironworks is in fact the only one along the canal to be shown on Bradshaw's map of 1830, where it is given as 'foundry'. Any furnaces here in the early days had disappeared by 1852, when the Gothersley Iron Co. were only operating the mill, and by 1882 the works had closed down.

The works was to the west of the canal and separated from it by two mill ponds, drained early this century and now mere depressions in the fields behind the wharfhouse. Unlike its counterpart at Gailey, the round house is in a sorry state and will soon be gone for ever unless steps are taken to arrest the decay.

Not far from the wharf and on the opposite side of the canal is an area of low-lying swampy land that is marked as a small basin on early maps. It may have been used by boats waiting to be loaded at Round House wharf, leaving the main channel clear, and it certainly served as a winding hole. Not so many years ago the Company's 42-ton dredger used to turn here and the entrance was cleared out for the purpose.

Of the ironworks itself nothing remains save grassy mounds, the large weir across the Smestow and the manager's house. Around the site of the works is a series of elaborate diversions and manipulations of brook courses that are typical of the Smestow valley. The main river follows an artificial channel on the opposite side of the valley from the canal and used to pass through the middle of the works, after first supplying the mill ponds. The old course of the Smestow became the 'Back brook' that bypassed the works, probably to conform with ancient water rights. A smaller mill stream, the Philley brook from the Enville estates, supplied some water to the Gothersley ponds and the remainder passed under the diverted Smestow to join the Back brook. There were many conflicting interests in these fast-flowing streams and it seems that landowners, millers and others had difficulty in agreeing amongst themselves. It is hardly surprising that the Canal Company had to search elsewhere for water. These tantalising fragments are the only indication that industry has ever invaded Gothersley.

32⅝-33⅞   *Prestwood Bridge (No. 34), Stourton*   13½-12¼
             Aqueduct, Bridge (No. 33) & Junction

One of the loveliest lengths of the Staffs & Worcs lies between Gothersley and the river Stour, where the canal follows the edge of Prestwood Park. The hall here, for many years the home of the Foley family and hidden from the canal by woodland, is now a sanatorium. Long before industry became concentrated in the Black Country, the Foleys owned ironworks, mills and forges along the Stour valley and it is surprising that they were not among the original shareholders in the canal. However, by the end of the 18th century the Foleys were among the leading iron-masters of the Midlands and earlier had given their backing to the Dudley and Stourbridge Canals.

Not only is this stretch of canal of surpassing beauty, but it also has the most perfect of all the bridges on the canal—Prestwood (No. 34, Plate 45). Beyond the reach of the County Council and ignored by ambitious farmers, it carries the back drive to Prest-wood Hall exactly as it did when built by Brindley. It has all the usual stone and brick features of bridges contemporary with the canal and is set against the red sandstone bank and lodge house among the trees. Attractive at any time, it is seen at its best in the late spring when the rhododendrons are in bloom and the wood-lands are carpeted with bluebells. The Canal Company under-standably called No. 35 'Prestwood bridge', but locally it it known by the intriguing name of 'Trickett's'. There is a pleasant and popular walk along the towpath from Stourton to bridge No. 35, returning along a path through Colbourn's Rough on the opposite side of the canal.

The valley narrows beyond Prestwood bridge and the canal is sandwiched between the sandstone ramparts of the park and the slopes of Enville Common with the alder swamps of the Smestow in between. The Upper Mottled Sandstones were left behind near Round House wharf and here the canal bank is of the older Bunter Pebble Beds. There is no clear cut division between the two types of rock and in spite of their name, there are still large areas of red sandstone in these beds. On the side of the towing path along here are long mounds of ancient dredgings, the work of the steam dredger and now with mature trees growing in them. The mounds contain bits of coal fallen from the boats, various types of fresh-water shells and other bric-à-brac that found its way into the canal in years gone by. How different is the story told by recent dredgings from our urban canals!

High on the hillside across the valley and some distance from the canal is Prestwood pumping station, another owned by the SSWCo. Unlike others we have met, the siting of this station was in no way influenced by the presence of the canal. It was built in 1926 and had electric pumps from the start, being the first station built by the company to use this new form of power. Its yield of about 3 million gallons a day is fairly typical of stations along the

Smestow and there are two boreholes that pass through the Pebble Beds into the Dune Sands or Lower Mottled Sandstone. Although both beds contain inexhaustible supplies of 'fossil' water of unknown origin, the Dune Sands have by far the greater yield. Prestwood still has its original pumps, two 'in-line' on each shaft with a pumping head of 790ft to the reservoir at Shaver's End, Dudley. The Brown-Boveri motors driving the pumps were replaced recently after about 45 years of continuous service. Once civic authorities in the Black Country had decided to provide a public water supply, it was inevitable that many of them should turn to the Triassic rocks of the Stour and Smestow valleys for their water. Ashwood and Hinksford stations were the first to feed into the rising main to Dudley and, as sanitation improved and demand increased, these were supplemented by Prestwood and later by Kinver.

Canal and river double back on themselves to negotiate a steep spur between the Smestow and Stour valleys. These hardly widen at all around the junction, a consequence of the 'rejuvenation' brought about by the Severn and in marked contrast to the meeting place at Stafford of the Penk and Sow. Brindley had little room for manoeuvre and he took the canal straight across the Stour and then turned sharply to follow its eastern bank. This may not be what he had in mind originally, for the 1766 Act specifically prevented him from making 'the said navigable Cut or Canal on the same Side of the River Stour with Stourton Castle, between the Junction of the Rivers Stour and Smestall, and a Bridge called Stourton Bridge'. The alternative route would have avoided several sharp bends, much rock cutting and a short tunnel, but would have required an aqueduct across the Smestow as well as the Stour.

The Stour aqueduct and its elevated approach are protected by stop narrows and a sluice at the Devil's Den (Plate 46). This is another picturesque spot, with the murky depths of the Den standing out against the sandstone cliff. A punt used to be kept here so that the owner of Prestwood and his guests at shooting parties could cross to the swamps on the other side of the canal. It has been suggested that the cave was excavated as a hovel for the 'navvies', but it is more likely to have been a boathouse from the start, a result of landowners' rights to navigate the canal. The two-arched aqueduct over the Stour is another classic example of Brindley's river crossings. The river passes through the eastern arch, the western normally being dry, and 90yd upstream is a low weir. The original course of the Stour left the present line near the weir and its swampy bed can still be seen until it is truncated by the canal embankment. The purpose of the weir was to divert and control the river while the aqueduct was being built and was perhaps retained to relieve pressure on the arches when the river is in spate. The sandstone arches are original, though eaten away by the corrosive effluent that passes for the river Stour. The river rises on the flanks of the Clent Hills and immediately plunges into areas that have been heavily industrialised for two centuries or more—Halesowen, Cradley, the Lye and Stourbridge itself—so its highly polluted waters are not unexpected. As occurred on the two aqueducts at Haywood, the parapet here was added at a later date and so also were the massive iron bars that protect the brick edging to the narrow channel.

Immediately after the Stour aqueduct we meet another of the canal's mysteries. Leading from the sharp bend is an immense stretch of water, 200yd long and recently separated from the main canal by an unsightly fence. It heads in the direction of the Stour-bridge Canal and almost gets there, so perhaps the intention was to build a staircase from that canal down to the Staffs & Worcs at Halfcot rather than the present flight of four locks at Stourton. It could have been a reservoir to conserve as much water as possible from the Stourbridge, for Stewponey lock comes immediately after the junction, or it may simply have been a fish pond for the Prestwood estate. The attempt to obscure the view of the lake has not been too successful, for not all boats negotiate the bend at the first attempt!

There are two small quarries in the Bunter Sandstone beyond the bend. These are part of the canal and probably provided stone during the construction of it, though Bunter Sandstone was not widely used for the purpose. Here, however, the rock is a parti-cularly massive freestone and may have been suitable for large blocks such as those used for hanging lock gates. At Stourton the canal is joined by another important branch, the Stourbridge, opened in 1779. The earlier branch from the Black Country, the Birmingham Canal, was only of limited benefit to Lord Dudley and other industrialists on the western side of the coalfield. Long before the Staffs & Worcs came into being there was a steady flow of trade along the Stour valley and a hundred years earlier Andrew Yarranton had attempted to make the river navigable. Coal was brought to Kidderminster and works along the Stour and so was iron for rolling and slitting at the forges and mills. When the works were linked by the Staffs & Worcs, proposals for a canal to Stourbridge and Dudley were not long to follow. The waterway was in fact built by two separate companies, but with mostly the same subscribers. The Staffs & Worcs had mainly been launched by landowners along its line, but the Stourbridge and Dudley canals were promoted by people like Lord Dudley, who supplied the materials needed by industry, and by chainmakers, glassmen, nailers and others who used the materials. The junction provided a very much shorter route to the Stour valley for local trade and to towns along the Severn and Bristol. The Stourbridge rapidly rivalled the Birmingham Canal in its importance as a feeder to the Staffs & Worcs and by the early years of this century had surpassed it.

From the outset most of the traffic from the Stourbridge turned south at the junction and for many years there was no building here, loads being gauged at Stewponey. About the middle of the 19th century a small toll office was built near the roving bridge and tolls were collected there from northbound boats. The office was in use until nationalisation, but there was no toll clerk here towards the end. The last boats to use this office regularly were those of Thomas Bantock. These carried steel strip and plate from the GWR transit basin at Stourbridge to the Swindon works of Richard Thomas & Baldwin. Tickets were left in a box at the office to be collected each day at 4 o'clock by George Wood's wife, Margaret, who was toll clerk at Stewponey during the war years. Stourton office has since been demolished and the roving bridge to the Stourbridge Canal has been damaged by vandals and has lost its brick parapet. Stourton bridge (No. 33) was built in 1777/9 by the Stourbridge Company and what remains is typical of bridges on that canal. The main feature that differs from bridges on the Staffs & Worcs is the use of shaped-brick springers to support the arch.

The bottom lock of the 'Stourton Four' is at the junction and is quite different from locks on the Staffs & Worcs, though barely a decade separates the two canals. Immediately above the bottom lock is a basin running parallel to the older canal for almost 100yd. This is now badly silted and overgrown and there are no signs of wharves along it. The basin was probably used for the delivery and collection of local goods to avoid paying tolls to the Staffs & Worcs and may have been used as a 'lay-by' for boats awaiting crews.

The flow of water down the Stourbridge can be considerable, for this is one of the outlets from the BCN, and Stourton locks have large overflow weirs. The Staffs & Worcs wanted all the water it could accommodate from the Stourbridge, but a sudden surge could have been an embarrassment. As a safety measure there is a long overflow weir next to the towpath on the main canal and opposite the lowest weir on the Stourbridge. Storm-water then flows straight across the Staffs & Worcs and into the river Stour before it can damage the embankments or aqueduct. The Staffs & Worcs has followed the Smestow almost from its source until the brook slips unobtrusively into the Stour, and Stourton is a geographical limit on the canal. Today this is only of passing interest, but a consequence, as we shall see, was that Stourton used to be an important control point for traffic along the canal.

6

The Stour Cut

STOURTON TO STOURPORT

Miles
from
Haywood

Miles
to
Stourport

The river Stour is never far away along the remaining 12 miles of
the Staffs & Worcs and for years boatmen have called this section
the 'Stour Cut'. Although the name came to be applied to the
entire canal, it probably originated from the heavy traffic that
flowed between the Black Country and works between Stourton
and Stourport. The canal continues its rapid descent through
splendid scenery in a region steeped in history, until it plunges
into the Severn in a blaze of glory at Stourport. The course is still
along sandstones of Triassic age and the lowest point in the series
is reached about a mile below Stourton. For the rest of the journey
the canal crosses beds of progressively younger rocks. There are
abundant relics of industry along the canal, both 'cottage' and
'heavy', but the remains are often hard to find, so well has nature
camouflaged man's violation of the Stour valley. The canal also
passes through the centre of Kidderminster, providing a brief
urban interlude amidst the rurality of the southern section.

34 *Stewponey Wharf, Lock & Bridge (No. 31) (Plate 47)* 12⅛

Whatever may be lacking at Stourton Junction in the way of
'atmosphere' is more than compensated for at Stewponey wharf.
Throughout most of the working life of the Staffs & Worcs,
this was the hub of the system. Along the northern section, the length between Aldersley and Autherley was always
busy, but otherwise trade declined after the opening of the Bir-

mingham & Liverpool Junction in 1835. Traffic originating on the southern section and trade from the Stourbridge Canal were the lifelines that enabled the Company to pay a dividend to the end. Most of the boats passed through Stewponey lock and the toll office here was the busiest on the canal. An account of some of the boat movements and loads is included in *English Canals* by Gladwin & White. Some important traffics are omitted, but there are details of about 800 loaded boats that passed through Stewponey during a six-month period in 1932/3. Over half of these boats travelled on the Stourbridge Canal and the bulk of the traffic was in coal.

Throughout the canal system generally, there were two ways of working the boats. There was the 'long-haul' traffic between industrial centres and large towns or ports, operated by families who usually lived on a pair of boats. These were originally horse drawn and worked separately, but from the late 19th century onwards a powered boat towed a 'butty'. Initially 'steamers' were used and in the 1920s these were replaced by motor boats. Until about 12 years ago, boats operating in this way could regularly be seen on canals like the Shropshire Union and the Grand Union. The other traffic was 'short haul', typical of the BCN and Black Country carriers like Ernie Thomas. 'Day boats' or 'Joeys' were used for the purpose and the cabin, if any, was little more than a shelter, so as not to occupy too much cargo space. Joeys were drawn by mules or horses, or a line of them was hauled by a tug, and a few are still at work on the BCN. Although both methods of working could be seen on the Staffs & Worcs, its relation to the South Staffordshire Coalfield and industry scattered along the Stour valley gave rise to quite a different system. This may best be described as 'intermediate-haul' traffic. The distance from Hawkins's basin, Churchbridge, to Stourport, for example, was too great to be covered in one day and most boats on the canal were worked singly by men who usually lived on board and travelled home at weekends and mid-week whenever possible. The labour force was largely recruited from boating families of the Black Country, mainly Tipton, Oldbury and Langley, where the decline in mining had made jobs scarce.

'Intermediate-haul' only became possible when the Kinver Light Railway opened in 1901. Boatmen travelled by tram from

Dudley to the 'Fish Inn' at Amblecote and caught the first tram of the day to Stewponey, arriving at 5 o'clock. This system lasted for almost half a century, long after the trams had been withdrawn and replaced by buses. It so happens that there is still a flow of commuters along this route, though the direction of flow has reversed. Many people who work in the Black Country now prefer to live around Stourton and Kinver!

Typical of the men who worked the 'intermediate-haul' traffic on the Staffs & Worcs before and during the Second World War is Tom Heritage. Tom was born into a family that worked a pair of Clayton's 'tar' boats, operating between Stanlow on the Manchester Ship Canal and the Midland Tar Distillery at Oldbury. He married a girl from another boating family and went to live near Langley Forge, Oldbury. Tom then gave up long-distance boating for good and worked for T. & S. Element on the Staffs & Worcs. Every Monday morning he travelled to Dudley with his bag of provisions, very often on foot, to catch the bus for Stewponey at 5.20 a.m. This bus, a single-deck 'Midland Red', was provided specifically for boat crews from the Black Country and it was always crammed to capacity. The 'old 'uns' smoked twist interminably and the atmosphere was thick with smoke by the time the bus reached its destination. Elements had about 33 boats at work on the Staffs & Worcs, mostly horse drawn, for motor-pairs were much slower on congested waterways with heavy lockage, and when the bus arrived at Stewponey there was a scramble to be first away. Loaded boats moored there over the weekend would go down the cut to Stourport Power Station and empty boats would travel in the opposite direction.

In a typical week, Tom would collect his horse from the stables at Stewponey wharf—Elements did not use mules—and would take his boat up the canal to Ashwood basin. Here he would pick up a load of steel 'flats' for Swindon ironworks. After unloading these he would carry on to Littleton colliery basin at Otherton, Hawkins's basin on the Hatherton branch or Cannock & Leacroft colliery up Churchbridge locks, only stopping for an hour or so at Gailey to rest his horse and quench his thirst at the 'Plough'. After collecting a load of up to 38 tons of coal slack at one of the colliery basins, he returned to Compton or even Ounsdale on occasions, where he spent Monday night. After stabling his horse for the night, Tom still found time for a drink and game of bar skittles at the nearest pub.

On Tuesday morning Tom would carry on down to Stourport, stopping only at the Bratch and Kidderminster for toll checks. After unloading at the basin he returned to Ashwood for another load of slack and spent Tuesday night at Greensforge, Stewponey or Kinver. Only on the run from Ashwood were the boats gauged by Fred Wood at Stewponey office and this is the reason why the details in *English Canals* only cover a fraction of the traffic on the Staffs & Worcs. Tom and his fellow boatmen tried to reach Stewponey on Wednesday evening, when they returned home for fresh supplies of food and a change of clothing. First thing on Thursday morning they travelled back to Stewponey and the second half of the week was much the same as the first. The week's work usually finished about mid-day on Saturday. It was hard work, between 12 and 18 hours a day, and the pay was a mere £4 5s 0d a week. Boats often worked through the night, in pitch darkness during the war years, and in all weathers. Only when the cold was so intense that the Company's ice breakers failed to keep the channel clear did the traffic stop. On these occasions the Elements crews worked under contract at ice breaking on the BCN.

It was only the wartime measure known as 'Essential Orders' that kept Tom and many of his colleagues on the 'Light Run', as the traffic to Stourport Power Station was called. Immediately the war was over he left Elements, but not the canals. He joined Alfred Matty & Son of Coseley and has been with them ever since, working a pair carrying phosphatic waste from Albright & Wilson of Oldbury to a lagoon at Tividale. Old boatmen like Tom Heritage, many of whom can neither read nor write, have acquired a philosophical approach to life that only comes with years at a helm, summer and winter, following behind a plodding horse. Theirs is a diminishing race, an anachronism in this age of motorways, but their passing will be our loss.

Stewponey takes its name from an inn that was here long before the arrival of the canal. This was the 'Stewponey & Foley Arms' at the junction of two important highways, the roads between Wolverhampton and Kidderminster and between Stourbridge and Bridgnorth. The inn was demolished when the junction was improved in the late 1930s and a pretentious replacement was built on an adjoining site. At the same time a new road bridge was built across the canal on the site of the trestle bridge that carried the Kinver Railway. There was also an early ironworks nearby, across the river Stour in the grounds of Stourton castle. However, Stewponey's main importance lay in its association with the canal, as is evident from the assemblage of buildings around the wharf. There are a lock house, toll office and cottages, and at one time there were warehouses, stables and a small carpenter's shop operated by the Canal Company.

The wharf is now owned by Dawncraft whose showroom for small craft occupies the site of the stables and who also renovated the toll office. Along the towing path between the lock and Stourton Junction are more relics of days gone by—a number of iron rings where a score or more of boats moored at weekends in the days of the 'Light Run'.

The Kinver Light Railway was an institution in its day and had the section from Stewponey to Kinver survived, it would now doubtless be a major tourist attraction. The KLR was built at the end of the 19th century by the British Electric Traction Co. and was opened on Good Friday, 4th April 1901. Soon afterwards it was purchased by the Dudley, Stourbridge & District Electric Traction Co. and the trams ran between Colbournbrook, Amblecote, to Kinver, a distance of 4¼ miles. An overhead supply was used and the gauge was 3ft 6in. From the outskirts of Stourbridge to Stewponey the track was laid by the side of the road and it then crossed the Staffs & Worcs near the old bridge (No. 32). The tramway then took to the fields alongside the canal, passed through the site of the Hyde ironworks, and terminated at Kinver (Plate 53), after crossing the Stour four times and the Hyde mill stream once. The first river crossing is a little way along the Bridgnorth road from Stewponey and the bridge still has a short length of track, complete with sleepers. Further details and illustrations of the KLR may be found in *Black Country Tramways* by J. S. Webb. The first volume of this comprehensive work, covering the period 1872 to 1912, was published in 1974 and the second will follow shortly.

The tramway was very heavily used. Not only did it enable men from the Black Country to find jobs outside the area when canal trade was feeling the effects of the decline in mining and associated industries, but it also provided a link with the countryside. At the cost of a few pence, people could get away from the smoke and grime of industry, often for the first time, into the fresh air of Kinver. During the summer months there were many excursions, with through cars from all over the Black Country and Birmingham. Privately hired cars for parties on day outings were also very popular and of course the locals found the line of great benefit. George Wood used to travel on the tram from his home at Stewponey lock to school in Kinver and paid 1d for the pleasure. The Kinver Light Railway was closed on 8th February 1930, a few weeks before the closure of much of the Black Country system.

34⅜-35   *Dunsley Tunnel (No. 31) and Hyde Lock*   11¾-11⅛
& Bridge (No. 30)

The Staffs & Worcs is certainly not noted for its tunnels. Many canals have a long tunnel where the summit level crosses a watershed, but on this waterway there is only the shallowest of cuttings at Aldersley. The first tunnel in our journey along the Staffs & Worcs, and one of the earliest on any canal, is at Dunsley. This short drift is 23yd long, less than a boat's length, and might easily be mistaken for a long bridge; an early Ordnance map in fact has it as 'Dunsley Tunnel Bridge'. However, a tunnel it is, and a most attractive one at that, with unlined walls hewn through the Pebble Beds and unfaced portals festooned with ivy. It also has a towing path, a feature usually associated with tunnels built much later in the canal era. In Brindley's day and for many years afterwards boats had to be legged or shafted through tunnels and Dunsley is an exception only because it is short and cut through soft rock. There are similar examples at Cookley on the Staffs & Worcs and at Armitage on the Trent & Mersey, though this was opened out in 1971.

There is an exposure in the Pebble Beds near the southern portal of Dunsley tunnel, where harder strata have been supported on brick piers. The softer material underneath has been eroded away by wash from boats and the brickwork is to prevent the cliff from crumbling into the canal. A short distance beyond the tunnel the Kinver Light Railway joins the canal and then follows it to

Kinver. The fine row of trees near the bend was a familiar land-mark to the boatmen, who called this section 'The Beeches' (Plate 48). Ahead lies the Hyde, as idyllic a spot as anywhere on the Staffs & Worcs, though it was not always so. The woods to the west disguise the tips of ash and slag from the biggest iron-works along the canal.

Hyde ironworks (Plate 49) was one of the oldest of the Stour valley and for many years was owned by the Foley family. The works included a slitting mill operated by the Stour, where iron plate from the tilt hammers was cut into thin bars and strips for blacksmiths and nailers. Richard Foley introduced the process of slitting to the Midlands in 1628 and this may well have been the mill where he did so. The ingenious Foley is said to have set off to Russia with his grandfather's Stradivarius and to have posed as a mendicant fiddler from France to obtain details of the slitting process. Unfortunately this romantic tale of industrial espion-age is quite untrue. The slitting of iron originated in Flanders and was introduced into this country towards the end of the 16th cen-tury. However, the Foley myth makes interesting reading and is recounted in full in Griffith's *Guide to the Iron Trade of Great Britain*, published in 1873.

Although Hyde ironworks existed long before the canal, it was greatly extended when the waterway link with the Black Country made it easier to obtain plentiful supplies of iron. Towards the end of the 19th century, when the works was operated by Lee & Bolton, there was a frontage along the canal of about 400ft and to the north was an arm leading into the works. There were 20 puddling furnaces for producing wrought iron, over a quarter of all the furnaces along the Stour valley, and also 5 mills and forges. By 1873 steel was being produced by two Siemens open-hearth fur-naces, but in spite of this 'modernisation', Hyde ironworks was too remote to survive to the present day. In its heyday the works specialised in high quality iron, the Best Best, stamped 'BB'. Bars, rods, sheets and angle iron were produced and plating was also carried out. The works is shown on the 6in. Ordnance map of 1881 and it must have closed down soon afterwards, for the Kinver Light Railway of 1898 ran through the site of the works and its ash tip. Most of the tip was removed to provide ballast for the permanent way and a car depot was built in the space formerly occupied by the cinder and slag.

All that remains of the works is a solitary house (Plate 50) and this has been tastefully restored. Of the rest there is nothing except low mounds in the undergrowth, slag walls, mill ponds and dry beds of leats. Rather more is left of the slitting mill. The slitting of iron was superceded by rolling, a process that almost certainly originated in south Staffordshire. By 1880 the Hyde mill was forging spades and other tools, and it continued to do so well into the present century. The sites of the ironworks, mills and ponds are all on private land, but the approach road is a public track. The manager's house is the only building shown on the etching in Griffith's directory that can still be recognised. The main entrance to the works was next to the house, near where the tramway crossed the approach road, and beyond is a substantial bridge where the road crosses the tailrace of the spade mill. Although it is many years since industry departed from this isolated spot, there is still a community at the Hyde. The bungalows probably started life as holiday chalets shortly after the Kinver Light Railway opened. A row of workers' cottages was pulled down recently and there are a couple of modern houses and a farm with an ancient dovecote. The main sluice of the spade mill was where the track crosses the Stour. This provided a head of several feet to drive the mill, impounded many thousand gallons of water, and enabled water to be diverted into the ironworks ponds. A few yards along the track to the Bridgnorth road is a house that once was the 'New Inn', a pub that went out of use when the ironworks closed down. Another track leads to Kinver village and a public footpath starts near the Stour bridge and crosses the fields to Stourton and Stewponey.

Prestwood is a contender for the prettiest bridge along the canal and the Hyde is certainly a candidate for the most attractive lock (Plates 50 & 51). The natural setting of the wooded hillside and sandstone cliffs merge into more formal gardens and mown grass around the lock. The gardens are the work of Jim Hodgson, who lives at the lock cottage and goes to great lengths to keep the place neat and tidy. Jim works for the Waterways Board at Stourport depot and his wife, Mary, provides morning coffee, lunches and teas at the lock cottage. The Hyde is a haven for hikers, boaters and others who use the canal. It is by no means the only instance along the Staffs & Worcs of what can be done to transform a commercial canal into a recreational waterway, but it is one of the best examples.

As at many remote locks, there is no towpath under Hyde bridge (No. 30), though the arch has been largely rebuilt at some time. At the winding hole above the lock and also near the track leading down to the cottage are exposures of the oldest rocks along the Staffs & Worcs, the Dune Sands or Lower Mottled Sandstone of the Triassic series. The canal left the Pebble Beds near the Beeches and it continues on the underlying rocks, of a rich red colour, almost to Whittington. Close to the tail of the lock are a couple of bridges where the Kinver Light Railway crossed the mill tailrace and the Stour. Both bridges still have rails and sleepers and the line of the tramway between here and Kinver is now a public footpath. This makes a pleasant route for an evening stroll, returning along the towing path.

$35\frac{1}{2}$ *Kinver Lock & Kinfare Bridge (No. 29)* $10\frac{5}{8}$

Below the Hyde there are fine views of Kinver Edge, a vast expanse of open land that has attracted people from the industrial Midlands for a century or more. The cliff-like edge is formed of fairly soft Dune Sands, protected by a capping of more resistant Pebble Beds. The sandstone outcrops are riddled with man-made caves, some said to have been hewn by hermits. In the days of the Kinver Railway and the 'charabanc' outings that superceded it, the caves housed tea rooms and amusement arcades, but now it is the open space and extensive views that attract crowds from the Midlands during summer weekends. On a neighbouring hill is the fine Norman church of St Peter which has memorial windows to the Brindleys of Union Hall, Compton, a settlement on the outskirts of Kinver. James Brindley is said to have been related to this family and to have stayed at Union Hall while he surveyed the canal in this neighbourhood. It may seem surprising that James, a millwright of humble origin, should have had such distinguished relatives and even more so that he should have been their guest while working on the canal.

Nowhere along the Staffs & Worcs is the increasing enthusiam for canal boating more apparent than on the length between Paddock Cottage and Kinver. Here boats are moored stem to stern for several hundred yards, alongside the successful boatyard of Dawncraft Pleasure Cruisers. Broadly speaking, boating enthusiasts fall into two groups. There are those who enjoy the pleasure of cruising, alone or in the company of others, and those who like 'simply messing about in boats'. Occasionally a few gaps can be seen in the line at Kinver, but by and large the 'residents' here seem to belong to the second category. Their presence is becoming more and more of an inconvenience to other canal users, boaters, walkers and anglers alike, and Dawncraft plans to provide a marina to accommodate them. This large basin will be on land between the canal and the river Stour. The number of boats on our canals increases every year and of necessity, moorings away from the main channel are becoming a feature of the system. Already there are several along the Grand Union Canal, with a most impressive example at Braunston.

Dawncraft's is a success story that reflects the upsurge in the recreational use of canals. The proprietors, George Wilson and his son, Ralph, started the yard at the Paddock, Kinver, in October 1958 with a handful of boats for hire. They increased the size of the fleet over the years, business expanded and they began to build boats for inland navigation. In 1971 the hire fleet was sold, in February 1972 boatbuilding was transferred to a new factory near Caldwall lock, Kidderminster, and today Dawncraft is among the leading manufacturers of boats for canal and river cruising. The Paddock is now only used as a boatyard where craft are repaired and displayed, though the main showroom for smaller boats is at Stewponey. There is a slipway at the Paddock and extensive boating services are available for users of the canal.

The track of the Kinver Light Railway runs behind the boatyard and crosses the Stour for the fourth and last time. On the other side of the river from the canal is a children's playground that includes a most realistic model railway. On 'steam' days passengers are carried in diminutive trucks over an elaborate network of lines. Returning to the tramway, its track can be traced almost to the end, but the terminal loop and buildings (Plate 53) disappeared in 1938/9 to make way for Kinver pumping station. This all-electric station is a modern replica of the one at

Prestwood and here the boreholes penetrate about 750ft of the Dune Sands after passing through a few feet of alluvial material. As has been noted, the Dune Sands are an excellent source of water supply and at Kinver there was an appreciable artesian flow before pumping commenced. Kinver is the fourth and last station of the South Staffordshire Waterworks Company that pumps to the reservoir at Shard End, Dudley.

At one time Kinver was quite a busy place on the canal. There is an old warehouse alongside the lock (Plate 52) and a number of wharves nearby. On the offside are the wharf and buildings of the Wolverley Timber Company, now the property of Mitchells & Butlers. The narrow boat *Bellatrix* takes booked parties from here for day outings or evening trips along the beautiful southern portion of the Staffs & Worcs during the summer months. This boat has operated for some years now and, like the *Cactus* at Haywood Junction and other trip boats, is becoming increasingly popular. The *Bellatrix* has all the decoration and finery of a long-distance working boat, though such craft were the exception rather than the rule on the Staffs & Worcs. Grimy boats carrying coal or steel were the 'traditional' craft of this canal!

Kinfare bridge (No. 29) has been widened on two occasions and the alterations are similar to those at Penkridge and Gailey. The bottom gates of the lock have had to be cranked, owing to the reduction in space, and a separate arch has been provided for the towing path. The first widening may have been carried out prior to 1835, unless the builders carefully removed the nameplate from the earlier parapet and replaced it when they had finished. The plate, easily overlooked behind an unsightly clutter of pipes, bears the old name of Kinver—'Kinfare'. This is derived from kine fair, so presumably there was an important cattle market here. Until a few years ago there was another pub next to Kinfare bridge, appropriately called the 'Lock Inn'. This was on the opposite side of the road from the lock itself and was demolished, as it was a danger to traffic. The road over No. 29 passes the site of the tram terminus, crosses the Stour near the site of another spade works and then becomes the main street of Kinver village.

The wharf below Kinfare bridge was alongside a small gas-works. Coal was delivered here and 'gas liqueur' was taken in boats of Chance & Hunt to their works on the Chemical Arm at

Oldbury. Beyond bridge No. 29, the Dune Sands gradually disappear beneath the Pebble Beds again, and in rock outcrops to the
east of the canal are some cave dwellings that are typical of the
area around Kinver. This region has for many years been known
as 'Gibralter Rock' or simply 'Gibralter', and the caves are said to
have been occupied by the families of boatmen during the last
century.

36¼-36½   *Whittington Horse Bridge (No. 28)*   9⅞-9⅝
Whittington Lock & Bridge (No. 27) (Plate 54)

Whittington is another place with an industrial history spanning
several hundred years. Although industry was scattered throughout the Smestow and Stour valleys, works were closer together
along the stretch between Gothersley and Whittington, where the
line of the canal is closest to the mining areas of the Black Country.
Before the building of the canal, the overland carriage of iron
from the blast furnaces to the ironworks and forges was kept as
short as possible and a concentration of industry developed
around Kinver. There were an early ironworks and nailers' forges
in the woods near the Anchor Hotel, Whittington and, during the
brief period when the Stour was navigable in the late 17th and
possibly early 18th centuries, goods no doubt arrived and were
sent away by boat. However, pack horses were the main form of
transport, for few roads would permit the carrying of heavy loads
in carts, and trade to and from the ironworks probably accounted
for Whittington Horse bridge (No. 28). The bridle road across it
headed straight for Stourbridge and the Black Country. No. 28
was built at the same time as the canal and was a delightful little
bridge until its appearance was ruined by the removal of its
parapet and nameplate. The ironworks or its associated forges
presumably continued in use after the canal came, for there are a
wharf and winding hole near bridge No. 28, but by 1880 there
was little sign of a works here. The line of mill leats alongside the
Stour can still be traced and there is what may have been a mill
pond on the opposite side of the canal.

Along the track to the east of Whittington Horse bridge and
180yd from the canal is the Anchor Hotel. The 'Anchor', an
ancient inn dating from the beginning of the 15th century, was

part of a community associated with an early ironworks in the woods nearby. Iron from the works was made into nails here and these are said to have been dispatched along the river Stour in shallow-draughted boats or 'flats'. Adjoining the inn was a row of nailers' cottages and behind it are three sandstone caves with fireplaces. These caves are linked together and one is thought to have been used as a bar. A few years ago the inn and cottages were carefully converted into a hotel, an additional wing was built and the caves became a wine cellar. The hotel is open to non-residents and has a first-class reputation for English and continental fare. It can be reached from Kinver along Dark Lane and is about 500yd from the village. Those travelling the canal can obtain light meals at the 'Anchor', but it is more the place to linger awhile over good food and in pleasant surroundings, perhaps to give the 'galley slaves' a well-earned break during a boating holiday.

About ¼ mile across the fields from bridge No. 28 in the opposite direction, a little farther by the lane, is an even older inn. At one time the 'Whittington Inn' was a manor house and the home of the grandfather of Dick Whittington, becoming an inn towards the end of the 18th century, in the turnpike era. Now on the A449 trunk road, the inn is a good example of inter-tie half timbering and there is said to be a concealed staircase, 'priest's hole' and tunnel to the neighbouring Whittington Hall.

There was yet another ironworks at Whittington lock. Griffith's directory of 1873 records that there were 9 puddling furnaces here and a couple of mills and forges belonging to J. Williams & Co. The Stour was impounded to form a mill pond of several acres and the works was sited between the river and the head of the lock. The 1882 Ordnance map shows the works intact and apparently in use, though by then the pond had become partly silted. By 1906 it had gone completely except for the mill building to the north of the main works and this still exists.

Whittington lock is in an attractive and secluded valley, crossed by a very narrow lane running between the A449 and the upper part of Kinver village. Whittington bridge (No. 27) carries this lane and is one of the rare instances of an original road bridge on the canal that has not subsequently been altered. There is no towing path under No. 27 and as long as there were horse-drawn boats on the canal, the horses had to cross the road. It is therefore interesting to compare No. 27 with bridges at Swindon or the Bratch and Aw bridge, where a towing path has been added, or Kinver, Gailey and Penkridge, where a separate arch has been provided. The lane over No. 27 runs along the top of the dam of the ironworks pond.

37½-37¾   *Caunsall Bridge (No. 26)*   8⅝-8¾
and Clay House Bridge (No. 25)

About ½ mile below Whittington the canal enters Worcestershire, after journeying through just over 37 miles of Staffordshire countryside. There is nothing to indicate where the Staffs & Worcs 'crosses the line', though there surely ought to be! The boundary runs from Heath Barn on the A449, along the southern edge of a small wood to the canal and Stour, and then follows the river northwards for a short distance. The point at which the boundary crosses the canal is about 300yd south of an overflow weir. After Whittington lock the Stour valley levels a little and widens, and the downward plunge of the Staffs & Worcs is arrested for a distance of 2¼ miles. Another effect of the reduction in gradient was to confine mills to tributaries of the Stour, and the next works down the river was at Cookley.

Caunsall bridge (No. 26) has its original arch, but has lost its brick parapet. No. 26 used to be particularly dangerous for traffic, as it is on a bend on the road to Caunsall and near a cross roads on the busy A449, and the provision of an open parapet was a necessary step. Clay House bridge (No. 25), however, is one of the best examples of a Brindley accommodation bridge on the canal. After surviving road improvements and other alterations, it was in danger of being demolished about the same time as Ebstree (No. 50) and for much the same reason. Fortunately, Kidderminster R.D.C. intervened and it is now scheduled as an ancient monument. The name 'Clay House' may have the same origins as the neighbouring ostentatious residence known as Clee Hall.

Between bridges 25 and 26 there is a caravan park alongside the canal. Water seems to be an adjunct to camping sites and here the polluted waters of the Stour have driven the campers to the canal bank. This is a form of recreation that has received little attention as far as canals are concerned. With adequate control and the careful selection of sites, camping could introduce many new-comers to the pleasures of canals. Rowing boats, canoes and small motor boats could be provided and sites need not be restricted to canals that are fully navigable.

38-38½   *Austcliff Wharf & Bridge (No. 24)*   8⅛-7⅝
and Cookley Tunnel (No. 23)

Austcliff bridge (No. 24) is another example of a 'second genera-tion' bridge, built of red brick and with a sandstone keystone. Its style was identical to the demolished bridge at Ebstree and was probably built at the same time.

Near the bridge was the wharf for Caunsall village. The track between the two is now a public footpath and this crosses the Stour by an ancient iron bridge. There used to be a smithy in the village that was perhaps used by the boatmen and there is a small pub, the 'Rock Tavern', so called because the back of the house is built into a sandstone outcrop. In later years this was not a pre-ferred stopping place and it is doubtful if overnight mooring here was ever encouraged, for between Caunsall and Cookley are a series of tight bends on the canal.

The canal gets very narrow beyond bridge No. 24, as it squeezes between the spectacular Hanging Rock at Austcliff and a loop of the meandering Stour (Plate 55). The funnelling effect of the nar-rows at this vulnerable spot could be disastrous after heavy rain and a large weir has been installed as a safeguard. One wonders whether this was foresight on the part of the Company Engineer, or if it resulted from bitter experience! The 25ft of sandstone over-hanging the canal here is one of the best exposures of the Pebble Beds along the Staffs & Worcs, though close inspection of all but the bottom few feet is difficult, even from a boat. The Pebble Beds have a total thickness of about 400ft in this area, but the inclination of the strata in the direction of the canal is small. The canal crossed the lower part of the series almost 2 miles away, near Whittington, and the exposures around Cookley are towards the top of the Pebble Beds. The irregular bedding formed when the sand and pebbles were deposited can be seen very clearly in the Hanging Rock. Two hundred million years ago, most of what is now southern England was covered by desert uplands that had a high rainfall. Swift rivers descended rapidly to the Midland plain, bringing along sand and pebbles to form the sand banks, shoals and deltas that are now known as the Bunter Pebble Beds. The relatively recent downcutting of the rejuvenated Stour has provided us with a vivid picture of these events at Hanging Rock and elsewhere, and Brindley's navvies added the final touch, cutting back the base of the cliff to make room for the canal.

The cliff soon gives way to lower land and at Rock House on the outskirts of Cookley is another wharf. There is no sign of a works here and the site would not have been suitable for any industry that required water power. The wharf may simply have served Cookley village, for it is about the only place where there is reasonable access from the canal, but this does not explain the presence of the arched wall at the wharf. The village itself straddles a precipitous spur of sandstone, around which the Stour makes a lengthy detour. Brindley thought better of following the river and took the canal straight through the spur by way of Cookley tunnel (Plate 56). With a length of 65yd, this tunnel is easily the longest on the Staffs & Worcs and is very similar to the one at Dunsley. There is a towing path with a handrail and at some time after it was driven, the roof of the tunnel was arched with brickwork, leaving the sandstone walls unlined. The tunnel passes under the main street of Cookley and from each side a track leads to the centre of the village, where there are several shops and a couple of pubs.

Cookley developed along lines similar to Swindon, around an early ironworks. Of the works in operation along the Stour in 1873, Cookley was second only to the Hyde and had 18 puddling furnaces. It was then owned by J. Knight & Co. and the works later went over to the processing of steel. It was one of four works along the Stour to do so, a change that ensured its survival to the present day, and now steel stampings are produced there. Until about 40 years ago, Cookley ironworks relied on canal transport for supplies of coal for the boilers and iron 'pigs' for working into wrought iron. The long basin in the works has mostly been filled in, but the entrance still exists a few yards beyond Cookley tunnel. This is spanned by an iron roving bridge dated 1871.

38¾-39⅝   *Debdale (Cookley) Lock & Bridge (No. 22)*   7⅜-6½
            (Plate 57) and Wolverley Forge Bridge (No. 21)

The long pound from Whittington ends at an isolated lock near
Cookley. Although the only access to Debdale lock is along the
canal or by a field path from Cookley village, its house is still
inhabited. This building is more pretentious than most lock
cottages along the Staffs & Worcs and there is an octagonal bay
to give a clear view of boats travelling from either direction.
Houses at Botterham, Aldersley and Haywood had similar bays.
Debdale lock is cut from a low sandstone cliff which contains a
large rectangular cave, with a narrow entrance and stone benches
round the walls. The cave is said to have been excavated by the
navvies as a temporary home while they were working on this
section of the canal. The purpose of the stone set in the ground
near the house is uncertain. It may have been a distance marker,
but the lock is not an integral number of miles from Haywood or
Stourport.

There is a cast-iron footbridge across the tail of the lock and
Debdale bridge (No. 22) is also a footbridge. The latter carries a
path that connects the lower part of Cookley village with the lane
to Wolverley. Although the decking is recent, the abutments are
original and they are unusual in that the brick and stone walling
is vertical. The reason is probably that the original decking
consisted of two cantilevered sections, forming a split bridge,
similar to the existing one at Caldwall lock.

Below Debdale lock is a very sharp bend where the canal nego-
tiates a low rocky spur. On the 6in. Ordnance map of 1882 there
are a couple of small buildings marked on the offside of the canal,
about 300yd from the bend, labelled 'boiler works'. Industry
along the Staffs & Worcs is very varied, and there is usually an
obvious reason for the siting of it, but this cannot be said of the
boiler works at this spot; it must have received all its fuel and
iron plate by canal and the finished articles must have been
dispatched the same way.

Ahead is one of the canal's more recent bridges, a graceful arch
that carries the huge water mains of the Elan pipeline (Plate 58).
Many million gallons of water pass over this bridge daily for the

citizens of Birmingham and other parts of the Midlands. While Black Country boroughs were content to dig holes along the Stour and Smestow valleys, Birmingham Corporation set their sights on the mountains of Mid Wales. The Elan Valley project was authorised by the Corporations Water Act of 1892 and three dams and the 73-mile pipeline were completed in 1907. The scheme captured the imagination of the Midland author Francis Brett Young, whose evocative novel *The House Under Water* is set in the Elan Valley. The waterworks at Elan were thought at the time to be adequate for Birmingham's needs for ever more, but a fourth dam was built in a neighbouring valley half a century later. On Thursday, 23rd October 1952, HM the Queen inaugurated the Claerwen dam, a few months after her Coronation. More recently demand was again in danger of exceeding the supply and supplementary plant was installed at Trimpley to extract water from the Severn.

The canal is joined by a road beyond the pipeline for the first time since we left Wightwick, but this only follows the waterway for about a mile. The next section is another beautiful one. First comes an area known as Wolverley Lea or 'World's End', with a winding hole where boats from Wolverley forge and wharf used to turn and an old house that has been restored and modernised. The canal then passes through a genuine, if inconspicuous cutting —most cuttings along the southern section have been 'one-sided' affairs. Here there is an excellent example of 'false' bedding in an outcrop of Pebble Beds on the side of the towing path. Wind and rain have sculptured the layers of sandstone with great effect.

Wolverley forge is another corner where there has been a pocket of industry since the Middle Ages. In the 16th century there was a corn mill here and in the 17th it became a forge. Like other works along the valley, the canal gave Wolverley forge a new lease of life and a wharf was built, with a couple of short tramway tunnels connecting it with the works. Walls around the yard are built of slag that was hammered out of the iron and several of the buildings and remnants of the mill leat can still be seen. The ironworks closed down some time during the 19th century, but the mill came into use again early in the 20th. This time the wheel was coupled to a generator which supplied electricity to Woodfield House across the other side of the valley. The machinery was later taken to a mill at Broadwaters, Kidder-minster, and is still in working order. Originally there were nine workmen's cottages here and most have now been pulled down, but the final stage in the chequered history of Wolverley Forge was the conversion of two of the cottages into a fine half-timbered residence. The site of the forge is on private land, but the build-ings and the attractive gardens which surround them can be seen from a public footpath that crosses Wolverley Forge bridge (No. 21). After leaving the forge, the canal enters a delightful wooded cutting with distant views of Wolverley church framed by the trees.

$39\frac{7}{8}$-$40\frac{3}{8}$ *Wolverley Lock, Wharf & Bridge (No. 20),* $6\frac{1}{4}$-$5\frac{3}{4}$
Wolverley Court Lock & Bridge (No. 19)

There are two locks at Wolverley, one on the canal and the other next to it! The 'Lock Inn' has always been favoured by boatmen and there used to be stabling here. Now it is managed by Trevor and Ann Hardwick, themselves canal enthusiasts, and there is always a welcome for travellers along the Staffs & Worcs. The interior has recently been radically altered to accommodate the numerous boaters and others who descend on Wolverley. The car park on the opposite side of the lock occupies the site of Wolverley wharf and there is a small warehouse here, though a row of cot-tages has been demolished. Wolverley bridge (No. 20) has been rebuilt and widened, for the road (now the B4189) has always been a busy one, and the bottom gates of the lock have been fitted with cranked beams. The quaint village of Wolverley nestles against a sandstone cliff on the opposite side of the valley, with the 18th-century church standing high on the rock.

Wolverley is the third place along the canal where Brindley was specifically prevented by the 1766 Act from taking a particular route. Here he was not to cross to the opposite side of the Stour, but there was little point in so doing unless his original intention had been to join the Severn at Bewdley and had decided that Wolverley was the best place to leave the valley of the river Stour. This is the most widely-known myth about Brindley and the Staffs & Worcs, and there cannot be one iota of truth in it. The story is that Brindley wanted to terminate his canal at Bewdley, where there had been a port for several centuries, but the residents of the town would have none of his 'stinking ditch'. Brindley was a highly competent engineer and the line between Haywood and Kidderminster was the result of brilliant surveying. That he should suddenly saddle himself with a 2,500yd tunnel, a second Harecastle, is unthinkable. Aside from this, it would have been of considerable benefit to Bewdley to have been on the main canal system, and the residents would have welcomed such a scheme. There must be some substance in the story, since Nash mentions it in his history of Worcestershire, written about 30 years after the canal was built, and it probably originated among a group of local businessmen with vested interests and no knowledge of canal engineering.

Although the route taken by the canal between here and the Severn is almost certainly the one chosen by Brindley in the first place, it is interesting to speculate on what routes he could have taken if the promoters had insisted on a termination at Bewdley. One possibility would have been to follow the 125ft contour from Wolverley along the western side of the valley to Kidderminster, with a tunnel to Wribbenhall on the Severn. The alternative would have been to tunnel along the line taken about a century later by the Kidderminster Loop Line of the GWR, leaving the Stour valley near Caldwell. Either route would have entailed a long tunnel followed by at least six locks, crowded together in a steep flight. It is little wonder that Brindley joined the Severn at the mouth of the Stour!

As the canal gets farther from the Black Country, so the pattern of industry along it changes. There were still a couple of ironworks on the way to the Severn, but in general the industry is now 'lighter' and more diverse. The first mill below Wolverley was in fact used for drawing wire and its wharf is included in the Canal Company's Table of Distances. A little farther on is Wolverley Court lock, a shallow one with a fall of only 6ft. We left the Triassic sandstones behind at Wolverley and the canal now takes a more leisurely course alongside the alluvial flood plain of the Stour until the hills close in again at Kidderminster. Wolverley Court lock is a stark, untidy place compared with previous locks along the Stour valley. Its cottage has been demolished and the only items of interest are the unique footbridge across the tail of the lock and the paddle gear. The split bridge is without the usual nameplate, but 'Wolverley Court Bridge, No. 19' is cast in the ironwork. It is not like other bridges at locks tails, which often have the Company's initials cast in them, and it is a mystery why No. 19 should have deserved individual treatment, or why it should have had a number at all. Lock footbridges are not normally included in the numbering sequence and this one may have replaced an accommodation bridge.

The most important feature of Wolverley Court lock is the survival of the only complete set of S&WCCo. wooden paddle gear still in use on the canal. This may be preserved intact, though not necessarily at Wolverley Court.

$40\frac{5}{8}$-$41\frac{1}{2}$ *Bridge No. 18 (Demolished)* $5\frac{1}{2}$-$4\frac{5}{8}$
and Limekiln Bridge (No. 17)

Bridge No. 18, an accommodation bridge for Sionhill farm, disappeared many years ago and so did its name. The absence of the usual 'narrows' and bend in the towpath suggest an opening bridge and it is in fact shown as a swing bridge on the 1882 Ordnance map. The only obvious signs of its existence are parallel hedgerows leading to the canal, but brick foundations still lurk beneath the surface to trap unwary boaters, particularly on the offside. The only other opening bridge on the Staffs & Worcs, No. 108, was replaced by a brick arch about the middle of the 19th century and it is surprising that No. 17 survived as long as it did on such a heavily used canal.

The chimney and building ahead belonged to the Broadwaters iron and tinplate works. Broadwaters is on the outskirts of Kidderminster at the start of one of the few urban sections along the Staffs & Worcs. The name refers not to the canal, but to a chain of pools to the east. In years gone by these were mill ponds, linked by a small, but hard-working stream. A paper mill, forges and corn mills around Churchill and Blakedown were powered by it, as were the works and other mills at Broadwaters. The stream dives under the canal at a 'narrows' before joining the Stour and nearby is the silted arm that led to the tinplate works, disused for 50 years or more.

The Stouvale ironworks, a little farther along the canal on the

same side as the towpath, fared better. It was one of three on the
Staffs & Worcs belonging to the Baldwin family, later Richard
Thomas & Baldwin. As occurred at the others, steel was processed
here after the ironworks closed down and the premises are now
used by Miles Druce Ltd. A long cobbled wharf with iron plates
set into the canal edge at intervals has survived from the old
works. The 'Railway Boats' of Thomas Bantock brought steel
bars here from the GWR basin at Mitton until 1948.

Nearer Limekiln bridge (No. 17) is the old warehouse of the
Clensmore corn mill and beyond the bridge is the site of Clensmore chemical works. No. 17, a bridge more typical of the
Birmingham Canal than the Staffs & Worcs, no doubt obtained
its name from kilns on the neighbouring wharf, though in later
years the main commodity delivered here was coal. Lime was
probably burnt for use at the chemical works rather than for
agricultural purposes. Next to No. 17 is the 'Navigation', a pub
that has long outlived the industry it was built to serve.*

41¾-42⅜ *Kidderminster Wharf, Lock & Bridge (No. 16)* 4⅜-3¾
to Round Hill Bridge (No. 13)

At Kidderminster the river Stour slips through a gap between
low sandstone ridges and Brindley chose this valley as the obvious
route for the canal. Aside from its convenient contours, Kidderminster was also a source of trade, for there was industry here
long before work started on the canal. The gap must already have
been crammed with houses, as the 1766 Act gave the Company
powers to purchase compulsorily any property in Kidderminster
that stood in the way of the canal. The waterway through the
town now looks as though it has always been there and industry
along its banks is mainly of later date, but signs of Brindley's
battle for space remain to this day.

The sudden narrowing of the valley occurs near the parish
church of St Mary & All Saints and here the Stour swings from
the western side to the eastern, presenting Brindley with his first
obstacle. He had to take the canal across the Stour at this point,
since the alternative would have been a route through the centre
of the town. This he did by means of a three-arch aqueduct whose

* The 'Navigation' closed in 1973.

walls have recently been cocooned in concrete. Despite their disguise, the low arches are similar to those of other original aqueducts along the canal and are just visible from the towpath near the head of Kidderminster lock. The next obstacle was the Bridgnorth turnpike, no doubt with houses on each side of it, and Brindley took this in his stride by building a deep lock followed by a short tunnel (Frontispiece & Plate 62). Kidderminster lock, with a fall of almost 12ft, is one of the deepest narrow locks on the canal. This was necessary to keep pace with the rapid fall of the Stour as it passed through the gap, but it also had to leave adequate clearance under the Bridgnorth road and any property that was to be built over the tunnel. With the Stour now to the east of the canal, a turnover bridge was needed and this was squeezed in between the lock and tunnel.

Land for these works around the road was purchased under the powers of the Act and most of it is still in the ownership of the Waterways Board. The tunnel itself is one of the earliest on the canal system to have been built by the 'cut and cover' method and after it was finished, houses and shops were built on top of it. An account of a pleasure cruise along the Staffs & Worcs and other canals in August 1774, has the following comment for the 23rd: 'Passed . . . Kidderminster Tunal under the Street 120 feet,' so in those days the tunnel was evidently something of note. If this figure for the length of the tunnel is accurate, it has since been shortened, because its present length is only about 73ft. The narrow section immediately after the tunnel suggests that this might have been done and the southern portal is not as old as the canal, though from its style it seems to have been built not long afterwards. Although the tunnel is slightly longer than the one at Dunsley, the Company insisted on calling it 'Kidderminster Bridge' when the nameplate was added about 1835.

The canal was opened through Kidderminster in 1771 and played an important part in the life and commerce of the town until well into the present century. The centre of activity was at Mill wharf, off Church street (Plates 59, 60 & 61). Every inch of space around the Stour aqueduct and lock was utilised. By 1882 there were the wharf and warehouse of the Shropshire Union Canal Company on the main canal, the most northerly of the buildings at Mill wharf, and there were several other warehouses

between the canal and Church street, including the one of three
storeys that is shown in the photographs of the mid 1920s. There
was also a coal wharf for a carpet works on the opposite side of
the canal. By 1900 some of the property had been pulled down and
a basin had been built in front of the large warehouse. About
the same time the SUCCo. premises were extended and in the
early 1900s an order office for the Earl of Dudley's Baggeridge
colliery was added. Mill wharf became the main distribution
centre for Baggeridge coal in the area. The wharf was very busy,
but we must not be misled by the two prints. These were taken by
the Baggeridge company, probably for publicity purposes, and
each shows the same three carts, all carefully posed to display the
Company's name! Nor did the Earl have a monopoly of coal sales
in Kidderminster, for a merchant called Vaughan sold Littleton
coal and there were others. Being next to Kidderminster lock, the
basin could easily be drained after stop-planks had been inserted
at the entrance, and this was done periodically to recover coal
fallen from boats.

Coal was not the only traffic at Kidderminster, but it was the
most important one. Other loads included the world-famous
Kidderminster carpets that were carried from Mill wharf in
SUCCo. 'fly boats', a traffic that was later operated by the LMS
railway. The carpets were loaded during the daytime at the
warehouse which has a car parked outside in Plate 60. (It is
interesting to note that this car may have been the one owned by
the Canal Manager and also that the Company's steam dredger is
moored near the entrance to the basin.) The horse-drawn fly-
boats left promptly at 6 o'clock in the evening and travelled
speedily through the night to Wolverhampton, where the carpets
were transferred to a train early next morning. This traffic was
worked by the Shropshire Union Company until they ceased
carrying in 1922 and after the railway grouping, it was run by the
LMS to get a foothold in Great Western territory. The Shropshire
Union did not pass through any industrial areas and the company
sought trade by becoming carriers as well as canal proprietors.
They set up basins and wharves at strategic points throughout the
Midland system at Brierley Hill, Netherton, Birmingham,
Stourport and Kidderminster, for example—and worked fast
boats drawn by two horses. The number of boats dwindled in

post-war years, but the carpet traffic lasted until October 1950 and one of the boats, the *Saturn*, can still be seen around the canal system.

Next to Kidderminster lock was a cottage (Frontispiece) and one of the principal toll offices on the canal and opposite, where the electricity substation now stands, was stabling for ten horses. These have all gone, but the cobbled track between Mill street and the wharf still runs by the side of the lock and has rows of larger setts to prevent undue wear from cart wheels. The basin has been infilled and landscaped to provide a new home for Richard Baxter, a 17th-century Puritan, evicted a few years ago when Kidderminster's ring road was built. Unfortunately the Shropshire Union warehouse was demolished by the Local Authority in 1972, though its neighbour survives. Perhaps Mill wharf will be restored one day to provide canal users with pleasant moorings near the town centre and the townspeople with a 'waterfront'. The canal bank below the church was improved not long ago, but a great deal needs to be done before Kidderminster attains the standard set by neighbouring Stourport.

For some distance beyond the tunnel, the canal is little wider than the boats which used it. This dramatic gorge-like section is flanked on one side by the ancient warehouse of Park Wharf Works, now belonging to the Carpet Manufacturing Company, and on the other is a tall building with an unusual bay window overlooking the canal (Plate 63). Both buildings are later than the canal and neither would seem to account for the narrowness at this point. After this brick 'cutting', the canal assumes more normal dimensions near Kidderminster gas works. There were usually two basins at gas works to ensure an uninterrupted flow of materials. One was for the delivery of coal, and tar or 'tar water' (ammoniacal liquid) was loaded at the other. However, Kidderminster was a fairly small works and, though there was a coal basin, tar passed through pipes into boats moored in the main canal. Most of the works has been dismantled, but the waterless gasholder is still a landmark on the Kidderminster skyline and next to the canal is what surely must be one of the finest chimneys in the Midlands. The corners have alternate courses of blue and red bricks and the sides are yellow and blue—the Cleopatra's Needle of the Kidderminster Embankment!

Between the gas works and the 'Sling', a narrow alley that led
from the canal to the town centre, was the skew-basin of Lee's
carpet works where coal slack was delivered, and beyond was the
basin for the famous carpet works of Brintons. The public have
right of way along the towing path between the Sling and Caldwall Hall bridge (No. 15), for this was the town's public wharf. A
whole variety of goods was unloaded or collected here and timber
from Stourport was brought to the saw mill opposite. Next to the
saw mill and backing on to the canal is the 'Old Parker's Arms'.
Until recently a faded sign on the gable end proclaimed 'Hy.
Richards: Pure Home Brew'd Ales & Wines'. Unfortunately this
no longer applies, as Banks Brewery now owns the house. The
site of Kidderminster castle, near bridge No. 15, is now occupied
by the Public Baths, and is commemorated by the 'Castle Inn' on
the opposite side of the canal. There was another coal basin near
Caldwall Mill bridge (No. 14) at the 'Light Works'. Electricity has
not been generated here for many years and now the MEB have a
switching station on the site. Separated from the canal by the
river Stour is the Castle Spinning Mill, part of Brinton's works.
No. 14 is one of the few original bridges surviving on this section
of canal. Opposite Caldwall Mill was another coal wharf and near
Round Hill bridge (No. 13) is an iron and brass foundry. The
carpet industry of Kidderminster is still very much alive, but it
comes as a surprise to find a foundry still in use here, when
kindred works along the Stour valley disappeared long since.*

The profusion of wharves and basins in Kidderminster show
how dependent the town was on the Staffs & Worcs. The canal
was fortunate in never really being supplanted by the railways of
the area. The first line to reach the town was the Oxford, Worcester & Wolverhampton in May 1852, but it only passed through
the outskirts in deep cuttings and on high embankments. The
venture was not a success, partly because the line crossed the no-
man's land in the Battle of the Gauges, and it thoroughly earned
the nickname of the 'Old Worse & Worse Railway'. It became
part of the short-lived West Midland and on 1st March 1863 was
taken over by the Great Western Railway Company. The story
might have been very different if this company had built the line in
the first place. Instead, Kidderminster relied heavily on canal

* The foundry closed down in 1972/3.

transport almost until the waterway was nationalised in 1948. The length through the town in fact was probably the busiest of the entire canal towards the end of its independent life.

The foundry near Round Hill bridge (No. 13) marked the end of the urban interlude and the canal is rural again for the rest of the journey to Stourport. The only signs of the vital contribution made by the Staffs & Worcs towards the prosperity of the town are a few rusty mooring rings among the weeds, furrowed brickwork and grooved bollards, and numerous 'stanked off' arms. What is basically a section packed with interest and memories of the canal in its heyday is in reality one of the few blemishes on a near-perfect waterway. Fortunately the age of conservation and concern for our environment has arrived just in time as far as Kidderminster is concerned, for there is still plenty to conserve. Perhaps in years to come the canal here will be an attractive place to linger awhile, away from the noise and bustle of the town centre.

$42\frac{1}{2}$-$43\frac{3}{8}$ *Caldwall Lock & Bridge (No. 12)* $3\frac{5}{8}$-$2\frac{3}{4}$
and Falling Sands Lock & Bridge (No. 11)

The Stour valley below Kidderminster is wide, but initially the river insists on clinging to the western side, leaving little room for the canal. The valley sides are cut into Triassic sandstone, though the surrounding hills are capped by gravelly river terraces, relics of the drainage system that existed before the youthful Severn reached its present level. Caldwall lock is cut into one of the sandstone cliffs, the last exposure of the Bunter Pebble Beds along the canal. Until a few years ago there was a delightful whitewashed lock cottage, nestling against the cliff (Plate 64), but it was severely vandalised and had to be demolished. This is a pity, for it made an attractive picture with the split accommodation bridge in the foreground, and would have been an ideal weekend cottage.

There are several small cantilever footbridges along the canal, usually bearing the initials 'S. & W. Co.', and there is in fact one at Caldwall, but No. 12 is the only full-sized bridge of this type. Caldwall bridge has sandstone quoins and iron cantilever sections and railings, with a slot to allow the towline to pass. This technique was widely used on the Stratford Canal, to avoid having to span the towing path, and the BCN has one example at Spon Lane locks. The bridge at Caldwall may have been 'experimental', for no other bridges on the Staffs & Worcs were built in this way, except perhaps Debdale (No. 22). Caldwall lock was the first to have its wooden gate quoins replaced by iron and for some reason the date '1925' is cast upside down.

Embedded high in the sandstone cliff at the head of Caldwall lock is an eye-bolt, a relic of an extraordinary experiment in electric haulage. About 1924, when motor-driven boats were still something of a novelty, trials were carried out on an electrically propelled barge operating between the lock and the centre of Kidderminster. The experiment was one of several schemes for speeding up traffic between the Midlands and the sea, via the river Severn, and this particular section was chosen because of its sharp bends and difficult bridges.

Power was supplied by two overhead trolley wires with supporting poles on each side of the canal for a distance of about ½ mile. The bases of a few poles can still be seen along the towing path and the eye-bolt anchored a support wire. The coal boat *Stourport* from the fleet of the Shropshire, Worcestershire and Staffordshire Electric Power Co. of Smethwick was adapted for the tests. (Soon afterwards this company built the power station at Stourport, the destination of the 'Light Run'.) The power unit was a 250 volt, 750rpm shunt wound, vertical-spindle motor driving a 10in. centrifugal pump specially designed for the purpose by the Gill Propeller Co. of King's Lynn and London. Propulsion was by means of a jet of water and steering was effected by rotating the jet. (For reversing the boat, the jet was rotated through 180°.) A speed of 3½mph was obtained with the power unit developing 12hp and the full rated horse-power was 18. The cost of operating the system was 1s 10d per ton-mile, said to be half that of a horse-drawn boat, and the trolley wires cost about £600 per mile.

Complete success was claimed for the experiment and it aroused considerable interest at the time. However, nothing came of it and traffic on the Staffs & Worcs continued to be predominantly horse-drawn for many years.

Companies were naturally anxious to get traffic moving on their canals as soon as sections became navigable and often it is by no means certain when a particular canal was completed and open throughout. The date generally accepted for the opening of the Staffs & Worcs to through navigation is 28th May 1772, when its completion was reported to the Committee. To celebrate the bicentenary of this event, the Staffs & Worcs Canal Society cruised the entire canal using two boats, a traditional narrow boat to represent the commercial life of the canal and a cruiser of the new 'Canal Era'. The cruise ended at Caldwall, where a rally of boats was held on 28th May 1972. The Bicentenary Rally was opened by Lord Hatherton, whose ancestors directed the running of the canal for almost two centuries and were among its leading promoters. Like the cruise that preceded it, the purpose of the rally was to commemorate the life of the canal as a successful commercial venture, coupled with the pioneering work of James Brindley and his assistants, and at the same time to demonstrate and encourage leisure uses of the canal.

Near Caldwall lock is an area of light industry that has recently moved to Kidderminster, including the factory of Dawncraft Pleasure Cruisers. The canal then passes Foley Park, where it is crossed by the fine seven-arch viaduct of the Kidderminster Loop Line. This was built by the GWR and opened to passenger traffic on 1st June 1878, to provide a link between the OW&WR at Kidderminster and the Severn Valley Railway at Bewdley, lines acquired from the West Midland in 1863. It is interesting to note that the Loop Line follows the 'easiest' route between the two towns. Although it crosses the canal at a high level, there are several deep cuttings and a tunnel before the line reaches Bewdley, yet this is the country through which Brindley intended to take his canal, according to the 'stinking ditch' legend. The line is still usable, though at present it is rarely used. The section of the Severn Valley Railway between Hampton Loade and Bridgnorth has been preserved by the SVR Company and it is hoped that one day trains will steam through the beautiful Wyre Forest again and over this viaduct into Kidderminster.*

On the offside of the canal near the viaduct is an old gravel-pit wharf where the Merchant family kept their boats and opposite is an unsightly scrapyard. The canal then continues along the edge

* Trains now operate between Bridgnorth and Bewdley.

of Oldington Wood, past the site of Falling Sands rolling mill, whose wharf is listed in the Table of Distances. Access to the mill was over Falling Sands bridge (No. 11), alongside the viaduct. The next lock (Plate 65) is also called Falling Sands and the instability of the strata hereabouts has obviously been a feature of the area for many years. The sand in question is only indirectly connected with the Triassic cliffs we have encountered along the southern section of the canal. It is a more recent deposit of brown wind-blown sand, perhaps derived from material brought down by the ancestral Stour. A large area of Hartlebury Common on the other side of the Stour valley is covered by blown sand which is still drifting. There are a number of smaller pockets around Foley Park and one of these is in Oldington Wood, extending from bridge No. 11 to the lock. Underlying this blown sand is the Upper Mottled Sandstone, forming a low scarp between abandoned levels of the river Stour, and the canal follows the outcrop of these rocks down to Stourport basins.

Also in Oldington Wood and about 100yd below Falling Sands lock there used to be a narrow loop that ran parallel to the canal for a further 80yd. It is shown on the Ordnance map of 1882 and many years ago it contained the hulls of old boats, but there is no sign of it now.

43⅞   *Pratt's Wharf & Stour Branch (1 mile)*   2¼

There is a side lock into the Stour at Pratt's Wharf (Plate 66), an arrangement similar to that at St Thomas, near Baswich. (The name 'Platt' on maps is an error that appeared on the first large-scale Ordnance Survey and has been perpetuated ever since.) The Stour was made navigable for a mile by a large sluice across it at Wilden ironworks. Little, if any straightening was carried out, though the river was dredged under contract from time to time by the Canal Company's steam dredger. Working 'down the brook' with a loaded narrow boat must have been a tricky operation, for there were several sharp bends to negotiate and the river is fast flowing. There was a steam saw mill at Wilden, but most of the traffic was coal and iron to the ironworks.

According to Griffiths, Wilden ironworks is one of the oldest in Worcestershire and it was certainly there long before the lock was built between the Staffs & Worcs and the Stour. Pratt's Wharf obviously predates the lock, for there would be no need for a wharf after the connection was made, and goods were transhipped to smaller boats on the river. This was the most convenient place for such an arrangement, as it was for the later lock. Here the Stour passes within a few yards of the canal before swinging away to Wilden on the opposite side of the valley.

The wharf was almost certainly named after Isaac Pratt of Henwick, near Worcester, who was deeply involved in canal matters towards the end of the 18th century. In the 1780s we find him a prominent member of the Stourbridge and Dudley companies and in 1787 he took charge of the building of the southern end of Dudley tunnel. Evidently he was more of a businessman than engineer, for his efforts on the tunnel were singularly lacking in success, and he left the Dudley Committee abruptly to become one of the biggest shareholders in the Worcester & Birmingham Canal in 1791. An activity of Isaac Pratt more directly concerned with the story of the Staffs & Worcs was his chairmanship of a subsidiary company of the Stourbridge. This subsidiary was established in Stourport about 1783 to promote the sale of coal from the Stourbridge Canal. The venture was not a success and the Company was wound up in March 1792, when Isaac Pratt purchased the boats and other assets. Pratt added carrying to his other interests and perhaps Wilden ironworks was one of his principal customers. Pratt's wharf is only a couple of miles from Stourport and the traffic could well have been negotiated by Pratt. These events give us a fairly reliable indication of the date of the wharf, but it is less certain when the lock was built. It is not shown on Bradshaw's map of 1830 and the link may have been made about 1840, since this was a period of expansion when the Hatherton branch was built and other improvements were carried out.

Pratt's Wharf lock has not been used for about 20 years and is now overgrown and derelict, but it still has the typical S&WCCo. paddle gear that has mostly disappeared from the main canal. There used to be two houses at the junction, probably built for a lock keeper and wharf clerk, but these have been demolished. It is possible to walk along the towing path between the wharf and Wilden, returning to the main canal at Oldington or Upper

Mitton, but the navigation does not belong to the Waterways Board and the usual towpath permit does not apply. Just before the works is a sluice that controlled the flow of water to Wilden pool. Although the entire waters of the Stour pass through the middle of the works, it was not always possible to use them without disrupting traffic and the pool was used as a reserve. There is a wharf along the whole length of the works and the navigation ended in a covered basin near the boiler house.

The works was operated by the Wilden Iron Company in 1852, when there were eight puddling furnaces, and by 1873 it was controlled by the Baldwin family. Sheet iron of 'BBB' quality was produced, one 'best' better than other works along the Stour, and tin plate was specially prepared for gas meters. Like the other works of E. P. & W. Baldwin, Wilden eventually changed to steel rolling and stamping and became part of the Richard Thomas & Baldwin group. Coal slack and cobbles from Highley Colliery and steel bars from South Wales were carried from Mitton Railway Basin to Wilden in Merchant's boats. Occasionally an LMS boat visited Wilden and there were infrequent deliveries of timber made by the Severn & Canal Carrying Company to the saw mill, where crates were made. These boats were always taken over by Merchant's crews at Pratt's wharf, for they were experienced in navigating the sharp bends and shoals of the Stour. Traffic 'down the brook' ceased about 1949 and the ironworks closed down a few years later. The buildings are now the Wilden Industrial Estate, the bridge at the main entrance has been lowered and the main sluice no longer maintains the Stour at a level high enough for navigation. However, the Stour still disappears into the midst of the works, an impressive sight when the river is in spate.

| $44\frac{1}{8}$-$45\frac{3}{8}$ | *Oldington Bridge (No. 10)*
to Mitton Chapel Bridge (No. 7) | 2-$\frac{3}{4}$ |

Oldington bridge (No. 10) is the last original one along the canal, with walls of red brick and sandstone string course and coping, all the standard features we have attributed to James Brindley. The fact that original bridges all the way along the canal

173

from Haywood to Stourport are nearly identical is significant. Sections of the canal differ in detail and no doubt reflect the contributions from various assistants working under Brindley, but the uniformity of bridge design indicates that this was the work of one man, and this can only have been Brindley himself. The removal of a service pipe in 1974 has greatly improved the appearance of Oldington bridge. This commendable development is a consequence of a greater awareness of Worcestershire County Council and its successor in canal conservation.

The soft Upper Mottled Sandstone, quarried at Wightwick and Wombourn for Black Country foundries, was worked along this section mainly for local use, though occasionally a load of sand was taken to a foundry at Worcester. We have already passed an iron and brass foundry on the outskirts of Kidderminster and there was another foundry in Stourport. The sandpits and their wharves were next to Bullock Lane bridge (No. 9) and around Upper Mitton bridge (No. 8). Upper Mitton was one of the two villages that merged to form Stourport after the canal came, the other being Lower Mitton. There was a public wharf in the village that may also have been used by the neighbouring wire mill on the Stour.

The Severn Valley Railway crosses the canal at Upper Mitton. This line was opened to passengers on 1st February 1862 as part of the West Midland and it was taken over by the GWR just over a year later. Next to the viaduct is the only interchange basin between railway and canal along the main line of the Staffs & Worcs, aside from those fed by mineral lines. The Railway Basin was built early this century and soon became fairly busy, though the Severn Valley was little more than a branch line. Most of the canal traffic originating here was steel from South Wales for Wilden and Stourvale works and coal from Highley colliery, to the north of Bewdley. There is a roller opposite the basin to assist boats in entering and leaving, and beyond the viaduct the canal widens to form a 'layby' for boats waiting to be loaded. The track is still laid as far as the viaduct so that coal trains can reach the siding to Stourport Power Station, but the rails beyond have been lifted as far as Bewdley.

Stourport did not exist before the Staffs & Worcs came and therefore has no 'traditional' industry. Instead a wide variety of trades have been established here over the last two centuries. On the outskirts of the town were a couple of carpet mills, 'overspill' from Kidderminster, a tin works near Mitton Chapel bridge (No. 7), and an iron foundry and tannery nearer the town centre. The tin works later became the Anglo Enamel Company, whose goods were shipped from the wharf next to the 'Bird in Hand'. This was an early form of container traffic and there was a crane at the wharf. Two boats a week worked between here and the firm of Kendrick at West Bromwich. Opposite the wharf is a winding hole where boats from this and other wharves in the neighbourhood could turn. Boats also turned at the entrance to the Railway Basin, in spite of a notice informing boatmen that they were 'liable' if they did so. By the sharp bend at Mitton Chapel bridge are the foundations of St Michael's church, where at one time the Canal Company rented a pew.

$45\frac{1}{2}$-$45\frac{7}{8}$ *Stourport: Gilgal Bridge (No. 6)* $\frac{5}{8}$-$\frac{1}{4}$
to Wallfield Bridge (No. 4)

The canal makes a sudden turn to the north-west at Mitton Chapel bridge, following the sandstone scarp between river terraces along the fringe of the Stour valley, and then resumes its southerly course at Gilgal bridge (No. 6). The wharf and warehouse here belonged to the iron foundry and sand from the pit near Bullock Lane was delivered until about 40 years ago. The foundry itself has gone to make way for Stourport's new police and fire stations. Next comes the tannery, followed by bridge No. 5. This is Lower Mitton bridge, known locally as 'Black Star bridge', and it lost the nameplate when the present concrete structure was built. The canal joins the Severn at what used to be called Lower Mitton and the name was dropped in favour of Stourport. However, the name is preserved in bridge No. 5 and, if no other missing plates are replaced, this one surely ought to be.

A consequence of Stourport having been a canal town and port is the abundance of pubs. There is the 'Black Star' near bridge No. 5, next door to each other at Wallfield bridge (No. 4) are the 'White Lion' and the 'Bell', and there are more in York Street. The Company owned a large house near No. 5 and the principal maintenance depot occupied both sides of the canal between this bridge and No. 4. The yards were connected by a wooden footbridge, but the eastern one and the bridge have now disappeared. All repairs to the canal were arranged from here, but work on the northern section was carried out from Penkridge until about 1924/6. The surviving yard has old workshops and a crane* and was used until about 1956, when the maintenance depot was transferred to the Middle Basin. York Street Depot is now used by Canal Pleasurecraft Ltd, founded by H. E. Abbott in premises formerly owned by the Severn & Canal Carrying Company. This firm were pioneers in the design and building of canal cruisers and were the first hirers to operate on the Staffs & Worcs and among the first in the country. Not only is York Street an ideal base from which to explore the canal, but the Severn and recently-restored Avon Navigation are also within easy reach.

The deep lock at York Street marks the end of the canal, for the land between here and the Severn is occupied by the terminal basins. There is a toll office next to Stourport lock (Plate 67) where hand-painted 'traditional' canal ware and books may be purchased. The office was built in 1853, much later than the ones at the Bratch and Stewponey. The earlier toll office was next to the barge locks and the building of the one at York Street may have been connected with the Company becoming carriers in 1851. The towing path ends at Wallfield bridge and the centre of Stourport is nearby, at the other end of York Street. Next to Wallfield bridge is a store where boaters can obtain most of the provisions they are likely to need.

46⅛   *Stourport Basins*   o

So different from the rest of the Staffs & Worcs is the scene from Wallfield bridge that it hardly seems part of the same canal. Few waterways start and end in such dramatic surroundings as does the Staffs & Worcs and nowhere is the changing rôle of our canals better demonstrated than at Stourport. The vast complex of basins always has plenty of boats, ranging from dinghies to large river craft, amidst a delightful collection of buildings dating from 1768 onwards. At Kidderminster the Staffs & Worcs slips almost apologetically past the town, but the canal dominates Stourport.

* Moved from Giggetty Wharf, Wombourn, about 1930.

Without it there would have been no town and the Local Council is becoming conscious of the fact. The character of Stourport as an 18th century canal town is being preserved as far as possible and many buildings now carry plaques proclaiming them to be 'ancient monuments', irrespective of whether or not they are directly connected with the waterway. Other local authorities would do well to note that Stourport considers buildings erected between one and two hundred years ago are old enough to be ancient. Although the flotilla in the basins is a welcome sight, few boats cruise the canal and their owners regard the basins as an appendage to the Severn, providing safe moorings off the river. There is nothing new in this, of course. Throughout their history, the basins have been a haven for river craft as well as a terminal to the canal.

Although development around the basins now obscures the reasons for the route chosen by Brindley for the last few hundred yards of his canal, the motive is shown clearly in Sheriff's print of Stourport made in 1776 (Plate 68). Here we have another example of Brindley's skill as a surveyor and his innate 'feel' for canal engineering. He carried the canal on the level as far as he was able and then at York Street he descended 12ft to a terrace about 30ft above the normal level of the river. The Severn rises suddenly after prolonged rain in the Welsh mountains and only recently have attempts to control the flow and prevent serious flooding of the lower reaches been successful. In Brindley's day and for many years afterwards, the land near the junction of the Stour and Severn frequently flooded to a depth of several feet. So that boats and cargoes could be handled safely at all times, he sited the terminal basin on a river terrace to the north of the junction and well above the level of the highest floods.

Immediately after Wallfield bridge the canal enters the Middle Basin, now better known as the upper one. This basin is the largest and also the oldest, being built between 1768 and 1771 by Thomas Dadford senior. Much of the original sandstone edging exists and buildings to the south are of the same age as the basin. There are a couple of arms giving additional wharfage along the northern edge and in the north-east corner is the site of a weighing station. The draught of a narrow boat increases by about 1in. for every ton of load and at the weighing station the exact amount was recorded for each boat. This was done by lowering standard weights on to a boat by means of a crane. The results of the 'weighings' were then sent to all toll clerks along the canal, who measured the amount of freeboard or 'dry inches' at four points on the boat. Reference to tables of weighings would then tell the clerks how much load was being carried by a particular boat and what toll was payable. The weighing station was pulled down about 1938/9 when Wallfield bridge was rebuilt and widened, but by then it had not been used for many years.

Next to the station is the warehouse of the Shropshire Union Canal Company that was taken over by the LM&SR in 1922. 'Shroppie' fly boats set out from here and one of the more unusual cargoes, the main one in later years, was vinegar. This was brewed at Holbrooks, a firm established early in the 19th century and still in business down by the Severn, though it is no longer a family concern.

Another building along the eastern side of the Middle Basin one of the earliest warehouses, known as the 'Long Room'. A few years ago this became unsafe below the water level and had to be demolished. Another long warehouse, the premises of the Severn & Canal Carrying Company, occupied the southern side of the basin. Its site, together with the earlier building near the upper barge lock, is now used as a maintenance depot by British Waterways. In the yard are two intriguing pieces of cast iron, interlocked by an elaborate joint. Beams like this supported the arches of early bridges on the canal and this one probably came from Round Hill. Both the L-shaped building on the corner near the entrance to the basin and the 'Long Room' are shown on the 1776 print.

Severn barges may have been built at Lower Mitton before the canal came, for when Thomas Monk, a pioneer of canal transport, was born there on 13th April 1765, his father's trade was boat building, so it is said. The building and repairing of boats certainly went on in the basins as soon as they were opened and has continued to the present day. The 1776 print shows a boatyard in the north-west corner of the basin, with a boat under construction on the slipway. Who knows? This may have been the very yard where Thomas learnt his trade. As a boy, Thomas Monk witnessed the building and opening of the Staffs & Worcs and during the early years of the canal he carried on his father's business. However, he grew to be an ambitious man and before long moved to Tipton on the Birmingham Canal, in an area where industry was expanding rapidly. He set up boatyards at strategic points throughout the Midlands and became established as a carrier. Thomas is credited with introducing living accommodation on narrow boats and also the technique of 'breasting up', where a pair of boats were tied together, side by side, when working the tidal Thames. The name of this famous son of Stourport is remembered to this day in the canal world, for the craft of the narrow canals are still sometimes known as 'Monkey Boats' in memory of Thomas Monk.

The most famous boat kept in the basins and perhaps even built there is the *Lady Hatherton*, known along the canal as the 'Committee Boat'. She was launched in the 1890s, not long after the 3rd Lord Hatherton became Chairman of the Committee. The *Lady Hatherton* had a very distinctive line, quite different from a traditional narrow boat, and she was used by the Committee for annual inspections of the canal. The furnishings and fittings were magnificent, particularly the panelling of rosewood and Spanish cane, and the Company's emblem was engraved on each of the front windows. The *Lady Hatherton* was named after Charlotte Louis, wife of the 3rd Baron.

Before each tour, many weeks of preparation were spent in cleaning and painting the boat in a dock at Stourport. The inspections often started at Compton, where the boat was moored before she moved to Stourport, and other traffic on the canal kept well out of the way while they were in progress. Two horses from the LMS boats towed the *Lady Hatherton* and a bell attached to a spring was mounted amidships to ensure smooth running. If the bell rang, the steerer was in serious trouble!

A motor was fitted to the boat after nationalisation and she has since changed hands several times. In recent years the wooden hull was found to be in a very bad condition and a new one was built at the boatyard of Les Allen in Oldbury. The entire cabin and superstructure were skilfully fitted to the new hull in one of the locks at Lapworth and *Lady Hatherton* now cruises the canals as a pleasure boat. Although the Hathertons were always involved in the affairs of the Staffs & Worcs, the most outstanding

179

contributions to the running of the canal were made by the 1st and 3rd Barons. As we have seen, the memory of the 1st Baron is perpetuated in the Hatherton Branch. The 3rd Lord Hatherton, who served on the committee for 62 years and was Chairman for 42 years, did not have a branch named after him. Instead he is commemorated in a most fitting manner, through his wife, by a boat that provides a link between the commercial era and age of recreation on our canals.

Before we leave the Middle Basin there is one surprising feature that ought to be mentioned. This is the clay 'tump' that used to occupy the centre of the basin. There was deep water round the wharves, but the tump was only about 9in. below the surface. When it was removed about 1956/7 it seemed as though it had been there since the basin was built. Prior to its removal it acted as a useful indicator of the level in the basin. If the bank broke the surface due to too much water passing down the locks to the Severn, then the deep-draughted trows were in danger of settling on the bottom. The channel round the tump and the other basins were cleared regularly by the Stourport hand dredger. This boat was built at about the same time as the *Lady Hatherton* and had a similar hull. Unfortunately her subsequent career was less distinguished, for she ended her days rotting away at the end of Ashwood basin.

There were once six basins at Stourport and two of them were reached through a bridge under Mart Lane. This bridge was No. 3 in the sequence, indicating that the first basin beyond it was there before 1835. This was known as the 'Furthermost' Basin, though there was an even remoter one leading from it. Coal slack from Littleton, Hawkins's and Ashwood basins was unloaded at the Furthermost Basin for use at Stourport Power Station. The coal wharf ran the entire length of the eastern side, including an arm at the northern end. Coal was unloaded by two electric grabs and was then conveyed to the power station in hoppers along a short length of aerial ropeway, the line of which can still be traced. Most of the boats on the 'Light Run' were owned by the Shropshire, Worcestershire & Staffordshire Electric Power Co. (SWS) who operated the station, but Element's boats also brought coal here. The traffic commenced when the station started generating in April 1926 and was withdrawn in June 1949, shortly after a rail link with the Severn Valley line had been completed. Work on the railway started about 1939 and was discontinued during the war years. The delay prolonged the life of the 'Light Run' for a while and about 30 boats a day passed through Stourport lock until just after the war. This was in fact the only traffic of any consequence to use the basins for almost half a century. Coal delivered by canal had dropped to 55,000 tons by 1948, a mere 10% of the total used by the station, and in the following year only 20,000 tons were unloaded at the wharf.

There were three dry docks along the southern edge of the Furthermost Basin. The outer ones were open and the middle one had the 'Black Shed' over it. New gates were fitted to the farthest dock from the entrance so that power station boats could be repaired there, but it was hardly ever used. Between two of the docks was a wide lock down to a lower basin, an inconvenient arrangement that was wasteful of water. Suitable land in Stourport was at a premium when the lower basin was built early in the 19th century and nowhere else was available for building additional wharfage. The basin is only a few yards from the Severn and if the intention was to create another connection with the river, it was never carried out. The basin had a short life and in 1866 Stourport Gas Works was built on the site. The lock later acted as a weir to carry away surplus water from the upper basins and the three dry docks drained into it.

The Furthermost Basin was infilled after the withdrawal of the power station traffic and the site is now a timber yard. Bridge No. 3 was demolished, though its approach exists near Mart Lane, and very little remains of the basin and wharves. Traces of the wide lock and the basin below can be seen from the bridge that spanned the lock tail. This is along a footpath that leaves Mart Lane at a corner of the stables opposite the 'Tontine'.

The 'Tontine', standing between the Middle Basin and the Severn, was the Canal Company's commercial hotel. Of the many fine buildings in Stourport, this is the most impressive and best represents the early days of the town (Plates 68, 69 & 70). It was built at about the same time as the basin and was a hotel for merchants on business in Stourport and passengers on the river and canal. The Committee and shareholders of the S&WCCo. met there and it was the scene of much revelry in the early days, when the 'gentry' and their ladies came from far and wide to patronise regattas on the Middle Basin. Stourport's days as a fashionable resort were short lived. Growth of commercial traffic saw to that, particularly after the opening of the Stourbridge and Dudley Canals in 1779, and water fêtes soon became impracticable. The heyday of the 'Tontine' did not last much longer. By the middle of the 19th century, canals had been robbed of their passenger traffic by the railways and the hotel's importance dwindled. It had become an insignificant inn by 1880, when its large number of rooms, with accommodation for a hundred beds, were mostly let as flats. The 'Tontine Hotel' is much the same today, but outwardly it still looks proudly over the Severn, exactly as it did two centuries ago. Even the gardens in front of it have hardly altered since the 1776 print was made and neither has the long block of stables next to the hotel. The 'Tontine' is not the only canal hotel to survive from the days of the packet boats, but it is without doubt the finest example. Most of the flats were vacated in 1971/2, and the future of the 'Tontine' is uncertain.

'Tontine' is an unusual name, though several hotels and pubs are called by it throughout the country, including one at Ironbridge. A tontine was an investment or loan made by a group of shareholders, the shares increasing as subscribers die, till the last survivor gets all. Perhaps this arrangement existed among a group of shareholders of the Staffs & Worcs Company and the 'Tontine' was where they met.

Stourport barge locks, the original link with the Severn, sweep majestically down to the river at the side of the 'Tontine' (Plates 68, 69 & 70). Amid the architectural splendour surrounding the basins, they could perhaps be dismissed as ordinary, but could never be overlooked. They were in fact quite a feat of engineering for their day, being built very solidly to withstand the turbulent floodwaters of the river and large enough for the Severn trows to use them. The barge locks are 75ft 10in. long and 15ft 4in. wide, with a minimum depth of 5ft 5in. over the sill, making them by far the biggest and deepest locks along the Staffs & Worcs. Although the barge locks were adequate for the traffic that used the river until the present century, the Severn & Canal Carrying Company tried to persuade the S&WCCo. to enlarge them just before the last war. Nothing became of their request and the locks have remained much the same as they were when built in 1768/71.

It is interesting to note that there is no bridge across the barge locks, nor does there appear ever to have been a permanent one, though there are footways along the top of the gates. The lack of a bridge enabled the tall-masted trows to reach the Middle Basin without difficulty. Although sails were used whenever possible and the current assisted boats travelling downstream, the trows often had to be hauled by men in the early days and they crossed the canal at the lock gates. This arrangement was far from satisfactory and an improved track was laid along the banks of the Severn so that horses could be used. The section between Bewdley and Worcester was known as the 'Severn Horse Towing-path Extension', and was built in 1803/4 with financial backing from the S&WCCo. The path was on the eastern side of the river below Stourport and it changed sides at the bridge in the town. There was still no need for horses to cross the barge locks, since it is quite likely that teams were changed at Stourport.

The earlier toll office was on the side of the upper barge lock, between it and the 'Tontine'. The building was identical to those at Stewponey and the Bratch, with iron-framed windows and a central stone chimney, and it was needlessly destroyed a few years ago. A lock cottage is built against the older warehouse at the top of the barge locks, on the site of the first overflow weir of the basins. Prior to 1816, working of the locks was more or less restricted to the hours of daylight, but increasing competition caused the Company to try various schemes for extending the period. After 1830 the locks were open day and night and the house may have been built about this time so that the lock keeper would always be available. Nowadays the gates are kept padlocked and operation is again restricted to normal working hours, under the supervision of the lock keeper. This can cause some inconvenience to people using the locks, but it ensures that the basins are not drained inadvertantly.

The Middle Basin was the only one built at about the same time as the canal and the irregular pond between the barge locks is of later date, if the 1776 print is accurate. The etching does show a river basin that was quite separate from the canal and there is some evidence that this existed. It was from the mouth of the river

basin that a second flight of locks was built (Plate 71), in anti-
cipation of a sudden increase in traffic following the opening of
the Dudley and Stourbridge canals. The sandstone masonry of
the present approach is very similar to the entrance shown on the
print and appears to be earlier than the locks (Plate 72). The
brickwork of Lower Severn bridge (No. 1) is keyed into the
sandstone walls and so are the lock tails. As further evidence of
the existence of the river basin, there is a depth of about 9ft of
water on the sill of the bottom narrow lock, whereas the others
have the usual depth of 4ft 6in.

There are four locks in the later flight, arranged as two pairs of
staircase locks or 'risers', and this second connection between the
Staffs & Worcs and the Severn was opened in 1781. The flight
uses less water than the earlier one, for there are more locks and
they are narrow. The saving would have been even greater if four
separate locks had been built, but there was not sufficient space
and the double locks were a compromise. A single loaded boat
travelling down the narrow locks takes with it in the region of
15,000 gallons of water, about three times that quantity pass to the
Severn when the boat is going uphill and the same boat draws
about 100,000 gallons from the basins when using the barge locks.
In actual fact, several boats would have used the locks simultaneously when the canal was busy and the situation was not quite
as bad as is implied by these figures, but considerable quantities of
water were drawn from the basins. Only a limited amount came
from the main canal and water was pumped from the river to
replenish the upper basins. The site of the pumping engine is near
the present funfair and water was pumped along wooden troughing to the Clock Basin above the narrow locks. The engine is
thought to have been dismantled to provide scrap iron during the
First World War, when it had been disused for some time, and the
troughing was filled in about 1950, after it had collapsed. The
shell of the engine house still remains, though part of the upper
storey has gone, and the Upper Severn bridge (No. 2) is sometimes called 'Engine bridge'.

The irregular Lower Basin was possibly built at the same time as
the narrow locks, as were bridges 1 and 2. The main purpose of
the basin was to provide an area for docking and mooring boats
that was separate from the main wharves and warehouses. There

were three dry docks in the basin, all draining into the Severn. One has been filled in, but the others are still used, though the workshops are derelict or have been demolished. As would be expected, bridge No. 2 has none of the features of Brindley's bridges, but there is a string course of small bricks, and it is similar to the southern portal of Kidderminster tunnel. It is perhaps of interest that the numerous bridges along the Teddesley feeder and supply from Pottall reservoir are scaled-down versions of bridge No. 2.

The narrow locks lead to the large Clock Basin, built at the same time as the flight and connected to the earlier Middle basin by a short channel. On the promontory of land between them stands the crowning glory of the basins—the Clock warehouse (Plate 73). This long warehouse was built after the narrow locks and may date from the early 19th century, as its clock was installed in 1812. The clock was a gift from the inhabitants of Stourport and the Canal Company donated £25 to the fund. Originally grain and general merchandise were stored in the Clock warehouse and during the war years it was part of a timber yard. In recent years it has been the headquarters of Stourport Yacht Club. There is another fine building in York Street whose front faces the Clock Basin, though there is no longer any access from the wharf. Workmen loading and unloading boats used to eat their meals in the basement of this house and it probably belonged to a wharfinger.

Our tour of the basins is now complete and we have seen how the system developed in three stages until Stourport was one of the biggest interchange ports in the country during the early part of the 19th century. The Middle Basin and barge locks were the original terminal of the Staffs & Worcs, the building of the parallel set of narrow locks and the Clock Basin formed the second stage and the basins beyond Mart Lane bridge were the final phase. However, development was not confined to the basins, for it also took place along the waterfront and this too is worth a visit before leaving Stourport.

The present bridge over the Severn is the third on the site and dates from 1870. The first bridge was built in 1775 to connect the new town with the village of Arley Kings and probably replaced the ferry at Redstone. It was at Arley Kings that the ill-fated

Kingston, Leominster & Stourport Canal would have joined the
Severn, had it been completed. Next to the bridge and on the
same side of the river as the town is the Engine or Crown Basin.
This is not shown on the 1776 print and it may have been built
by way of 'compensation' when the earlier river basin was used for
the narrow locks. The intake for the pumping engine was in the
Crown Basin and it was also used as a dock. The entrance is
spanned by a swing bridge and was fitted with gates. The dock
was filled through a 'broken back' or inverted syphon from the
Lower Basin and trows were floated on to the land now occupied
by the car park for repair. Like all towns along the Severn that
can be reached easily from the industrial Midlands, Stourport has
for many years been a popular venue for day outings. There is a
small amusement park for the visitors next to the Engine Basin
and river boats ply from here in the summer months.

The present riverside walk was once the Severn Horse Towing-
path Extension and all along it are wharves, steps and moorings
for boats that did not use the basins (Plate 74). Although the
importance of Bewdley and other ports on the Severn declined
rapidly after the opening of the Staffs & Worcs, trows continued
to travel as far as Bridgnorth until the end of the 19th century and
many of them called at Stourport. In the shadow of the 'Tontine'
is the 'Angel Hotel', which was probably connected with this
traffic, for the Company's hotel would not have welcomed boatmen. One can imagine unruly gangs of hauliers drinking away the
profits of previous tows at the 'Angel' while awaiting the next
trip. Wharves and warehouses line the river beyond the 'Angel',
ending at the mouth of the Stour with the mill and maltings of
Holbrook's vinegar works. The Stour itself is crossed by one of
the bridges of the 1803/4 horse path.

Beyond the Stour is the power station, built on a low river
terrace and sited here because of the unlimited supply of cooling
water. The station can take up to 14,000,000 gallons of cooling
water an hour and this seems to be drawn mainly from the Stour.
The water is returned to the Severn at the other end of the station,
with an increase in temperature of about 13° F. In spite of pollution, fish seem to prefer this warmer water, judging by the fishermen that congregate around the outflow! The earliest part of the
station faces the river and was opened in 1927 by Earl Baldwin,

then Stanley Baldwin, MP for Bewdley and Stourport and Prime Minister. Compared with many power stations, the building has some character and an attempt was made to emulate the style of the original buildings when the 'B' station was built in the late 1940s. The station started generating on 1st April 1926, several months before it was 'opened', and originally it supplied parts of Shropshire, Worcestershire and Staffordshire with electricity from two 18,000 kilowatt turbo-generators. (This is the significance of the initials 'SWS' above the main entrance.) Further plant was added over the years and the present generating capacity is about 300,000 kilowatts, making it a small station by today's standards. The coal store, for many years stocked by canal traffic, is between the station and the Stour. The brickwork of the earlier part of the station still has faint traces of camouflage, a wartime effort to make it look like something else from the air. One wonders what was the reaction in the German High Command when pilots reported that the British had painted their power stations in green and yellow stripes!

There are a couple of old cottages next to the power station. One is called the 'Stack House' and the other, now a café, used to be the 'Cross Inn', a hostelry very much older than Stourport or the Staffs & Worcs. The newspaper notice seeking support for the canal (page 19) mentioned that the proposed terminal was to be at Redstone's Ferry. The names of the inn and neighbouring cottage suggest that this was the site of the ferry, since Redstone rock is not far away, on the opposite bank. Lower down the river, inns and ferries usually occurred at points that could be reached by boats on successive tides. High tides reached Worcester before locks were built to improve navigation on the river, but Redstone was well beyond the tidal limit. Along the upper reaches, inns are often to be found at places where the river could be forded when conditions were favourable and a ferry operated when they were not. The 'Cross' was probably such an inn, as Redstone was an old-established crossing point and iron from the Forest of Dean was also unloaded here for Wilden ironworks.

Redstone rock is a majestic cliff of Upper Mottled Sandstone, rising sheer from the fast-flowing, turbid waters of the Severn. About half-way up the cliff is an inaccessible cave that was once the home of a hermit who is said to have received alms from

passing boatmen. On the opposite side of the river are wharves
where Severn barges delivered petrol, aluminium ingots and
timber until a few years ago. A little farther along the horse path
is the last link with the Staffs & Worcs. The southern limit of the
long stretch of river where the 1766 Act permitted the Company
to terminate the Staffs & Worcs is Titton brook, and this stream
joins the Severn near Lincomb lock. The lock can easily be
reached by boat from Stourport, but the journey is best made on
foot along the old horse path, as there is much to see and linger
over. It is about 1¼ miles from the basins to Lincomb lock and the
return journey could include Hartlebury Common, or even the
Worcestershire County Museum at Hartlebury Castle.

7

The Hatherton (Churchbridge) Branch
HATHERTON JUNCTION TO CHURCHBRIDGE

Miles
from
Hatherton Junction

Miles
to
Churchbridge

The Hatherton or Churchbridge Branch, mentioned briefly during
our journey down the main line of the Staffs & Worcs, will now
be described in detail. Although the branch is no longer navigable, parts of the towpath are accessible and the intrepid walker
will find plenty of interest along the branch. Even those content
to 'bridge hop' by car cannot fail to notice the marked contrast
between the main line and its most important branch. These
canals were built at the beginning and end of the canal era, for
vastly different reasons and through widely differing terrain.

While railways were being built along the beds of some canals
and others were being robbed of their long-distance trade, the
Birmingham Canal Navigation embarked on an orgy of construction reminiscent of the 'Mania' years of the 1790s. About 30 miles
were added to the BCN system between the years 1840 and 1860
and the reason for this surprising turn of events was coal. The
Birmingham Canal was built to carry coal, its fortunes followed
those of the coal industry and the disappearance of commercial
traffic coincided with the decline in mining. Now the main reason
why the 'Black Country' acquired prosperity and its name was the
presence of a 30ft seam known as the 'Thick Coal'. Much of the
readily accessible coal in this and other seams had been worked
out by the middle of the 19th century and industrialists anticipated the inevitable decline in their fortunes by turning their
attention to the less prolific and partly concealed coalfield around
Cannock. Proprietors of canals, among them the Staffs & Worcs,

189

immediately started to extend their waterways in this direction. It was in the interests of the BCN to do so because many customers requiring coal had premises along the old Birmingham Canal. For the Staffs & Worcs, a branch to Cannock would be another source of coal traffic and one that enabled carriers to avoid paying tolls to the Birmingham company.

Some coal was worked in the region between Cannock and the Black Country during the early days of the Staffs & Worcs and in 1798 there were proposals to build a tramway from collieries at Wyrley to the canal. Nothing became of them, but when work started on the Hatherton Branch in 1839, the line of the proposed tramway was followed as far as Bridgtown, not far from Cannock. The 1st Lord Hatherton, Chairman of the S&WCCo. at the time, was one of the main instigators of the scheme, and the branch, completed in April 1841, was named after him, though it was sometimes known as the Churchbridge Branch. The only place where a valley of any size runs from the Cannock Coalfield to the main line of the Staffs & Worcs is at Calf Heath and this was chosen as the starting point. Although the line of the branch followed closely the Saredon and Wyrley brooks, eight locks were required to get the canal to Churchbridge, $3\frac{1}{8}$ miles away.

In the early 1860s, Churchbridge locks linked the Hatherton Branch with the Cannock Extension Canal of the BCN. The branch enabled the Staffs & Worcs to penetrate the Cannock Coalfield with its established mines, and also to acquire links with several new pits and a 'back door' to the BCN system. The fact that the affairs of the company were in good order when the Staffs & Worcs was nationalised in 1948 was in no small measure due to the foresight of Lord Hatherton and his committee over a century earlier. Unfortunately, the Hatherton Branch had served its purpose and its last load locked down shortly afterwards. The branch has since been quietly sinking into the void left by the coal that was responsible for its very existence (Plate 75), but it is unlikely to disappear completely. The Hatherton Branch still supplies water to the main line, a rôle that will become increasingly important in years to come, and it plays a vital part in draining the region through which it runs (Plates 76 & 77).

o   *Hatherton Junction: Calf Heath Bridge (No. 1)* $3\frac{3}{8}$
                         & Locks

The region around Hatherton Junction is described on pages 76 to 79.

$\frac{3}{8}$ *Dog Bridge (No. 2)*   3

The pound above Calf Heath locks is $1\frac{1}{2}$ miles long and is severed by the M6 motorway near the site of Dog bridge (No. 1). At the culverted section is the 'Dog & Partridge', a pub that has hardly changed since the days when boatmen used it. Also near Dog bridge is a shop where people from the boats bought provisions, but the bridge itself disappeared completely when the motorway was built and the channel was culverted. If there is any connection between the 'dog' in each case, one wonders which came first, the pub or the bridge.

$\frac{5}{8}$ *'Scrawper's End' Bridge (No. 3)* $2\frac{3}{4}$

The third bridge along the Hatherton Branch is near Saredon, but the post office nearby claims it to be Calf Heath and the region around the bridge is known locally as 'Scrawper's End'. It would be interesting to know who scrawped what and when! There are a couple of lengthsman's cottages on one side of the bridge. In addition to the branch, there was also the feeder to Calf Heath reservoir to maintain. This feeder leaves the canal on the opposite side of bridge No. 3 from the cottages. It is not many years since it was used regularly and could be again if it were cleared of rushes and silt.

$\frac{7}{8}$-$1\frac{1}{8}$ *Saredon Mill Bridge (No. 4) and Bridge No. 5* $2\frac{1}{2}$-$2\frac{1}{4}$

Saredon Mill bridge (No. 4), or what is left of it, is typical of bridges along the Hatherton Branch. There is uniformity in the design of original bridges along the branch, just as there is along the main canal. About 70 years separate the two canals, the entire canal era, and bridges on the branch are purely functional with little dressed stone or ornament. They were usually built of red bricks with an arch edged with bull-nosed brindled bricks. Bridge No. 4 has three cavities in the brickwork on the offside and underneath the arch. These probably supported the centring when the bridge was built and were retained for drainage or maintenance purposes. The wharf near No. 4 served Saredon mill, a Georgian building that was razed to the ground in 1971.

The canal has a peculiar pond-like appendage between bridges 4 and 5. This is about 50yd wide and was excavated when the canal was built. Its purpose is uncertain, but there are a number of possible explanations for this excrescence from the canal. The hole could have been where marl was dug to puddle the bed of the canal, or a small reservoir to increase the capacity of the pound, or even a 'layby' for boats not in use. The first of these seems the most plausible explanation, though by tradition it is a fish pond. There was no Act of Parliament for the Hatherton Branch, which meant that the consent of all landowners along the line had to be obtained before work commenced. This was readily given, but the landowner hereabouts is said to have insisted that the Company provide him with a fish pond, with water supplied by the canal.

No. 5 is a skew bridge carrying the lane between Saredon and Four Crosses. No original bridges on the main line are skewed. In Brindley's day, if a road approached a canal obliquely, the bridge was set square to the waterway, and the road, or occasionally the canal had sharp bends on the approaches. The technical difficulties in building a skew arch had been mastered long before the Hatherton Branch was built and skew bridges are commonplace along later canals and on railways.

$1\frac{3}{8}$-$2\frac{1}{8}$ *Cat's Bridge (No. 6) to Wedge's Mill Lock* 2-$1\frac{1}{4}$
& Bridge (No. 9)

There is doubt about the correct name of No. 6, the variations being Cat's and Catch bridge, shown on Ordnance maps, and Four Crosses bridge, preferred by the Canal Company. 'Cat' may have had some association with the 'dog' of No. 2, Four Crosses referred to a hamlet on the neighbouring Watling Street and 'Catch' could have arisen from a mine nearby. (Catch pits were shafts for drainage purposes.)

Triassic sandstones and marls underly the entire main line of the Staffs & Worcs, but these rocks only extend along the Hatherton Branch until just beyond bridge No. 5. A fault then brings the older Coal Measures to the surface and the rest of the branch is in the Cannock Coalfield. This sudden change in strata has had a dramatic effect on the appearance of the canal, for all around are areas of low-lying, swampy land due to the collapse of old workings. For over a mile the canal banks have been raised repeatedly to counter the effects of subsidence or 'swagging', and bridge No. 6 is in danger of disappearing altogether (Plate 75). The arch is supported on huge baulks of timber and the crown is now too low for a narrow boat to pass, even if navigation were not obstructed by the timbering. The canal bank to the east of No. 6 has given way completely and wasteland around the canal is permanently flooded. As a result, Meadow lock and the accommodation bridge nearby are almost marooned by swamps. It was trouble from subsidence that hastened the closure of the Hatherton Branch and other canals in the Cannock area. The towing path between bridges 6 and 7 is no longer owned by British Waterways and Meadow lock can only be approached from Wedge's Mill.

A brook now joins the Hatherton Branch near an accommodation bridge (No. 8, Plate 76) and this is one of the principal sources of water at the northern end of the summit level of the main line (Plate 77). It used to flow under the canal and into the Wyrley brook, and the 1882 Ordnance map shows an overflow weir at the aqueduct. For the next 300yd there is hardly any trace of the branch. Wedge's Mill bridge (No. 9) went when the Wolverhampton–Cannock road (A460) was widened and a large cranked pipe marks its site. Factories have been built over the fourth lock and on the site of Wedge's Mill, which was to the north of the lock.

$2\frac{3}{8}$-$2\frac{7}{8}$ *Jovey's Lock to Walkmill Lock & Bridge (No. 12)* $1\frac{1}{2}$

Beyond the infilled section at Wedge's Mill, the canal is almost navigable for a short distance. A few years ago the Wyrley brook was diverted to provide land for sewage treatment and it now joins the canal near bridge No. 10 and flows along the channel for ¼ mile. This section includes Jovey's lock, the fifth on the branch and the 'odd one out'. Long before the Hatherton Branch came, locks had been built having an equal fall wherever possible, usually about 6ft. 6in. This applied to other locks along the branch, but Jovey's lock was a shallow one. Now there is no change in level and the brook flows unimpeded between the walls of the lock. Like many locks on the branch, Jovey's has been affected by subsidence and the original sandstone edging has been replaced here and there with blue bricks. However, unlike the others, it still has some of its paddle gear. The ground paddle and post are still *in situ* on the offside of the lock. As on the main line, many wooden quoins along the Hatherton Branch were replaced with cast-iron ones in the late 1920s and 1930s and the top-gate quoins at Jovey's lock date from 1933.

No. 10 was an accommodation bridge across the tail of Brick Kiln lock, the sixth along the branch. Although the arch has collapsed, the side walls are standing and show clearly how canal bridges were constructed. The brickwork is a thin shell enclosing a fill of rubble and soil. The name of the lock arose from the proximity of Hawkins's Longhouse brick and tile works. The Company regarded it as the third and bottom lock of the Bridgtown flight, for the top-gate quoins have 'B3 1931' cast in them.

Above the lock are the rotting timbers of an old day boat, typical of the craft that used the branch, and beyond are the abutments of bridge No. 11. (This bridge was built after the canal, but it has been included in the numbering sequence to avoid confusion.) No. 11 carried the tramway that linked the Longhouse works with a marl pit to the south of the canal. Bricks and tiles have been made along this section for many years and there were once a number of collieries. Shafts were sunk as soon as the canal reached the area. Beete Jukes, in his account of the South Staffordshire Coalfield published in 1853, describes a 'newly-sunk pit at the Waterloo colliery at Longhouse, near the Walk Mill'. Coal was found at 136ft from the surface and a boring to 526ft passed through several seams, having a total thickness of about 35ft of coal. At greater depths were more coal seams and an abundance of fireclay. It is little wonder that Lord Hatherton was so enthusiastic about building the branch and that it was an immediate success after it was opened.

Next comes Rosemary lock, the middle one of the Bridgtown flight and named after the Rosemary tile works. Oddly enough, this works, whose products are still famous throughout the country, is ⅜ mile to the south of the canal, where it has been since 1882 at least. Perhaps the works next to the lock, the Walkmill Tileries, belonged to the same Company. This works was replaced by plant for washing and grading sand and gravel, but its wharf can still be seen below the lock. At the back of the wharf is an unusual wall that is built entirely of tiles.

Walkmill lock (Plate 78) is at the top of the Bridgtown flight and is also the summit lock of the branch, the canal having risen 45 ft from the main line. The striking feature of Walkmill lock is that few repairs have been carried out on it, whereas most of the others show signs of frequent maintenance. The reason for this is probably the large complex of basins above the lock. Although the area around the branch was riddled with mine workings, the coal-masters would soon have faced bankruptcy if the basins had gone out of use for any length of time and Walkmill was probably avoided. The lock still has many of its original features, including its eight rubbing plates. These oval iron plates, keyed to the brickwork in pairs at each end of the lock, prevented boats from damaging the walls when the lock was full. They are occasionally to be found on the main line in locks and under bridges, where they probably also date from about 1840. There is a lock cottage at Walkmill that is still inhabited and at one time there were stables where horses were left while boats were loading in the basins. At the head of the lock is a pulley that facilitated the handling of horse-drawn boats.

To the north of the canal, between the lock and the site of Walkmill bridge (No. 12), is Great Wyrley basin, the earliest on the branch. This basin was opened towards the end of 1842 and the Cheslyn Hay tramway from collieries at Wyrley ended here. The tramway fell into disrepair after it had been in use for about 30 years. It was restored in 1880 and coal was still being loaded at the basin early in the present century, when the 'Bass' boats worked from it. The coal carried by these boats was probably destined for breweries at Burton, but the name could equally have applied to the coal they were carrying, for the Bass coal is one of the thicker seams of the Cannock Coalfield.

Great Wyrley basin was quite small compared with the later Hawkins's basin, whose entrance was on the opposite side of the canal. Access to it was under a small bridge near Walkmill lock and along a narrow, 140yd channel. The side walls of the roving bridge are still there but the arch has gone and the basin and its approach channel have been infilled. The channel had an aqueduct over the Wyrley brook and was crossed by the track to Walkmill Tileries. Originally there was a swing-bridge at this point, but this was replaced by a lift-bridge whose flame-cut uprights can still be seen.

Hawkins's basin covered over 2 acres (Plate 79) and turning loaded boats in a high wind was hazardous. Element's boats carried as much as 38 tons from here to Stourport Power Station and there were only a few inches of freeboard. One careless move and the boat was on the bottom! Earlier, this was one of the basins where the Glosters delivered their hay for pit ponies and loaded with 'big' coal for their return journey down the Severn. The coal came from the neighbouring Cannock Old Coppice colliery of J. Hawkins & Sons, a highly successful mine that had a life of almost a hundred years. It was a 'family' concern until it came under state ownership and was always known as 'Hawkins's' to the boatmen. It is interesting to note that in the 1900s it was managed by Joshua Hawkins, with Elijah Rowley as Under-Manager. Biblical names had long been popular in the Black Country and when miners moved to the developing coalfield around Cannock, perhaps this tradition accompanied them.

A rail connection was made with the colliery towards the end of its life, but for many years the bulk of the output left Cannock Old Coppice by canal. In addition to coal, bricks and tiles from the Rosemary works were also loaded at Hawkins's basin. Element's 'Light Run' was one of the most important traffics during the years of decline. In 1949 7,000 tons of coal slack left Hawkins's for Stourport Power Station, and in the following year the quantity had fallen to 2,000 tons. The traffic ended in June 1949 and the pit itself closed down in the early 1960s. Gaunt buildings and towering tips are all that remains of Cannock Old Coppice, but an anonymous official of the National Coal Board has had the

foresight to provide a new coppice to replace the old. The land
that was once occupied by the basin is now covered by young
trees. Hawkins's has gone, but its name, once a byword along the
Staffs & Worcs, is still remembered with feeling by old boatmen.

The traffic originating on the ½-mile summit of the Hatherton
Branch was considerable and a substantial supply of water had to
be provided. Aside from lockage water at Churchbridge, the
principal feed was from Walkmill reservoir. This was near the
Rosemary tile works, on the opposite side of the Wyrley brook
from the canal. The supply joined the arm leading to Hawkins's
basin and entered the canal at the summit lock. The reservoir
continued to supply the branch until the basin was closed and it
has since been infilled.

Walkmill bridge has disappeared completely and has been replaced by a culvert. Gone too have all traces of the mill to the
south of the canal that gave the bridge its name. The old Urban
Manure Works to the north has fared better, for this still operates
as Cannock Fertilizers Ltd. The green and white enamel signs of
this firm are a familiar sight on buildings and along main roads in
south Staffordshire. This may seem a surprising industry in an
area where for many years mining has been the main activity.
Perhaps the works originally processed and distributed manure
provided by the pit ponies!

3⅜   *Churchbridge*   o

The summit follows the line of the Walkmill leat as far as the
weir where it leaves the Wyrley brook, and it may be that the leat
was realigned to make room for the canal. The mill was certainly
in existence before the canal, for the latter had an overflow weir at
the start of the leat. The canal and brook are spanned at this point
by a two-arch accommodation bridge (No. 13). Next to it is the
bridge that carried a branch of the South Staffordshire Railway,
built about 20 years after the canal, assuming that the Hatherton
Branch extended this far originally. The SSR built a small interchange basin at Churchbridge in 1860, the Staffs & Worcs Company contributing to the cost. This basin was for the transhipment
of goods between railway and canal and was connected to the
railway by a long siding. The Wyrley brook was diverted to

provide land for the wharves, basin and bridges, a sluice was in-stalled to enable water to pass into the canal, and Churchbridge basin became another important source of trade on the Staffs & Worcs. Although the basin is now drained, its outline can be traced and the remains of the sidings and the base of a crane can still be seen.

The Hatherton Branch ended at Churchbridge (No. 14) where it is crossed by Watling Street (A5). In the early 1850s the BCN decided to extend their system along the 473ft contour towards Cannock about 90ft above the summit of the Hatherton Branch. It was in the interests of the two companies to link their canals and in 1854 agreement was reached to build the interconnecting flight of locks. The land needed was purchased jointly by the two com-panies, but the building of the locks was paid for by the Staffs & Worcs. The Churchbridge flight was built in 1858/9 and opened in 1860, but did not come into use until the Cannock Extension Canal was completed three years later. The thirteen locks, crowded into a distance of ⅝ mile and each with a rise of 6ft 10in., were a magnificent spectacle. They swept up the hillside in a perfectly straight line to Rumer Hill Junction on the Extension Canal. According to boatmen who used them, their exposed position also made them the windiest flight in the country! In addition to having the 'standard' rise adopted by the BCN many years earlier, Churchbridge locks were among the last narrow ones to be built. Their construction was almost identical to the flight built at the same time and still in use at the Delph on the Dudley Canal.

The S&WCCo. benefited immediately from their expenditure on Churchbridge locks. Coal from Cannock & Leacroft, Cannock & Rugeley and other pits around Hednesford passed down the flight to the Hatherton Branch and continued to do so until shortly after nationalisation of the canal system. In the end it was mining subsidence that closed the branch. A war against sub-sidence was waged for many years on the Cannock Extension Canal, culminating in the dramatic battle of July 1960. This was won, despite the embankment sinking 21ft in one week due to opencast mining, but a few years later the canal began to sink at a greater rate than the banks could be repaired. Stop planks were inserted in 1963, the northern end of the Extension was drained, and Churchbridge locks and the Hatherton Branch were abandoned. The surrounding land has since been worked opencast for coal and fireclay and the entire flight has been obliterated except for a fragment of masonry at the tail of the bottom lock, visible in a field near the A5 road.

Although this concludes the account of the Hatherton Branch, there is a postscript to the story. The complex of basins and the tramway connection at Walkmill had every appearance of being 'at the end of the line', and this was also the main point of water supply. Could it be that the branch originally terminated here? If the branch was continued to Churchbridge while the locks were under construction, the supplementary feed at the railway basin may have been a temporary measure to help maintain the level in the ½-mile extension.

8

Route Maps

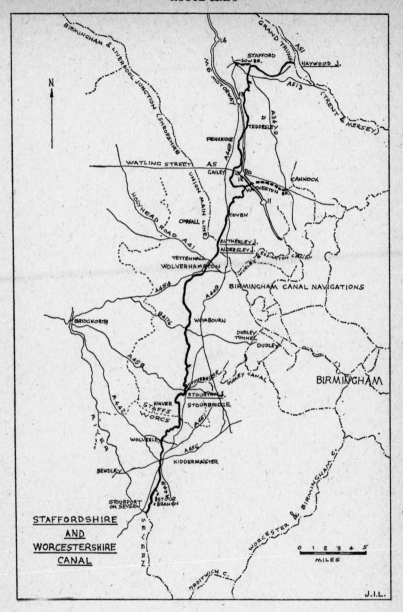

KEY TO DIAGRAMMATIC MAPS

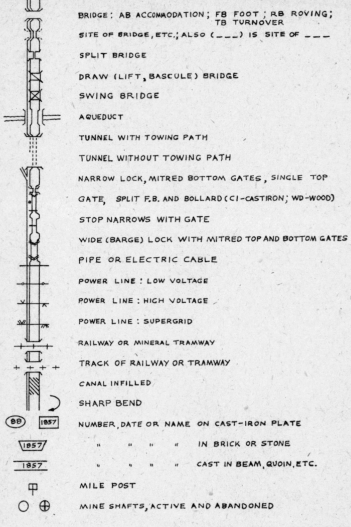

BRIDGE : AB ACCOMMODATION ; FB FOOT ; RB ROVING ; TB TURNOVER

SITE OF BRIDGE, ETC.; ALSO (___) IS SITE OF ___

SPLIT BRIDGE

DRAW (LIFT, BASCULE) BRIDGE

SWING BRIDGE

AQUEDUCT

TUNNEL WITH TOWING PATH

TUNNEL WITHOUT TOWING PATH

NARROW LOCK, MITRED BOTTOM GATES, SINGLE TOP GATE, SPLIT F.B. AND BOLLARD (CI-CASTIRON ; WD-WOOD)

STOP NARROWS WITH GATE

WIDE (BARGE) LOCK WITH MITRED TOP AND BOTTOM GATES

PIPE OR ELECTRIC CABLE

POWER LINE : LOW VOLTAGE

POWER LINE : HIGH VOLTAGE

POWER LINE : SUPERGRID

RAILWAY OR MINERAL TRAMWAY

TRACK OF RAILWAY OR TRAMWAY

CANAL INFILLED

SHARP BEND

NUMBER, DATE OR NAME ON CAST-IRON PLATE

"   "   "   "   IN BRICK OR STONE

"   "   "   "   CAST IN BEAM, QUOIN, ETC.

MILE POST

MINE SHAFTS, ACTIVE AND ABANDONED

SPR STOP-PLANK RACK; SG STOP GROOVES; SL STORMWATER SLUICE; OF OVERFLOW WEIR; IT INLET; B ORIGINAL BRIDGES, LOCKS, ETC.

J.I.L.

See page 50 for list of abbreviations.

STAFFORDSHIRE & WORCESTERSHIRE CANAL

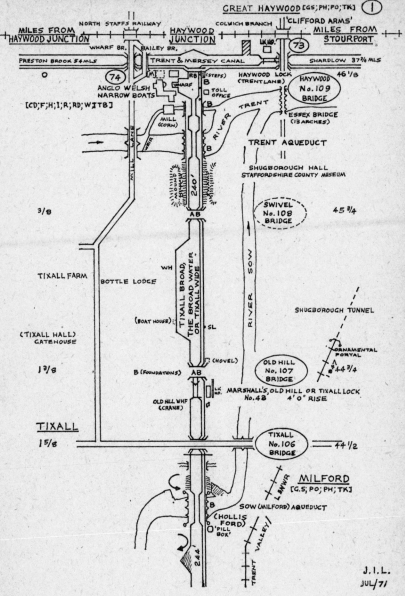

GREAT HAYWOOD [GS; PH; PO; TK]   ①

MILES FROM HAYWOOD JUNCTION

NORTH STAFFS RAILWAY

COLWICH BRANCH

'CLIFFORD ARMS'

MILES FROM STOURPORT

HAYWOOD JUNCTION

WHARF BR.   BAILEY BR.

LK.110.   73

PRESTON BROOK 54 MLS

TRENT & MERSEY CANAL

SHARDLOW 37¾ MLS

0   74

ANGLO WELSH NARROW BOATS

WHARF   (STEPS)

RB

TOLL OFFICE

HAYWOOD LOCK (TRENTLANE)

HAYWOOD No.109 BRIDGE

46⅛

[CD; F; H; I; R; RD; W; T B]

MILL (CORN)

WBR

TRENT

ESSEX BRIDGE (13 ARCHES)

TRENT AQUEDUCT

240'

SHUGBOROUGH HALL STAFFORDSHIRE COUNTY MUSEUM

3/8

AB

MOUND

SWIVEL No.108 BRIDGE

45¾

TIXALL FARM

BOTTLE LODGE

WH

(BOAT HOUSE)

TIXALL BROAD, THE BROAD WATER OR TIXALL WIDE

SL

RIVER SOW

SHUGBOROUGH TUNNEL

(TIXALL HALL) GATEHOUSE

(HOVEL)

OLD HILL No.107 BRIDGE

ORNAMENTAL PORTAL

44¾

1⅜

B (FOUNDATIONS)

AB

OLD HILL WHF (CRANE)

LK.No.

MARSHALL'S, OLD HILL OR TIXALL LOCK No.43   4'0" RISE

TIXALL

1⅝

TIXALL No.106 BRIDGE

44½

MILFORD [G.S; PO; PH; TK]

L&MWR

B

(HOLLIS FORD) 'PILL BOX'

SOW (MILFORD) AQUEDUCT

244'

TRENT VALLEY

J.I.L.
JUL/71

203

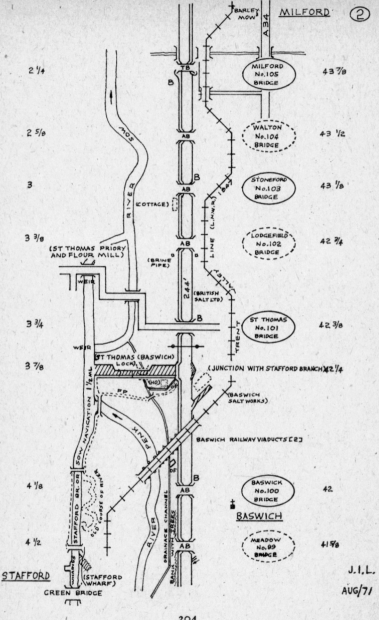

BARLEY MOW

MILFORD ②

2 ¼

2 ⅝

3

3 ⅜

3 ¾

3 ⅞

4 ⅛

4 ½

MOS

RIVER

(COTTAGE)

(ST THOMAS PRIORY
AND FLOUR MILL)

(BRINE PIPE)

2.44'

(BRITISH SALT LTD)

WEIR

WEIR

ST THOMAS (BASWICH)
LOCK)

(HO)

FP

SOW NAVIGATION 1 ½ ML

PENK

STAFFORD BR. OR

OLD COURSE OF RIVER

RIVER

DRAINAGE CHANNEL

BANK WITH TREES

CHIMNEYS

STAFFORD

GREEN BRIDGE

(STAFFORD WHARF)

TB

B

AB

B

AB

AB

B

ST THOMAS No.101 BRIDGE

(JUNCTION WITH STAFFORD BRANCH) 2 ¼

(BASWICH SALT WORKS)

DF

BASWICH RAILWAY VIADUCTS [2]

DF

B

AB

AB

LINE (L.N.W.R.) 1847

TRENT VALLEY

A34

MILFORD No.105 BRIDGE 43 ⅜

WALTON No.104 BRIDGE 43 ½

STONEFORD No.103 BRIDGE 43 ⅛

LODGEFIELD No.102 BRIDGE 42 ¾

42 ⅜

BASWICK No.100 BRIDGE 42

BASWICH

MEADOW No.99 BRIDGE 41 ⅝

J. I. L.

AUG/71

204

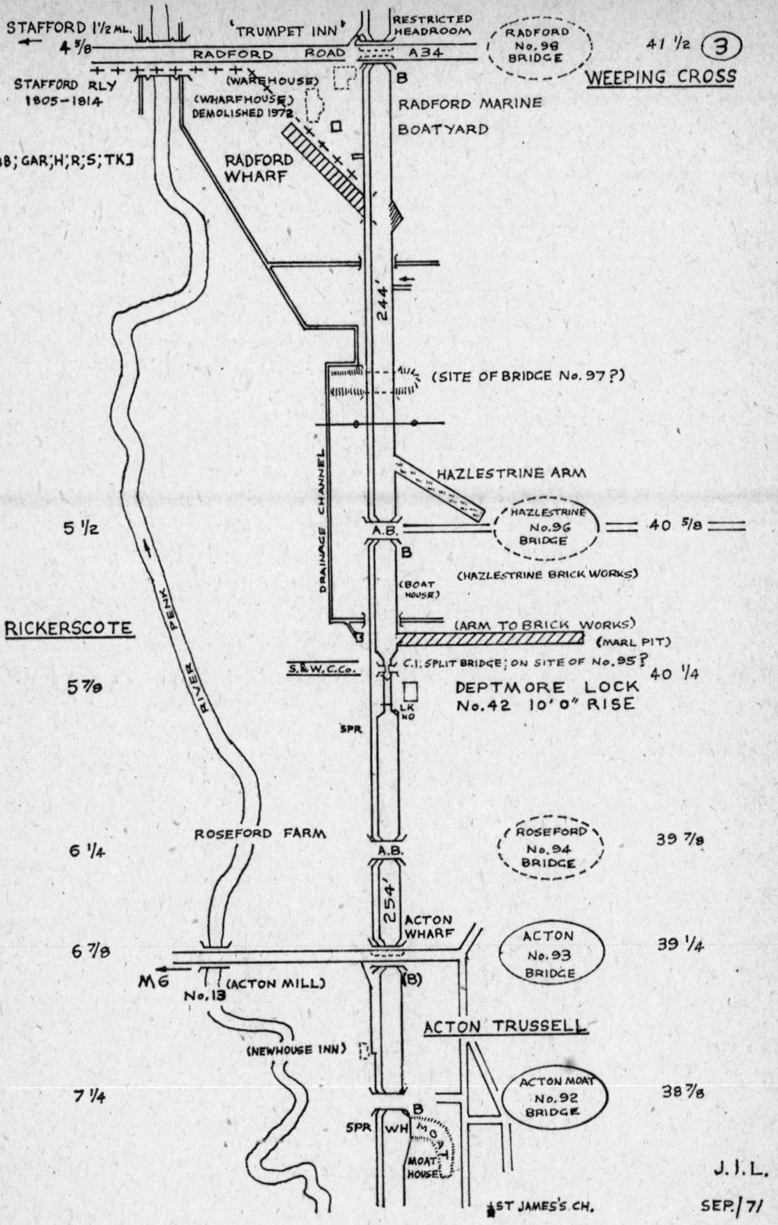
STAFFORD 1½ ML.
4 ⅝
'TRUMPET INN'
RESTRICTED HEADROOM
RADFORD ROAD A34
RADFORD No. 98 BRIDGE
41 ½
3
WEEPING CROSS
STAFFORD RLY 1805-1814
(WAREHOUSE)
(WHARFHOUSE) DEMOLISHED 1972
B
RADFORD MARINE BOATYARD
[BB; GAR; H; R; S; TK]
RADFORD WHARF
244'
(SITE OF BRIDGE No. 97?)
DRAINAGE CHANNEL
HAZLESTRINE ARM
5 ½
A.B.
HAZLESTRINE No. 96 BRIDGE
40 ⅝
B
(HAZLESTRINE BRICK WORKS)
(BOAT HOUSE)
RICKERSCOTE
RIVER PENK
(ARM TO BRICK WORKS)
(MARL PIT)
S.&W.C.Co.
C.I. SPLIT BRIDGE; ON SITE OF No. 95?
40 ¼
5 ⅞
DEPTMORE LOCK No. 42 10' 0" RISE
LK HO
SPR
ROSEFORD FARM
ROSEFORD No. 94 BRIDGE
39 ⅞
6 ¼
A.B.
254'
ACTON WHARF
6 ⅞
ACTON No. 93 BRIDGE
39 ¼
M6
No. 13
(ACTON MILL)
(B)
ACTON TRUSSELL
(NEWHOUSE INN)
7 ¼
ACTON MOAT No. 92 BRIDGE
38 ⅞
B
SPR
WH
MOAT
MOAT HOUSE
ST JAMES'S CH.
J.I.L.
SEP. /71

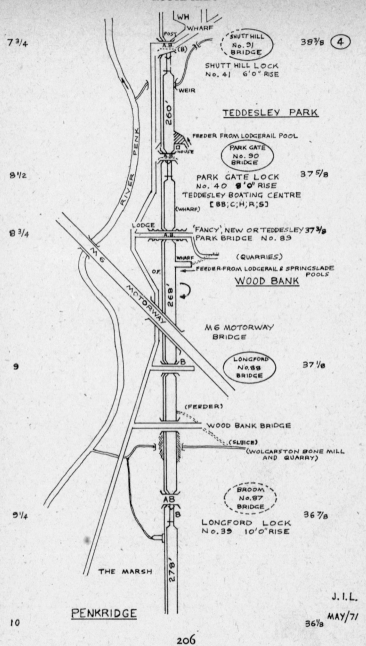

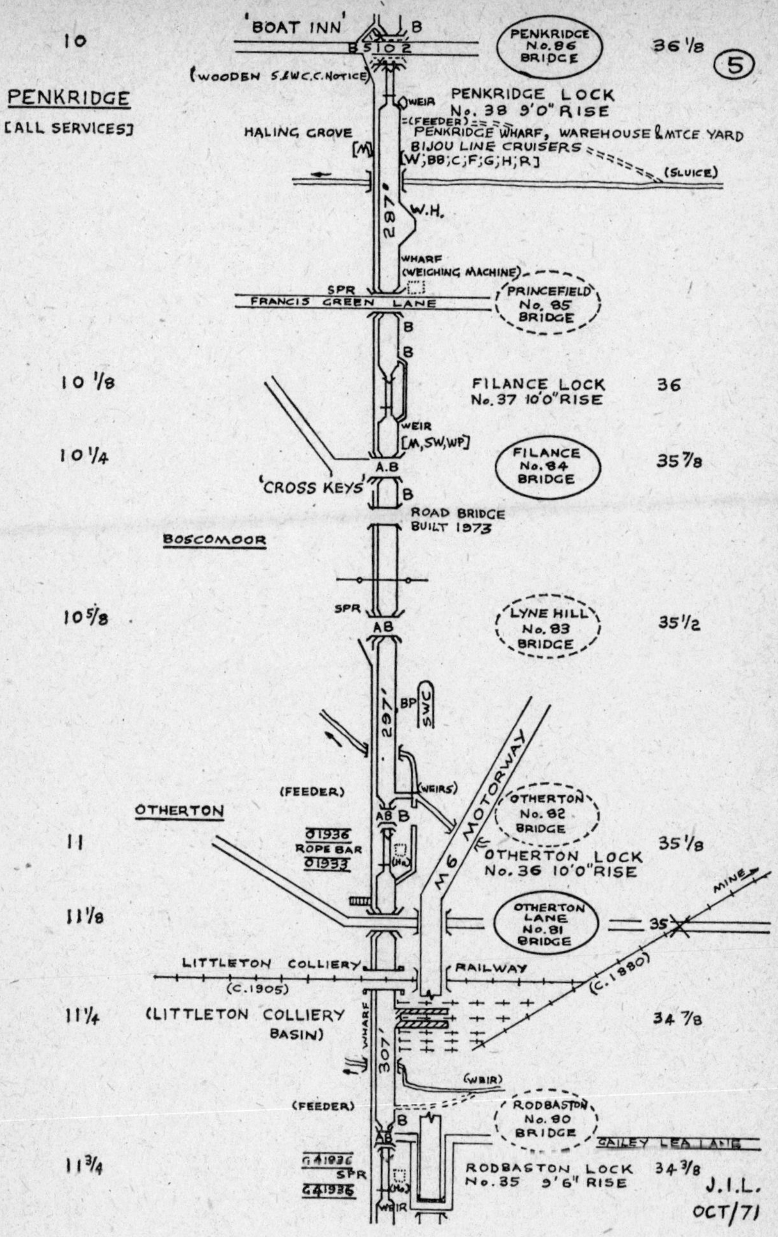
10
'BOAT INN'
B
B5102
PENKRIDGE No. 86 BRIDGE
36 1/8
5
(WOODEN S.&W.C.C. NOTICE)
PENKRIDGE
[ALL SERVICES]
WEIR
PENKRIDGE LOCK No. 38 9'0" RISE
(FEEDER)
HALING GROVE
PENKRIDGE WHARF, WAREHOUSE & MTCE YARD
BIJOU LINE CRUISERS
[M]
[W; BB; C; F; G; H; R]
(SLUICE)
297'
W.H.
WHARF
(WEIGHING MACHINE)
SPR
FRANCIS GREEN LANE
PRINCEFIELD No. 85 BRIDGE
B
B
10 1/8
FILANCE LOCK No. 37 10'0" RISE
36
WEIR
[M, SW, WP]
10 1/4
A.B
FILANCE No. 84 BRIDGE
35 7/8
'CROSS KEYS'
B
ROAD BRIDGE BUILT 1973
BOSCOMOOR
SPR
10 5/8
AB
LYNE HILL No. 83 BRIDGE
35 1/2
BP
SWC
297'
M6 MOTORWAY
(FEEDER)
(WEIRS)
OTHERTON
OTHERTON No. 82 BRIDGE
AB
B
11
O1936
ROPE BAR
O1933
35 1/8
OTHERTON LOCK No. 36 10'0" RISE
MINE
11 1/8
OTHERTON LANE No. 81 BRIDGE
35
LITTLETON COLLIERY
RAILWAY
(C.1905)
(C.1880)
11 1/4
(LITTLETON COLLIERY BASIN)
34 7/8
WHARF
307'
(WEIR)
(FEEDER)
B
RODBASTON No. 80 BRIDGE
AB
GAILEY LEA LANE
11 3/4
G.A1936
SPR
G.A1936
RODBASTON LOCK No. 35 9'6" RISE
34 3/8
WEIR
J.I.L.
OCT/71

⑥

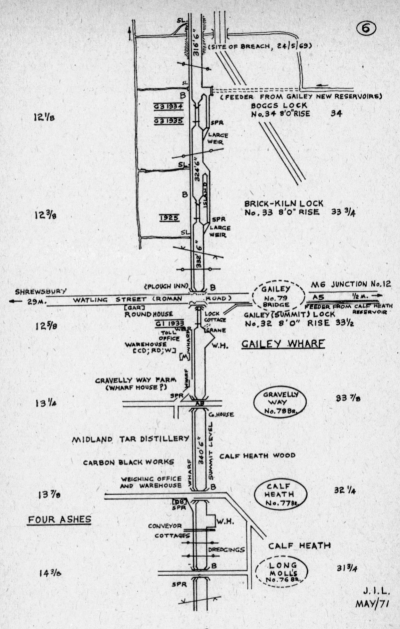

SL

316'6"

(SITE OF BREACH, 24/5/69)

(FEEDER FROM GAILEY NEW RESERVOIRS)

SL

B

G.3 1934

G.3 1935

SPR

LARGE WEIR

BOGGS LOCK
No.34 8'0"RISE   34

12 1/8

SL

324'6"

B

ISLAND

1925

SPR
LARGE WEIR

BRICK-KILN LOCK
No. 33 8'0" RISE   33 3/4

12 3/8

SL

332'6"

SHREWSBURY
29M.

(PLOUGH INN)   B

WATLING   STREET (ROMAN   ROAD)

[GAR]
ROUND HOUSE

GAILEY
No. 79
BRIDGE

M6 JUNCTION No.12

A5   1/2 M.

FEEDER FROM CALF HEATH
RESERVOIR

12 5/8

G.1 1933

WEIR

LOCK
COTTAGE

TOLL
OFFICE

CRANE

WHARF

WAREHOUSE
[CD; RD; W]   [M]

W.H.

GAILEY (SUMMIT) LOCK
No. 32 8'0" RISE 33 1/2

GAILEY WHARF

GRAVELLY WAY FARM
(WHARF HOUSE?)

13 1/4

WHARF

SPR

AB

GRAVELLY
WAY
No. 788a.

33 7/8

G. HOUSE

MIDLAND TAR DISTILLERY

CARBON BLACK WORKS

WHARF

340'6"

SUMMIT LEVEL

CALF HEATH WOOD

WEIGHING OFFICE
AND WAREHOUSE

B

CALF
HEATH
No. 778a.

32 1/4

13 7/8

[DB]
SPR

FOUR ASHES

W.H.

CONVEYOR
COTTAGES

DREDGINGS

CALF HEATH

14 3/8

B

SPR

LONG
MOLL'S
No. 76 Bg.

31 3/4

J. I. L.
MAY/71

208

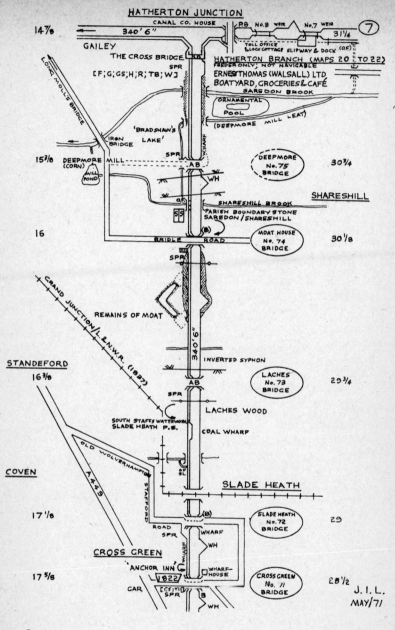

HATHERTON JUNCTION

CANAL CO. HOUSE

14⅞   ← 340'6"   PB No.8 WEIR   No.7 WEIR   31¼   ⑦

GAILEY   TOLL OFFICE
THE CROSS BRIDGE   LOCK COTTAGE SLIPWAY & DOCK (QF)
SPR   HATHERTON BRANCH (MAPS 20 TO 22)
[F;G;GS;H;R;TB;W]   FEEDER ONLY; NOT NAVIGABLE
          ERNEST THOMAS (WALSALL) LTD
          BOATYARD, GROCERIES & CAFÉ
          SAREDON BROOK

LONG MOLL'S BRIDGE   ORNAMENTAL POOL
          (DEEPMORE MILL LEAT)

'BRADSHAW'S LAKE'   WHARF

IRON BRIDGE

15⅜ DEEPMORE MILL   SPR   AB   DEEPMORE No.75 BRIDGE   30¾
(CORN)   MILL POND

          WH

          SHARESHILL BROOK   SHARESHILL
          PARISH BOUNDARY STONE
          SAREDON / SHARESHILL

16   (B)   MOAT HOUSE No.74 BRIDGE   30⅛
          BRIDLE ROAD

          SPR

GRAND JUNCTION / L.N.W.R. (1837)

REMAINS OF MOAT   340'6"

          INVERTED SYPHON

STANDEFORD   AB
16⅜   LACHES No.73 BRIDGE   29¾

          SPR

          LACHES WOOD
SOUTH STAFFS WATERWORKS
SLADE HEATH P.S.   COAL WHARF

OLD WOLVERHAMPTON & STAFFORD

COVEN   QF SL

          SLADE HEATH

17⅛   (B)   SLADE HEATH No.72 BRIDGE   29

A449   ROAD   SPR   WHARF
          WH
CROSS GREEN   WHARF

ANCHOR INN   WHARF-HOUSE
17⅝   1822   CROSS GREEN No.71 BRIDGE   28½
GAR   (CERING) SPR   B
          WH   J.I.L.
                    MAY/71

0   209

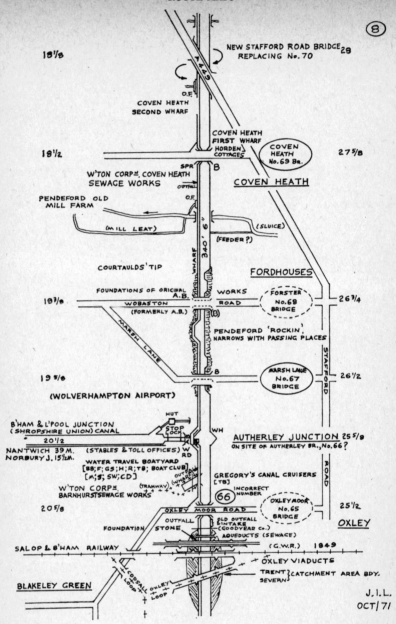

⑧

NEW STAFFORD ROAD BRIDGE 28
REPLACING No. 70

19⅛

O.F.

COVEN HEATH
SECOND WHARF

COVEN HEATH
FIRST WHARF
HORDEN
COTTAGES

COVEN
HEATH
No. 69 Br.

27⅝

19½

B

W'TON CORP⁰ COVEN HEATH
SEWAGE WORKS

SPR

OUTFALL

COVEN HEATH

O.F.

PENDEFORD OLD
MILL FARM

(MILL LEAT)

(SLUICE)

(FEEDER ?)

340' 6"

WHARF

COURTAULDS' TIP

FORDHOUSES

FOUNDATIONS OF ORIGINAL
A.B.

WORKS

FORSTER
No. 68
BRIDGE

26¾

19⅜

WOBASTON
(FORMERLY A.B.)

ROAD

MARSH LANE

PENDEFORD 'ROCKIN'
NARROWS WITH PASSING PLACES

B

MARSH LANE
No. 67
BRIDGE

26½

STAFFORD

19⅝

(WOLVERHAMPTON AIRPORT)

HUT

B'HAM & L'POOL JUNCTION
(SHROPSHIRE UNION) CANAL

STOP
LOCK

WH

AUTHERLEY JUNCTION 25⅝
ON SITE OF AUTHERLEY BR., No. 66?

20½

NANTWICH 39 M.
NORBURY J. 15½ M.

(STABLES & TOLL OFFICES)

W
RD

WATER TRAVEL BOATYARD
[BB; F; GS; H; R; TB; BOAT CLUB]
[M; S; SW; CD]

OUTFALL

W
(WHARF)

ROAD

W'TON CORP⁰
BARNHURST SEWAGE WORKS

(TRAMWAY)

GREGORY'S CANAL CRUISERS
[TB]

66

INCORRECT
NUMBER

OXLEYMOOR
No. 65
BRIDGE

25½

20⅝

OXLEY MOOR ROAD

OXLEY

OUTFALL
STONE

OLD OUTFALL
(INTAKE
(GOODYEAR Co.)

FOUNDATION

AQUEDUCTS (SEWAGE)

SALOP & B'HAM RAILWAY

(G.W.R.) 1849

OXLEY VIADUCTS

BLAKELEY GREEN

CODSALL LOOP

OXLEY
LOOP

TRENT
SEVERN } CATCHMENT AREA BDY.

J. I. L.
OCT/71

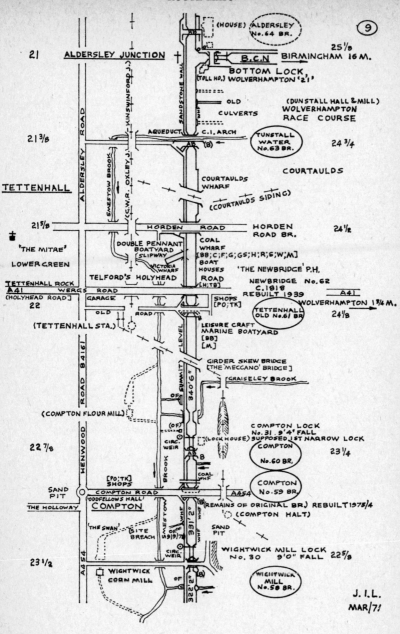

⑨

(HOUSE) ALDERSLEY No. 64 BR.

21   ALDERSLEY JUNCTION

25⅛
B.C.N   BIRMINGHAM 16 M.
BOTTOM LOCK
(TOLL HO.) WOLVERHAMPTON '21'

OLD
CULVERTS   (DUNSTALL HALL & MILL)
WOLVERHAMPTON
RACE COURSE

21⅜   AQUEDUCT   C.I. ARCH

TUNSTALL
WATER
No. 63 BR.   24¾

TETTENHALL   COURTAULDS

COURTAULDS
WHARF

(COURTAULDS SIDING)

21⅝   HORDEN ROAD   HORDEN
ROAD BR.   24½

COAL
WHARF
[BB; C; F; G; GS; H; R; S; W; M]
'THE MITRE'   DOUBLE PENNANT
BOATYARD
SLIPWAY   BOAT
HOUSES
LOWER GREEN   VICTORIA
WHARF   'THE NEWBRIDGE' P.H.
TELFORD'S HOLYHEAD ROAD   [H; TB]   NEWBRIDGE No. 62
C.1818
TETTENHALL ROCK   WERGS ROAD   REBUILT 1939   A41
A41   GARAGE   WOLVERHAMPTON 1¾ M.
(HOLYHEAD ROAD)   SHOPS
22   OLD   [PO; TK]   TETTENHALL
OLD No. 61 BR.   24⅛
ROAD

(TETTENHALL STA.)   LEISURE CRAFT
MARINE BOATYARD
[BB]
[M]

GIRDER SKEW BRIDGE
(THE 'MECCANO' BRIDGE)

CRAISELEY BROOK

(COMPTON FLOUR MILL)

COMPTON LOCK
No. 31 9'4" FALL
(LOCK HOUSE) SUPPOSED 1ST NARROW LOCK
CIRC.
WEIR   COMPTON
No. 60 BR.   23¼

22⅞   [PO; TK]
SHOPS   COAL
WHF.   COMPTON
No. 59 BR.
SAND
PIT   COMPTON ROAD   A454
THE HOLLOWAY   ODDFELLOWS HALL   (REMAINS OF ORIGINAL BR.) REBUILT 1973/4
COMPTON   (COMPTON HALT)
'THE SWAN'   SITE
BREACH   SAND
9|9|78   PIT
CIRC.
WEIR   WIGHTWICK MILL LOCK
No. 30   9'0" FALL   22⅝
23½   WIGHTWICK
CORN MILL   WIGHTWICK
MILL
No. 58 BR.

J. I. L.
MAR/71

211

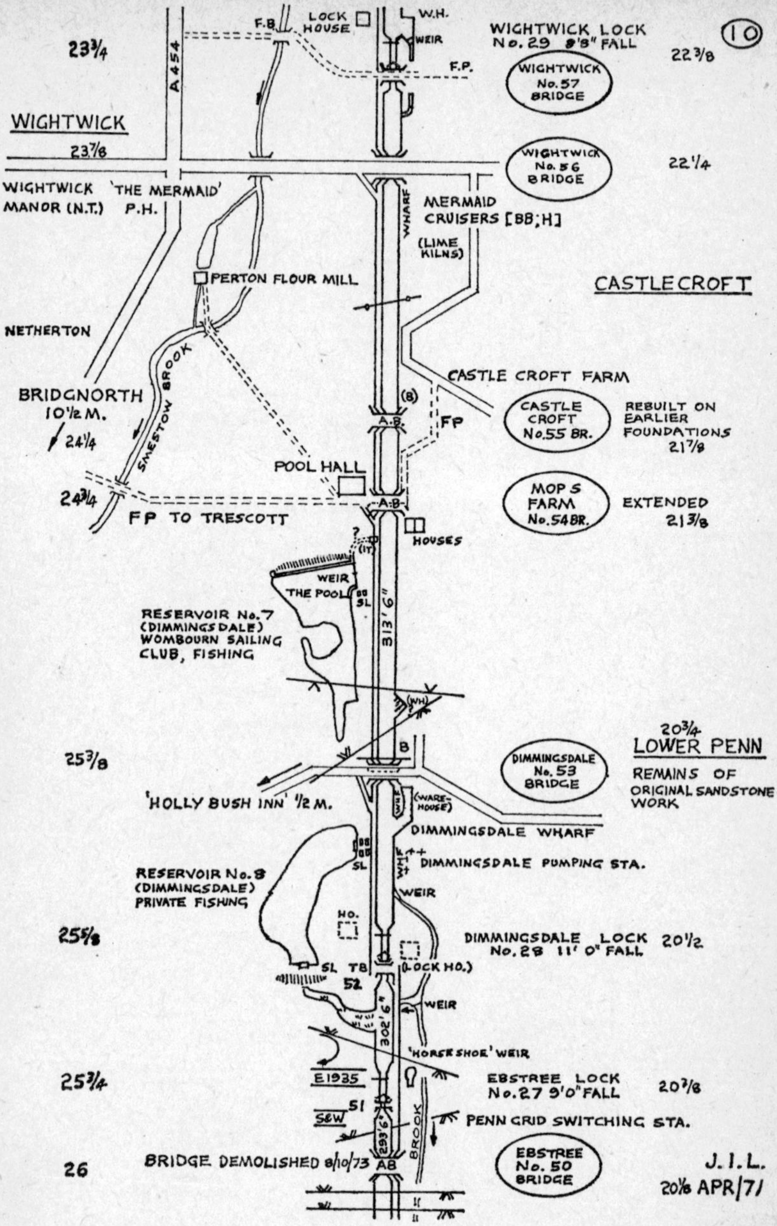
10
23¾
LOCK HOUSE
F.B.
W.H.
WEIR
WIGHTWICK LOCK No. 29 8'8" FALL
22⅜
A454
F.P.
WIGHTWICK No. 57 BRIDGE
WIGHTWICK
23⅞
WIGHTWICK No. 56 BRIDGE
22¼
WIGHTWICK MANOR (N.T.)
'THE MERMAID' P.H.
WHARF
MERMAID CRUISERS [BB; H]
(LIME KILNS)
PERTON FLOUR MILL
CASTLECROFT
NETHERTON
SMESTOW BROOK
CASTLE CROFT FARM
BRIDGNORTH 10½ M.
24¼
(8)
A.B.
FP
CASTLE CROFT No.55 BR.
REBUILT ON EARLIER FOUNDATIONS
21⅞
POOL HALL
24¾
A.B.
MOPS FARM No.54 BR.
EXTENDED
21⅜
FP TO TRESCOTT
HOUSES
WEIR
THE POOL
SL
313' 6"
RESERVOIR No.7 (DIMMINGSDALE) WOMBOURN SAILING CLUB, FISHING
(WH)
20¾
LOWER PENN
25⅜
B
DIMMINGSDALE No. 53 BRIDGE
REMAINS OF ORIGINAL SANDSTONE WORK
'HOLLY BUSH INN' ½ M.
WHF
(WAREHOUSE)
DIMMINGSDALE WHARF
SL
DIMMINGSDALE PUMPING STA.
RESERVOIR No.8 (DIMMINGSDALE) PRIVATE FISHING
WEIR
HO.
25⅝
DIMMINGSDALE LOCK No. 28 11' 0" FALL
20½
SL
TB
(LOCK HO.)
52
WEIR
302' 6"
'HORSESHOE' WEIR
25¾
E1935
EBSTREE LOCK No. 27 9'0" FALL
20⅜
51
S&W
PENN GRID SWITCHING STA.
293' 6"
BROOK
26
BRIDGE DEMOLISHED 8/10/73
AB
EBSTREE No. 50 BRIDGE
J.I.L.
20⅛ APR/71

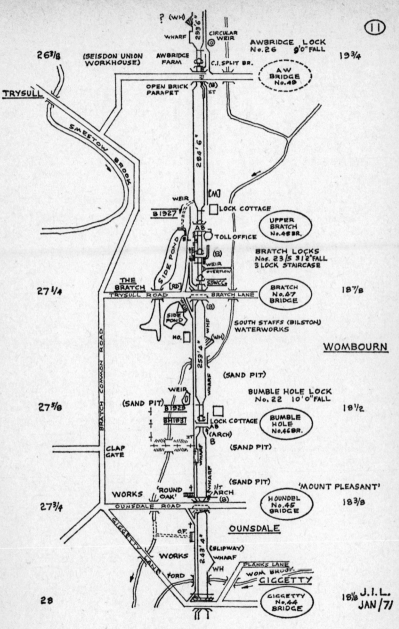

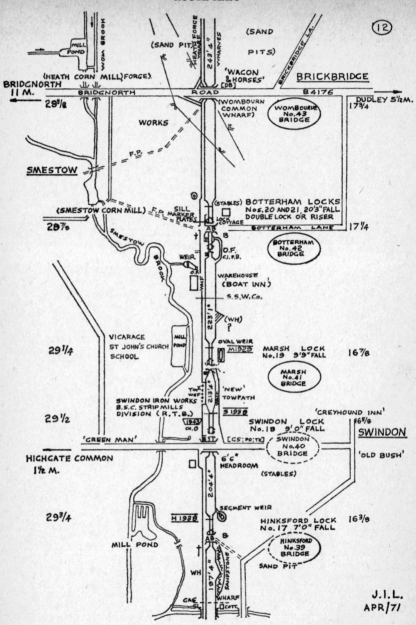

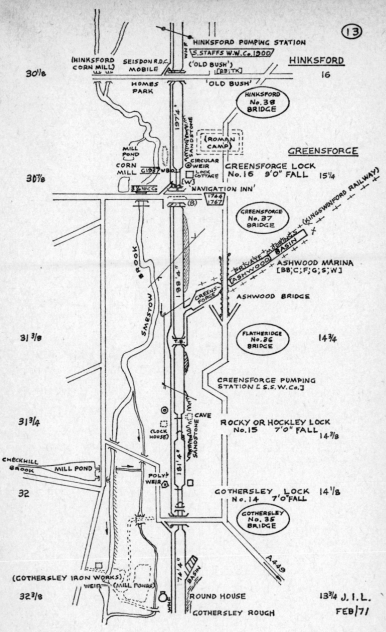

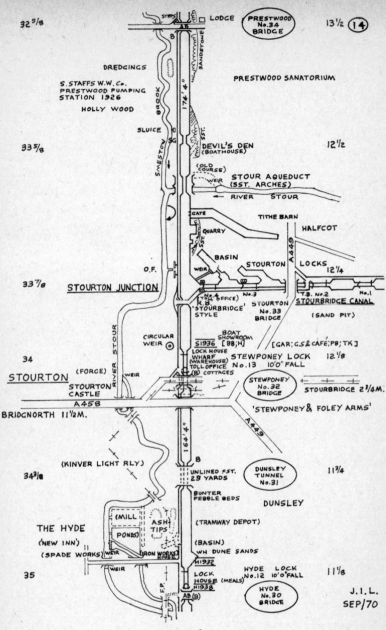

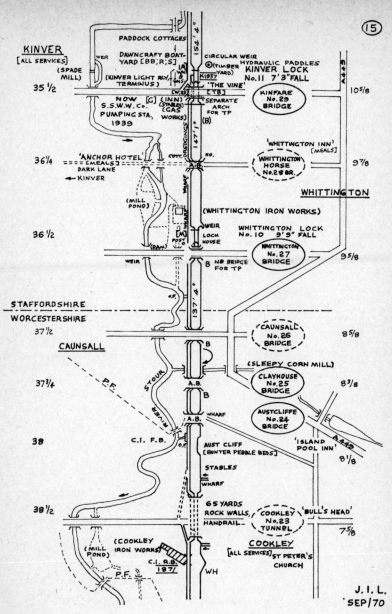

⑮

KINVER
[ALL SERVICES]

(SPADE
MILL)

35½

PADDOCK COTTAGES

DAWNCRAFT BOAT-
YARD [BB; R; S]

WEIR

(KINVER LIGHT RLY.
TERMINUS)

NOW [G] (INN)
S.S.W.W.Co. (STABLES)
PUMPING STA., (GAS
1939 WORKS)

154'4"

147'1"

K1937

CIRCULAR WEIR
⊙(TIMBER
YARD)

'THE VINE'
[TB]

HYDRAULIC PADDLES
KINVER LOCK
No.11 7'3"FALL

SEPARATE
ARCH
FOR TP
(B)

KINFARE
No.29
BRIDGE

10⅝

A449

36¼

'ANCHOR HOTEL'
==== [MEALS] ====
DARK LANE
← KINVER

COTT.

NO.

A.B.

WHITTINGTON INN'
[MEALS]

WHITTINGTON
HORSE
No.28 BR.

9⅞

WHITTINGTON

(MILL
POND)

WHARF

(WHITTINGTON IRON WORKS)

36½

(DAM)

[M]
POST
O.

WEIR
LOCK
HOUSE

WHITTINGTON LOCK
No.10 9'9" FALL

WHITTINGTON
No.27
BRIDGE

9⅝

WEIR

137'4"

A.F.

B NO BRIDGE
FOR TP

STAFFORDSHIRE
WORCESTERSHIRE

37½

B

CAUNSALL
No.26
BRIDGE

8⅝

CAUNSALL

P.F.

RIVER STOUR

B

(SLEEPY CORN MILL)

CLAYHOUSE
No.25
BRIDGE

8⅜

37¾

A.B.

B

38

C.I. F.B.

A.B. WHARF

O.F.

AUSTCLIFFE
No.24
BRIDGE

A449

'ISLAND
POOL INN'

8⅛

AUST CLIFF
[BUNTER PEBBLE BEDS]

STABLES

WHARF

39½

65 YARDS
ROCK WALLS,
HANDRAIL.

COOKLEY
No.23
TUNNEL

'BULL'S HEAD'

7⅝

(MILL
POND)

(COOKLEY
IRON WORKS)

C.I. R.B.
1871

P.F.

WH

COOKLEY
[ALL SERVICES] ST PETER'S
CHURCH

J. I. L.
SEP/70

217

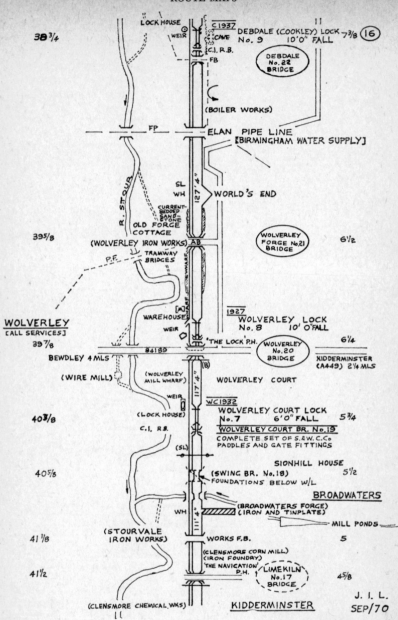

38¾

LOCK HOUSE

C1937

WEIR

CAVE

C.I. R.B.

FB

DEBDALE (COOKLEY) LOCK 7⅜ (16)
No. 9   10'0" FALL

DEBDALE
No.22
BRIDGE

(BOILER WORKS)

FP

ELAN PIPE LINE
[BIRMINGHAM WATER SUPPLY]

R. STOUR

SL
WH

127'4"

CURRENT-
BEDDED
SAND &
STONE

WORLD'S END

OLD FORGE
COTTAGE

39⅝

(WOLVERLEY IRON WORKS)

AB

WOLVERLEY
FORGE No.21
BRIDGE

6½

P.F.

TRAMWAY
BRIDGES

WHARF

[A]
WAREHOUSE

1927

WOLVERLEY LOCK
No. 8   10' 0" FALL

WEIR

'THE LOCK P.H.

WOLVERLEY
No.20
BRIDGE

6¼

WOLVERLEY
[ALL SERVICES]

39⅞

B4189

(B)

117'4"

BEWDLEY 4 MLS

KIDDERMINSTER
(A449) 2¼ MLS

(WIRE MILL)

(WOLVERLEY
MILL WHARF)

WOLVERLEY COURT

WEIR

WC1932

WOLVERLEY COURT LOCK
No.7   6'0" FALL   5¾

40⅜

(LOCK HOUSE)

WOLVERLEY COURT BR. No.19

C.I. R.B.

COMPLETE SET OF S.&W.C.Co
PADDLES AND GATE FITTINGS

(SL)

SIONHILL HOUSE

40⅝

(SWING BR. No.18)
FOUNDATIONS BELOW W/L

5½

BROADWATERS

WH

114'4"

(BROADWATERS FORGE)
(IRON AND TINPLATE)

MILL PONDS

41⅛

(STOURVALE
IRON WORKS)

WORKS F.B.

5

(CLENSMORE CORN MILL)
(IRON FOUNDRY)

41½

'THE NAVIGATION'
P.H.

LIMEKILN
No.17
BRIDGE

4⅝

(CLENSMORE CHEMICAL WKS)

KIDDERMINSTER

J. I. L.
SEP/70

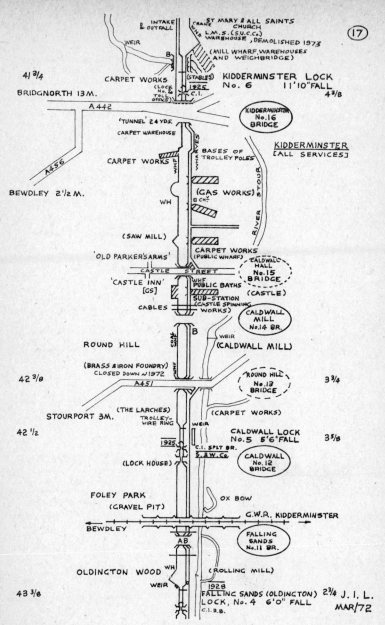

ST MARY & ALL SAINTS
CHURCH

INTAKE & OUTFALL

CRANE

L.M.S.(S.U.C.Co)
WAREHOUSE, DEMOLISHED 1973

WEIR

(MILL WHARF, WAREHOUSES
AND WEIGHBRIDGE)

(17)

41 3/4

CARPET WORKS

BRIDGNORTH 13M.

(STABLES)

(LOCK No.6 TOLL OFFICE)

1925

C.I.

KIDDERMINSTER LOCK
No. 6   11'10" FALL

4 3/8

A 442

KIDDERMINSTER
No. 16
BRIDGE

A 456

'TUNNEL' 24 YDS.

CARPET WAREHOUSE

CARPET WORKS

WHF

WHARVES

BASES OF
TROLLEY POLES

KIDDERMINSTER
[ALL SERVICES]

BEWDLEY 2 1/2 M.

WH

(GAS WORKS)

□ CH?

RIVER STOUR

(SAW MILL)

'OLD PARKER'S ARMS'

CARPET WORKS
(PUBLIC WHARF)

CALDWALL
HALL
No. 15
BRIDGE

CASTLE   STREET

'CASTLE INN'
[GS]

WHF

PUBLIC BATHS

(CASTLE)

SUB-STATION

CABLES

(CASTLE SPINNING
WORKS)

CALDWALL
MILL
No.14 BR.

ROUND HILL

COAL WHF

B

WEIR

(CALDWALL MILL)

(BRASS & IRON FOUNDRY)
CLOSED DOWN 1972

42 3/8

A451

WHF

ROUND HILL
No. 13
BRIDGE

3 3/4

STOURPORT 3M.

(THE LARCHES)
TROLLEY-
WIRE RING

(CARPET WORKS)

WEIR

42 1/2

1925

C.I. SPLT BR.
S. & W. Co.

CALDWALL LOCK
No. 5   5'6" FALL

3 5/8

(LOCK HOUSE)

CALDWALL
No.12
BRIDGE

FOLEY PARK
(GRAVEL PIT)

OX BOW

G.W.R. KIDDERMINSTER

BEWDLEY

FALLING
SANDS
No.11 BR.

AB

OLDINGTON WOOD

WH

(ROLLING MILL)

WEIR

1928

43 3/8

FALLING SANDS (OLDINGTON) 2 3/4
LOCK, No. 4   6'0" FALL

C.I.R.B.

J. I. L.
MAR/72

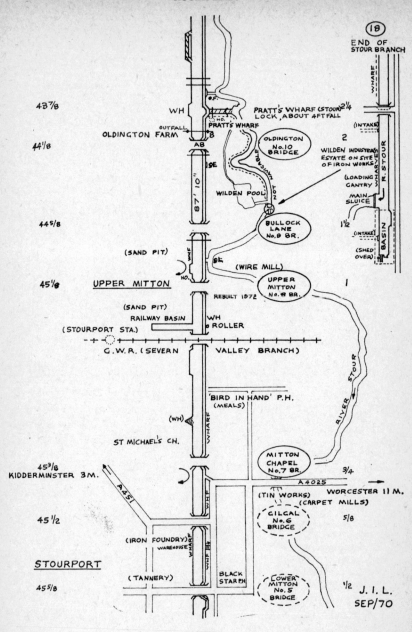

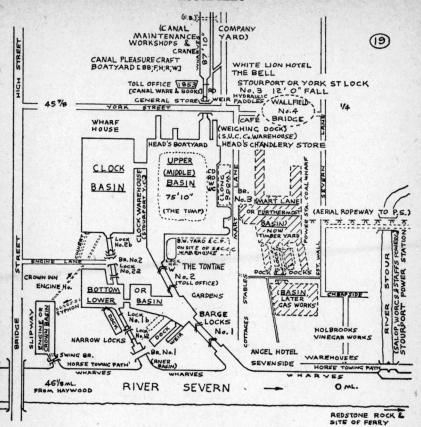

STOURPORT BASINS
LOCKS

No.	Name	Rise		Length		Breadth		Depth on Sill	
(a) *Wide locks*		ft	in.	ft	in.	ft	in.	ft	in.
1	Lower Barge lock	13	0 nom.	75	10	15	5	6	10 nom.
2	Upper Barge lock	11	10	75	10	15	4	5	5
(b) *Narrow Locks*									
1a	Lower Boat locks	13	0	75	0	7	2	4	6
1b	(Staircase pair)								
2a	Upper Boat locks	11	10	75	0	7	2	4	6
2b	(Staircase pair)								
–	Barge lock off Mart Lane basin, now infilled								

BRIDGES

No. 1 Lower Severn bridge   No. 2 Engine Lane or Upper Severn bridge

No. 3 Mart Lane bridge

221

HATHERTON (CHURCHBRIDGE) BRANCH
(NOT NAVIGABLE)

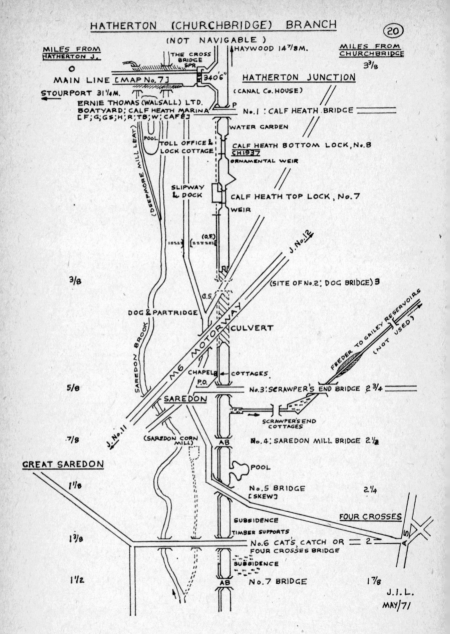

20

↑HAYWOOD 14⁷/₈M.

MILES FROM
HATHERTON J.

0

MILES FROM
CHURCHBRIDGE

3³/₈

THE CROSS
BRIDGE
SPR.

MAIN LINE [MAP No.7]   34'0'6"   HATHERTON JUNCTION

STOURPORT 31¼M.   (CANAL Co. HOUSE)

ERNIE THOMAS (WALSALL) LTD.   P   No.1 CALF HEATH BRIDGE
BOATYARD; CALF HEATH MARINA
[F;G;GS;H;R;TB;W;CAFE]

WATER GARDEN

POOL   TOLL OFFICE &   CALF HEATH BOTTOM LOCK, No.8
LOCK COTTAGE   CH1927

ORNAMENTAL WEIR

SLIPWAY
& DOCK   CALF HEATH TOP LOCK, No.7

WEIR

(O.F.)

J.No.12

3/8   (SITE OF No.2 DOG BRIDGE) ∃

G.S.

DOG & PARTRIDGE

MOTORWAY M6   CULVERT   FEEDER TO GAILEY RESERVOIRS (NOT USED)

CHAPEL   COTTAGES

5/8   P.O.   No.3 SCRAWPER'S END BRIDGE 2³/₄

SAREDON

SCRAWPER'S END
COTTAGES

7/8   J.No.11   (SAREDON CORN   AB   No.4 SAREDON MILL BRIDGE 2½
MILL)

GREAT SAREDON

1¹/₈   POOL   No.5 BRIDGE   2¼
[SKEW]

FOUR CROSSES

SUBSIDENCE

1³/₈   TIMBER SUPPORTS   No.6 CATS CATCH OR   2
FOUR CROSSES BRIDGE

SUBSIDENCE

1½   AB   No.7 BRIDGE   1⁷/₈

J.I.L.
MAY/71

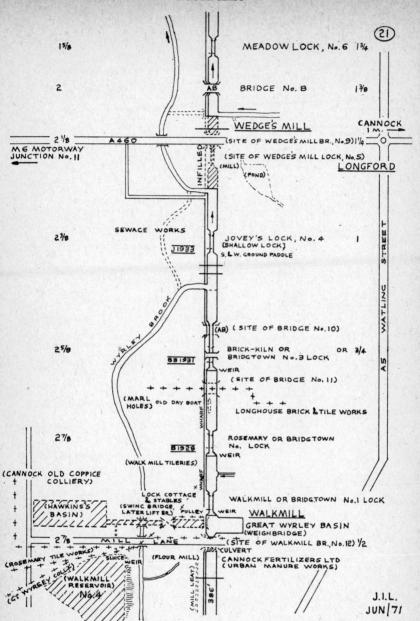

㉑

1⅝   MEADOW LOCK, No.6 1¾

2   BRIDGE No. 8   1⅜

CANNOCK
1 M.

2⅛   A460   WEDGE'S MILL
M 6 MOTORWAY
JUNCTION No. 11   (SITE OF WEDGE'S MILL BR., No.9) 1¼

(SITE OF WEDGE'S MILL LOCK, No.5)
(MILL)   LONGFORD
(POND)

SEWAGE WORKS
2⅜   JOVEY'S LOCK, No. 4   1
(SHALLOW LOCK)
J 1933   S. L. W. GROUND PADDLE

(AB) (SITE OF BRIDGE No. 10)

2⅝   BRICK-KILN OR   OR ¾
BB 1931   BRIDGTOWN No.3 LOCK

WEIR
(SITE OF BRIDGE No. 11)

(MARL
HOLES) OLD DAY BOAT
LONGHOUSE BRICK & TILE WORKS

2⅞   ROSEMARY OR BRIDGTOWN
No. LOCK
B 1928   WEIR
(WALK MILL TILERIES)

LOCK COTTAGE
& STABLES   WALKMILL OR BRIDGTOWN No.1 LOCK
(CANNOCK OLD COPPICE
COLLIERY)   (SWING BRIDGE
LATER LIFT BR.) PULLEY   WEIR   WALKMILL

(HAWKINS'S
BASIN)   GREAT WYRLEY BASIN
(WEIGHBRIDGE)

2⅞   MILL   LANE   (SITE OF WALKMILL BR., No.12) ½
CULVERT
(ROSEMARY TILE WORKS)   CANNOCK FERTILIZERS LTD
SLUICE   WEIR   (FLOUR MILL)   (URBAN MANURE WORKS)

(WALKMILL
RESERVOIR)
No.4   386'

WYRLEY BROOK

A5 WATLING STREET

WHARF

(MILL LEAT)

J.I.L.
JUN/71

223

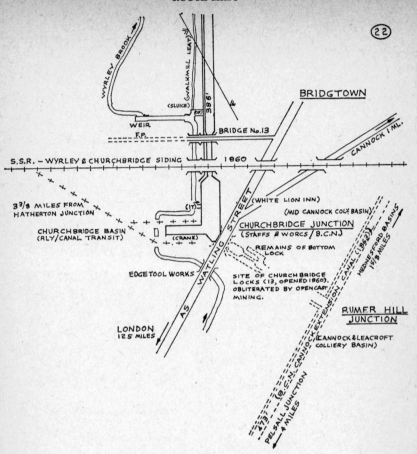

(22)

BRIDGTOWN

CANNOCK 1 ML.

BRIDGE No.13

S.S.R. - WYRLEY & CHURCHBRIDGE SIDING   1860

3 3/8 MILES FROM
HATHERTON JUNCTION

(WHITE LION INN)

(MID CANNOCK COL⁴ BASIN)

CHURCHBRIDGE BASIN
(RLY/CANAL TRANSIT)

CHURCHBRIDGE JUNCTION
(STAFFS & WORCS / B.C.N.)

(CRANE)

REMAINS OF BOTTOM
LOCK

EDGETOOL WORKS

SITE OF CHURCHBRIDGE
LOCKS (13, OPENED 1960).
OBLITERATED BY OPENCAST
MINING.

RUMER HILL
JUNCTION

LONDON
125 MILES

(CANNOCK & LEACROFT
COLLIERY BASIN)

HEDNESFORD BASINS
1 5/8 MILES

A5 WATLING STREET

WYRLEY BROOK

(WALKMILL LEAT)

(SLUICE)

386'

WEIR

F.P.

CANNOCK EXTENSION CANAL (1863)

4737   (8) S.N.

PELSALL JUNCTION
4 MILES

224

Appendices

APPENDIX I

Geology and the Staffordshire
& Worcestershire Canal

When James Brindley and his assistants set out the line of the
Staffordshire & Worcestershire Canal just over 200 years ago, the
science of geology was in its infancy, but these pioneers of civil
engineering had a remarkable aptitude for relating geology to
engineering principles. Now we have a fairly clear understanding
of the geological evolution of the West Midlands and can appreciate its close association with the route of the canal, the siting of
engineering works upon it and the means of securing a water
supply. Furthermore, local materials were used as far as possible
for constructing the canal. Building stone for locks and bridges,
clay for 'puddling' or lining the bed* and brick making, and sand
for mortar were all quarried along the waterway and later provided trade on the canal. To understand fully the story of the
Staffs & Worcs, it is advantageous to have an insight into the
geological background of the area, and this appendix gives a brief
account of the geology that is germane to the canal, summarising
features mentioned in the guide. A list of references is provided
for those who wish to delve deeper into this aspect of the Staffs
& Worcs.

A single group of rocks known as the Trias underlies the main
line of the Staffs & Worcs and the general picture is a relatively
simple one. (Recent workers have shown that the oldest rock of
the system, the Dune or Lower Mottled Sandstone, really belongs

* 'Puddling' of the Staffs & Worcs Canal was usually confined to exposed sections
such as embankments and aqueducts.

to the earlier Permian system. However, it is invariably included with the Trias on current geological maps and for convenience this classification is adopted here.) Although older coal-bearing strata do not occur at the surface anywhere along the main line, the South Staffordshire Coalfield is only a few miles to the east throughout its length and is traversed by part of the Hatherton Branch. The proximity of this coalfield was in fact one of the main reasons for the canal's prosperity. The southern portion of the canal also passes near the Wyre Forest Coalfield, but this did not make a significant contribution to trade on the waterway. The Staffs & Worcs bears few scars from the industrial revolution, though it was one of the main arteries of the Black Country, and the waterway passes through 46 miles of colourful, undulating and unspoilt scenery that is typical of the Trias.

The rocks of the Triassic system are mainly red or buff in colour, with occasional mottling or streaks of green and yellow, making a vivid contribution to the landscape. The red colouration and also a paucity of animal or plant remains are due to the inhospitable, desert-like conditions that existed when the Trias was laid down between 225 and 180 million years ago. The region now occupied by the west Midlands was then a slowly-subsiding basin, open to the north-west, but otherwise enclosed by a range of mountains known to geologists as the Mercian Highlands. Initially the climate was hot and arid with the landscape scoured by searing winds from the east. Occasional torrential rains swept down gravel fans from the enclosing mountains. Throughout the period the basin continued to sink, former mountains were reduced to low hills and conditions generally became less tempestuous. During the final stages of the Triassic era, the bulk of the material was deposited as fine sediment, possibly wind-borne dust, in the still waters of vast saline lakes. The accumulation of all this detritus has left us with at least 3,000ft of Triassic rocks in our area. In the lower part sandstones predominate, interspersed with layers of pebbles. The upper part of the formation, known as the Keuper Marl, is mainly a compact purplish-red clay. Many other types of rock were deposited on top of the Trias, but these have all been eroded away except for a partial cover of superficial, unconsolidated material known as 'Drift'. This veneer accumulated during the last 200,000 years, mainly as a result of fluctuations in the great ice sheets that covered much of Britain until their final withdrawal about 20,000 years ago.

The Trias is divided into a lower series known as the Bunter and an upper, or Keuper series. The Bunter is subdivided into three groups, the Dune Sandstone, the Pebble Beds and the Upper Mottled Sandstone, and the Keuper into the Keuper Sandstone and Keuper Marl (figure A1).

Dune (Lower Mottled) Sandstone

As its name implies, the Dune Sandstone was formed by shifting, wind-blown sand. The grains are rounded and polished, and the direction of 'currents' in the beds indicates that the prevailing wind was from the east. The Dune Sandstone is bright red in colour with occasional greenish-yellow streaks and blotches and until recently it was known as the Lower Mottled Sandstone. It is the oldest rock along the Staffs & Worcs and only occurs at the surface around Kinver. There are good examples of Dune Sandstone around Hyde lock and at Kinver Edge, where 'caverns' and 'rock houses' have been hewn in this rock.

Bunter Pebble Beds

Resting on the Dune Sandstone are the Bunter Pebble Beds. Their name is a little misleading, as there are many feet of brownish-red sandstone between the masses or bands of rounded pebbles. These beds are partly the delta-fans of intermittent torrential rivers that flowed into the Midland basin from the Mercian Highlands and partly due to a great river that entered the Midland desert area from the south. The directions of these rivers can be deduced from the 'false bedding' of delta-fans exposed along the canal. There is a particularly good example near Wolverley Forge bridge (No. 21) where the flow appears to have been from the south. Cannock Chase is formed by a vast tract of Pebble Beds and exposures along the fringe can be seen near Lodgefield (No. 102) and Baswick (No. 100) bridges. The Pebble Beds also contribute to the spectacular scenery along the southern section of the canal and there are many exposures between Hinksford and Kidderminster, including the unlined tunnel at Dunsley (No. 31) and the partly-lined tunnel at Cookley (No. 23). One of the best examples is the Hanging Cliff, near Cookley.

The Dune Sandstone and, to a slightly lesser extent, the Pebble Beds contain an abundance of water and stations along the line of the canal pump many millions of gallons daily into Black Country reservoirs. The occurrence of these beds along the canal was a fortunate accident. Until quite recently a plentiful supply of coal was needed to fire the boilers of the steam pumps and most of it was delivered by canal.

Upper Mottled Sandstone
The highest rock of the Bunter Series is the Upper Mottled Sandstone. The material forming it was mainly water-borne, but the rock is rather similar in general appearance to the Dune Sandstone. Small patches occur near Rodbaston lock and at Cross Green, but the main exposures are between Compton and Wightwick, around Wombourn and to the south of Kidderminster. There is also a spectacular example a short distance from the canal at Redstone Rock, on the Severn below Stourport. The Upper Mottled Sandstone was quarried extensively as moulding sand for brass and iron foundries and for making iron 'pigs'. There are numerous old wharves along the outcrop where the sand was loaded for shipment to the Black Country and elsewhere.

Keuper Sandstone
At the base of the Keuper Series is the Keuper Sandstone, mainly brown, yellow or white in colour and quite different from the Bunter sandstones. The Keuper Sandstone occurs over a fairly wide area and is usually evenly bedded, indicating deposition under more settled conditions than those under which the Bunter rocks were laid down. It is the only Triassic sandstone to be widely used as a building stone and it is to be found in canal works, churches and public buildings throughout the Midlands. A local variety known as Tixall stone was a source of building material for the canal and another, the Penkridge stone of the Teddesley Estate, was also used for the purpose. The Keuper Sandstone underlies the canal between Teddesley and Aldersley, but is mainly covered by a few feet of Drift and the only exposure of any consequence is the narrow cutting known as the 'Pendeford Rockin'. It was used extensively by Brindley to great effect and

most original bridges, locks and aqueducts along the canal include dressed blocks of Keuper stone.

Keuper Marl

The Keuper Marl, a thick formation occupying considerable areas of the counties surrounding the South Staffordshire Coalfield, is the highest bedded rock in the succession along the Staffs & Worcs Canal. Marl usually denotes a highly calcareous clay, but the Keuper is really a mass of purplish-red or brown mudstones. It is only slightly calcareous, making it suitable for brick making and for many years it has been quarried for the purpose. The deposit accumulated as sediment in extensive, but shallow lakes. At times these were highly saline and around Stafford the Keuper Marl contains beds of rock salt. The Marl occurs along the canal between Radford and Teddesley, but permanent exposures of this soft material are rare, for it soon weathers down to the reddish-brown soil that is typical of the Midland counties. Keuper Marl was quarried at Hazlestrine brickworks and there are numerous small excavations near the northern end of the canal which may have supplied material for the bricks used in its construction. Bricks were made locally from the Keuper Marl as work on the waterway progressed and they can usually be identified in all earlier bridges. Once the canal had been completed and had acquired its branches, the more durable engineering bricks of Etruria Marl were brought from the Black Country for later works and repairs.

Although saline springs occur near the line of the canal, salt was extracted some distance away, at Stafford Common. This was pumped as brine to works at Baswich for processing and shipment by canal and railway. There were also brine baths in Stafford, adjoining the end of the Sow Navigation.

Drift Deposits

A great thickness of rock was deposited on top of the Trias, but this has since been eroded away by the action of ice, wind and water and the geological record of this period has disappeared. This wearing down of the land surface is a continuing process and at present Triassic rocks are the foundation of the landscape along the Staffs & Worcs, though even these have been partly swept away. A greater part of this erosion probably took place during the ice age of the last million years, when glaciers formed in Scotland, the Lake District and Wales, and covered our area from time to time. Ice sheets dammed existing rivers to form lakes and these in turn overflowed to modify the channels or create new ones. A dramatic example is the reversal of the direction of the river Severn and its effect on streams that now run into it. The 'gap' at Aldersley and Tettenhall that provided Brindley with a convenient route for the summit of the canal was probably formed in this way.

Periods of intense cold were interspersed with warmer conditions, when retreating glaciers left behind boulders and clay that had been carried great distances by the ice. Sand and gravel were also laid down and often redistributed by torrential rivers of meltwater, and both are now quarried for building material along the line of the canal. Unlike the rounded grains of the Trias, this sand consists of angular fragments, a 'sharp' sand suitable for building purposes. Boulder clay would have made construction of the canal difficult, but like the marls, it formed a watertight bed without the need for 'puddling'. The waxing and waning of great ice sheets on the continents caused substantial changes of sea level. As the level rose, material accumulated in the valleys as rivers became more sluggish, and during periods of relative fall, the rivers cut their channels deeper. Gravelly terraces abandoned by the rivers in this way can be seen along most of the Staffs & Worcs and they often provide a convenient route for the canal, above the present flood plains.

A foundation of Triassic rocks was thus sculptured by ice and glacial meltwater to form the landscape of today. The present river system of the area was mainly initiated during the ice age and has since had little effect on the scenery, aside from spreading silt and other sediments over the floors of valleys. The above events decided the course of the Staffs & Worcs Canal, helped to provide trade when it was a commercial venture and made it one of the most beautiful of all canals during its retirement as a recreational amenity.

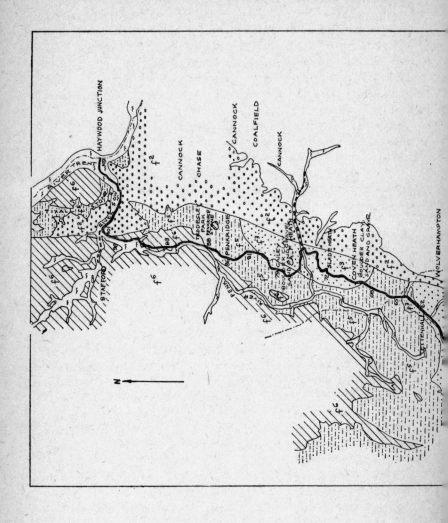

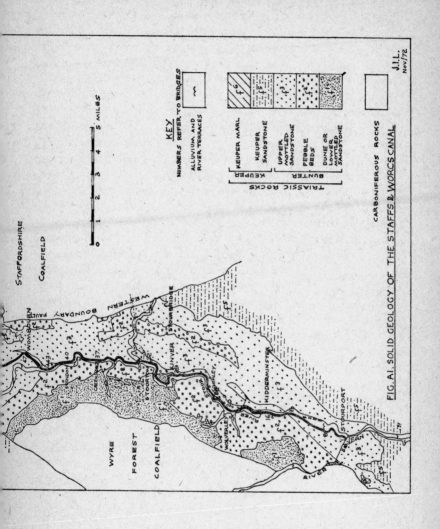

STAFFORDSHIRE
COALFIELD

WESTERN BOUNDARY FAULT

WOMBOURN

SWINDON

WYRE
FOREST
COALFIELD

CREEK

WOLVERLEY

COOKLEY

WHITTINGTON

KINVER STOURBRIDGE

KIDDERMINSTER

STOURPORT

RIVER

KEY

NUMBERS REFER TO BRIDGES

ALLUVIUM AND
RIVER TERRACES

f6	KEUPER MARL	KEUPER
f5	KEUPER SANDSTONE	
f3	UPPER MOTTLED SANDSTONE	BUNTER
f2	PEBBLE BEDS	
f1	DUNE OR LOWER MOTTLED SANDSTONE	

TRIASSIC ROCKS

CARBONIFEROUS ROCKS

0 1 2 3 4 5 MILES

FIG. A1. SOLID GEOLOGY OF THE STAFFS & WORCS CANAL

J.I.L.
Nov/72

The Landscape of the Staffs & Worcs Canal

The canal climbs in a leisurely manner from the valley of the river Trent at Haywood to the summit level at Gailey. It then traverses the main watershed of England with ease, compared with many canals, and finally descends rapidly to the river Severn at Stourport. Initially the canal runs in an easterly direction, but from Baswich to Stourport the general line is southerly.

After leaving Haywood, the line is along the edge of the first abandoned terrace of the river Sow, just above the level of the highest floods. To the south is the higher, wooded ground of Cannock Chase, formed by the more resistant Bunter Pebble Beds, and to the north are hills of Keuper Sandstone in Tixall Park. The canal crosses the Sow valley at Milford and continues along a terrace for several miles, following the foot of the slope formed by the Pebble Beds. Around Stafford and to the north and west of the canal are vast tracts of Keuper Marl. This gives rise to gently undulating scenery of mainly pastoral character, whereas the landscape of the Pebble Beds is generally wooded and poorly drained. Thus between Stafford and Gailey the canal is mainly flanked by woodland on the east and farmland on the west, following river terraces most of the way. The rising ground towards Cannock Chase was at one time one of the main sources of water for the northern section of the canal.

For a while the canal follows the natural gradient of the Penk valley, with widely separated locks at Tixall, Deptmore and Shutt Hill. However, the Keuper Marl thins to the south and disappears altogether at Teddesley, where the Keuper Sandstone comes to the surface and the canal and Penk part company. The sandstone is more resistant to erosion than are the softer marls and the ground rises rapidly towards Gailey. Starting with Shutt Hill, the locks are now necessarily closer together and there are ten of them before the summit is reached.

Keuper Sandstone underlies the greater part of the 10-mile summit level, but it is mainly obscured by a thin veneer of boulder clay or sands and gravels of glacial origin. The levelling of the sandstone by the movement of ice made it relatively easy to construct the section of canal between Gailey and Autherley, and the only major deviation from a straight line occurs where it crosses the valley of Saredon brook. The pebbly soil of this area is now mainly under cultivation, but it was not always so, as is evident from place names like Calf Heath, Slade Heath and Coven Heath.

At Autherley the entire character of the scenery surrounding the canal changes. The waterway suddenly enters a narrow valley with Wolverhampton on one side and Tettenhall on the other. This is the Aldersley or Tettenhall Gap, probably formed by over-flowing meltwater from a glacial lake to the north, carving a flat-bottomed valley through the Bunter sandstones. This was very convenient for Brindley, who was able to cross the watershed with the shallowest of cuttings before starting the descent to the Severn at Compton. So far the scenery has been fairly closely related to the underlying strata, but this is not the case for the rest of the journey. The influence of the Bunter sandstones on the scenery of the southern section is confined to local detail. The main factors were the diversion of the river Severn to its present southerly course and a lowering of the sea level. These caused the Stour and its tributaries, particularly the Smestow, to deepen their channels and the present rivers flow along flat bottomed, marshy valleys that are flanked in places by sheer cliffs of Bunter Sandstone.

These wet and winding valleys had been avoided by road builders and there were few settlements along them, so it is a credit to Brindley that he managed to steer a course for his canal with few major obstacles. The result is a waterway of great beauty through colourful and ever changing scenery. The process of downcutting of the Stour and Smestow took place in stages, each one being marked by an abandoned terrace. The canal drops steeply from one terrace to another until the valley levels out below Kidderminster, keeping above the flood plain and only deviating where rocky spurs required the cutting of tunnels at Dunsley and Cookley. In places the terrace was too narrow, or had been eroded away completely, and here the rock face had to be cut away to accommodate the canal. The vast complex of basins that terminate the canal at Stourport are also situated on a river terrace, out of reach of the highest floods of the Severn.

APPENDIX II

Table of Distances

The following list is based on the Staffordshire & Worcestershire Canal Company Table of Distances, with the correction of several inaccuracies in the tabulated mileages. The original table was issued to all toll clerks and it is perhaps no coincidence that many errors occur on sections that were heavily used. The table was probably published late in the 19th century from measurements made very much earlier. The original spelling has been retained, though this occasionally differs from the present form, and the distances given are correct to within 1 furlong ($\frac{1}{8}$ mile). Information that did not appear in the original table is given in brackets.

MAIN LINE OF STAFFS & WORCS CANAL

	Miles to Haywood	Miles from Stourport
STOURPORT, JUNCTION WITH THE RIVER SEVERN	46$\frac{1}{8}$	0
Lower Mitton Bridge (No. 5)	45$\frac{5}{8}$	$\frac{1}{2}$
Gilgal Bridge (No. 6) and Wharf	45$\frac{1}{2}$	$\frac{5}{8}$
Mitton Chapel Bridge (No. 7)	45$\frac{3}{8}$	$\frac{3}{4}$
Upper Mitton Bridge (No. 8) and Wharf	45$\frac{1}{8}$	1
Bullocks Lane Bridge (No. 9) and Wharf	44$\frac{5}{8}$	1$\frac{1}{2}$
Oldington Bridge (No. 10)	44$\frac{1}{8}$	2
Pratt's Wharf and Wilden Iron Works	43$\frac{7}{8}$	2$\frac{1}{4}$
Falling Sands Lock	43$\frac{3}{8}$	2$\frac{3}{4}$

	Miles to Haywood	Miles from Stourport
Falling Sands Bridge (No. 11) and Iron Works	42$\frac{7}{8}$	3$\frac{1}{4}$
Caldwall Bridge (No. 12) and Lock	42$\frac{1}{2}$	3$\frac{5}{8}$
Round Hill Bridge (No. 13)	42$\frac{3}{8}$	3$\frac{3}{4}$
Caldwall Mill Bridge (No. 14)	42$\frac{1}{4}$	3$\frac{7}{8}$
Caldwall Hall Bridge (No. 15) and Public Wharf	42$\frac{1}{8}$	4
KIDDERMINSTER LOCK, WHARF, WAREHOUSE AND MACHINE	41$\frac{3}{4}$	4$\frac{3}{8}$
Limekiln Bridge (No. 17) and Wharf	41$\frac{1}{2}$	4$\frac{5}{8}$
Stour Vale Iron Works	41$\frac{1}{8}$	5
Wolverley Court Bridge (No. 19) and Lock	40$\frac{3}{8}$	5$\frac{3}{4}$
Wolverley Mill Wharf	40$\frac{1}{8}$	6
Wolverley Bridge (No. 20), Lock and Wharf	39$\frac{7}{8}$	6$\frac{1}{4}$
Wolverley Forge Bridge (No. 21) and Wharf	39$\frac{5}{8}$	6$\frac{1}{2}$
Debdale Bridge (No. 22) and Lock	38$\frac{3}{4}$	7$\frac{3}{8}$
Cookley Tunnel (No. 23) and Iron Works	38$\frac{1}{2}$	7$\frac{5}{8}$
Austcliffe Bridge (No. 24) and Wharf	38	8$\frac{1}{8}$
Clay House Bridge (No. 25)	37$\frac{3}{4}$	8$\frac{3}{8}$
Whittington Bridge (No. 27), Lock and Iron Works	36$\frac{1}{2}$	9$\frac{5}{8}$
Whittington Horse Bridge (No. 28)	36$\frac{1}{4}$	9$\frac{7}{8}$
Kinver Bridge (No. 29), Lock and Wharf	35$\frac{1}{2}$	10$\frac{5}{8}$
Hyde Bridge (No. 30), Lock and Iron Works	35	11$\frac{1}{8}$
Dunsley Tunnel (No. 31)	34$\frac{3}{8}$	11$\frac{3}{4}$
STEWPONY WHARF, LOCK AND WAREHOUSE	34	12$\frac{1}{8}$
Stourton Bridge (No. 33), STOURBRIDGE CANAL JUNCTION	33$\frac{7}{8}$	12$\frac{1}{4}$
Round House, Wharf and Iron Works	32$\frac{3}{8}$	13$\frac{3}{4}$
Gothersley Bridge (No. 35) and Lock	32	14$\frac{1}{8}$
Gothersley or Hockley Lock (Rocky)	31$\frac{3}{4}$	14$\frac{3}{8}$
(Flatheridge Bridge (No. 36) and Ashwood Basin)	31$\frac{3}{8}$	14$\frac{3}{4}$
Green's Forge Bridge (No. 37), Lock, Wharf and Basin (i.e. Ashwood)	30$\frac{7}{8}$	15$\frac{1}{4}$

	Miles to Haywood	*Miles from Stourport*
Hincksford Bridge (No. 39) and Lock	$29\frac{3}{4}$	$16\frac{3}{8}$
Swindon Forge, Bridge (No. 40), Wharf, Lock and Iron Works	$29\frac{1}{2}$	$16\frac{5}{8}$
Marsh Lock	$29\frac{1}{4}$	$16\frac{7}{8}$
Botterham Bridge (No. 42) and Two Locks	$28\frac{7}{8}$	$17\frac{1}{4}$
Wombourne Common Bridge (No. 43) and Wharf	$28\frac{3}{8}$	$17\frac{3}{4}$
Heath Forge Wharf	$28\frac{1}{4}$	$17\frac{7}{8}$
Bumble Hole Bridge (No. 46) and Lock	$27\frac{5}{8}$	$18\frac{1}{2}$
BRATCH BRIDGE (NO. 47) AND THREE LOCKS	$27\frac{1}{4}$	$18\frac{7}{8}$
Awebridge (No. 49) and Lock	$26\frac{3}{8}$	$19\frac{3}{4}$
Ebstree Lock	$25\frac{3}{4}$	$20\frac{3}{8}$
Dimmingsdale Lock and Reservoir	$25\frac{5}{8}$	$20\frac{1}{2}$
Dimmingsdale Bridge (No. 53), Wharf and Warehouse	$25\frac{3}{8}$	$20\frac{3}{4}$
Mops Farm Bridge (No. 54)	$24\frac{3}{4}$	$21\frac{3}{8}$
Castle Croft Bridge (No. 55)	$24\frac{1}{4}$	$21\frac{7}{8}$
Whightwick Bridge (No. 57) and Lock	$23\frac{3}{4}$	$22\frac{3}{8}$
Whightwick Mill Bridge (No. 58) and Lock	$23\frac{1}{2}$	$22\frac{5}{8}$
COMPTON WHARF, LOCK AND BRIDGE (NO. 60)	$22\frac{7}{8}$	$23\frac{1}{4}$
Tettenhall Bridge (No. 62) and Wharf	22	$24\frac{1}{8}$
(Hordern Road Bridge and Wharf)	$21\frac{5}{8}$	$24\frac{1}{2}$
Dunstall Water Bridge (No. 63)	$21\frac{3}{8}$	$24\frac{3}{4}$
BIRMINGHAM CANAL JUNCTION AT ALDERSLEY AND ALDERSLEY BRIDGE (NO. 64)	21	$25\frac{1}{8}$
SHROPSHIRE UNION CANAL JUNCTION	$20\frac{1}{2}$	$25\frac{5}{8}$
Marsh Lane Bridge (No. 67)	$19\frac{5}{8}$	$26\frac{1}{2}$
Coven Heath Bridge (No. 69) First Wharf	$18\frac{1}{2}$	$27\frac{5}{8}$
Coven Heath Bridge (No. 70) Second Wharf	$18\frac{1}{8}$	28
Cross Green Bridge (No. 71) and Wharf	$17\frac{5}{8}$	$28\frac{1}{2}$
Slade Heath Bridge (No. 72) and L. & N.W. Railway Bridge	$17\frac{1}{8}$	29
Laches Bridge (No. 73)	$16\frac{3}{8}$	$29\frac{3}{4}$

TABLE OF DISTANCES

	Miles to Haywood	Miles from Stourport
Moat House Bridge (No. 74)	16	$30\frac{1}{8}$
Deepmore Bridge (No. 75) and Wharf	$15\frac{3}{8}$	$30\frac{3}{4}$
The Cross Bridge & HATHERTON BRANCH TO OLD COPPICE, GREAT WYRLEY—Cannock & Hednesford Collieries	$14\frac{7}{8}$	$31\frac{1}{4}$
Calf Heath Bridge (No. 77) and Wharf	$13\frac{7}{8}$	$32\frac{1}{4}$
Gravelley Way Bridge (No. 78)	$13\frac{1}{4}$	$32\frac{7}{8}$
GAILEY WHARF, BRIDGE (No. 79), LOCK AND WAREHOUSE	$12\frac{5}{8}$	$33\frac{1}{2}$
Brick-Kiln Lock	$12\frac{3}{8}$	$33\frac{3}{4}$
Boggs Lock	$12\frac{1}{8}$	34
Rodbaston Bridge (No. 80) and Lock	$11\frac{3}{4}$	$34\frac{3}{8}$
(Littleton Colliery Basin, Otherton)	$11\frac{1}{4}$	$34\frac{7}{8}$
Otherton Lane Bridge (No. 81)	$11\frac{1}{8}$	35
Otherton Lock	11	$35\frac{1}{8}$
Lyne Hill Bridge (No. 83)	$10\frac{5}{8}$	$35\frac{1}{2}$
Filance Lock	$10\frac{1}{8}$	36
PENKRIDGE BRIDGE (No. 86), WHARF, LOCK AND WAREHOUSE	10	$36\frac{1}{8}$
Longford Bridge (No. 87) and Lock	$9\frac{1}{4}$	$36\frac{7}{8}$
Longford Bridge (No. 88)	9	$37\frac{1}{8}$
Teddesley Bridge (No. 89)	$8\frac{3}{4}$	$37\frac{3}{8}$
Park Gate Bridge (No. 90), Wharf and Lock	$8\frac{1}{2}$	$37\frac{5}{8}$
Shutt Hill Bridge (No. 91) and Lock	$7\frac{3}{4}$	$38\frac{3}{8}$
Acton Bridge (No. 93) and Wharf	$6\frac{7}{8}$	$39\frac{1}{4}$
Roseford Bridge (No. 94)	$6\frac{1}{4}$	$39\frac{7}{8}$
Deptmore Lock	$5\frac{7}{8}$	$40\frac{1}{4}$
Hazlestrine Bridge (No. 96)	$5\frac{1}{2}$	$40\frac{5}{8}$
RADFORD BRIDGE (No. 98), WHARF AND WAREHOUSE	$4\frac{5}{8}$	$41\frac{1}{2}$
Baswich Bridge (No. 100) and SALT WORKS	$4\frac{1}{8}$	42
STAFFORD BRANCH CANAL AND LOCK	$3\frac{7}{8}$	$42\frac{1}{4}$
Lodgefield Bridge (No. 102)	$3\frac{3}{8}$	$42\frac{3}{4}$
Stoneford Bridge (No. 103)	3	$43\frac{1}{8}$

239

TABLE OF DISTANCES

	Miles to Haywood	Miles from Stourport
Millford Bridge (No. 105)	$2\frac{1}{4}$	$43\frac{7}{8}$
Tixall Bridge (No. 106)	$1\frac{5}{8}$	$44\frac{1}{2}$
Old Hill Bridge (No. 107), Wharf and Lock	$1\frac{3}{8}$	$44\frac{3}{4}$
HAYWOOD WHARF AND JUNCTION with the Trent and Mersey Canal	0	$46\frac{1}{8}$

HATHERTON BRANCH

	Miles to Churchbridge	Miles from Hatherton Junction
HATHERTON JUNCTION	$3\frac{3}{8}$	0
Saredon Mill Bridge	$2\frac{1}{2}$	$\frac{7}{8}$
Four Crosses Bridge	2	$1\frac{3}{8}$
Wedges Mills	$1\frac{1}{4}$	$2\frac{1}{8}$
Walk Mill, Old Coppice and Great Wyrley Collieries	$\frac{1}{2}$	$2\frac{7}{8}$
CHURCHBRIDGE	0	$3\frac{3}{8}$

APPENDIX III

Engineering Works

The Staffs & Worcs is one of the earliest canals and follows the contours of the land for most of its length. Consequently, locks are unevenly spaced, usually occur singly and have irregular heights, and there are none of the major engineering works that are to be found on later canals. Tunnels are short, embankments are low and cuttings are shallow, but all are nevertheless representative of the work of James Brindley and his contemporaries.

1   Locks and Levels
The rise and fall of locks and the levels of intervening pounds given in the following table are based on a section of the canal published by the Company and kindly made available by British Waterways Board, and also on the Canal Returns in volume 3 of the Report of the Royal Commission on Canals (1908, pages 162 to 165). Minor changes in levels have been made since the Canal Returns were compiled, but these only amount to a few inches.

Miles		*Locks*	*Fall*		*Level*‡		*Notes*
Main Line			ft	in.	ft	in.	
$46\frac{1}{8}$	1	Stourport Bottom Barge Lock*	about 29	0	75	10	Original connection with river Severn
	2	Stourport Top Barge Lock					
	1a 1b	Stourport Bottom Boat Locks (Riser†)					1781 connection with river Severn
	2a 2b	Stourport Top Boat Locks (Riser)					
	–	Barge lock off Mart Lane Basin					Infilled
$45\frac{7}{8}$	3	Stourport or York Street	12	0	87	10	
$43\frac{7}{8}$	–	Pratt's Wharf	about 4	0			Side lock down to river Stour (derelict)
$42\frac{7}{8}$	4	Falling Sands or Oldington	6	0	93	10	
$42\frac{1}{2}$	5	Caldwall	5	7	99	5	
$41\frac{3}{4}$	6	Kidderminster	11	11	111	4	
$40\frac{3}{8}$	7	Wolverley Court	6	0	117	4	
$39\frac{7}{8}$	8	Wolverley	10	0	127	4	
$38\frac{3}{4}$	9	Debdale or Cookley	10	0	137	4	
$36\frac{1}{2}$	10	Whittington	9	9	147	1	
$35\frac{1}{2}$	11	Kinver	7	3	154	4	
35	12	Hyde	10	0	164	4	
34	13	Stewponey	10	0	174	4	Junction with Stourbridge Canal
32	14	Gothersley	7	0	181	4	
$31\frac{3}{4}$	15	Rocky or Hockley	7	0	188	4	
$30\frac{7}{8}$	16	Greensforge	9	0	197	4	
$29\frac{3}{4}$	17	Hinksford	7	0	204	4	
$29\frac{1}{2}$	18	Swindon	9	0	213	4	
$29\frac{1}{4}$	19	Marsh	9	9	223	1	
$29\frac{7}{8}$	20 21	Botterham Two Locks (Riser)	20	3	243	4	
$27\frac{5}{8}$	22	Bumble Hole	10	0	253	4	
$27\frac{1}{4}$	23 24 25	Bratch Three Locks	31	2	284	6	Deepest narrow lock on canal
$26\frac{3}{8}$	26	Awbridge	9	0	293	6	
$25\frac{3}{4}$	27	Ebstree	9	0	302	6	
$25\frac{5}{8}$	28	Dimmingsdale	11	0	313	6	
$23\frac{3}{4}$	29	Wightwick	8	8	322	2	
$23\frac{1}{2}$	30	Wightwick Mill	9	0	331	2	
$22\frac{7}{8}$	31	Compton	9	4	340	6	First narrow lock to be built. Summit level; junction with BCN, Shropshire Union and Hatherton Branch
		Total fall: Summit Level to river Severn	291	8			

Miles		Locks	Rise		Level‡		Notes
Main Line cont.							
			ft	in.	ft	in.	
12⅝	32	Gailey	8	0	332	6	Bradshaw (1830) gives rises of 14ft 5in. for locks 32 & 33 and 19ft 0in. for locks 34 & 35
12⅜	33	Brick-kiln	8	0	324	6	
12⅛	34	Boggs	8	0	316	6	
11¾	35	Rodbaston	9	6	307	0	
11	36	Otherton	10	0	297	0	
10⅛	37	Filance	10	0	287	0	
10	38	Penkridge	9	0	278	0	
9¼	39	Longford	10	0	268	0	
8½	40	Parkgate	8	0	260	0	
7¾	41	Shutt Hill	6	0	254	0	
5⅞	42	Deptmore	10	0	244	0	
3⅞	–	Baswich or St Thomas					Side lock down to river Sow (infilled)
		Fall of about	6	6			
1⅜	43	Tixall	4	0	240	0	Shallowest lock on canal. Junction with Trent & Mersey Canal

Total rise: Trent & Mersey
Canal to Summit Level   100   6

Hatherton Branch

1	Calf Heath Bottom Lock
2	Calf Heath Top Lock
3	Meadow
4	Wedge's Mill
5	Jovey's
6	Brick-kiln or Bridgtown No. 3
7	Rosemary or Bridgtown No. 2
8	Walkmill or Bridgtown No. 1

Total rise of about 45ft to bottom of Churchbridge locks (BCN)

* See map 19 for the lock arrangement at Stourport.

† A riser is a pair of locks built as a staircase, with the top gates of the lower lock forming the bottom gates of the upper one.

‡ Approximate level of pound above lock (above OD).

The average rise of the 12 locks between Haywood Junction and the summit level is 8ft 4in. and the average fall of the 31 locks between the summit and the river Severn is 9ft 5in. The average distance between locks on the ascent is 1 mile and on the descent it is ¾ mile.

Stourport barge locks are 75ft 10in. long and 15ft 4in. wide, with a depth of 5ft 5in. on the sill of the top lock. The depth on the sill of the bottom lock depends on the level of the Severn and is normally about 6ft 10in. All narrow locks on the canal are 75ft 0in. long, have a nominal width of 7ft 2in. and, except for the bottom lock at Stourport, have a depth of 4ft 6in. on the sill. The river lock of the narrow flight at Stourport has a depth of about 9ft on the sill.

2 Bridges

Over-bridges are described in the guide as they occur. When the cast-iron bridge plates were added about 1835 there were 109 bridges across the canal and now there are 122, some serving more than one purpose. (This number does not include the numerous small footbridges at the tail of locks.) 53 bridges carry roads, 48 are accommodation bridges (on farms, estates, etc.) or carry footpaths, 9 are railway bridges, and 4 convey water or sewage effluent across the canal. There are also 6 turnover bridges where the towpath changes sides and 6 roving bridges carrying the towpath of an arm or branch canal. A further 7, including 2 swing bridges, have been demolished. About 50 bridges are contemporary with the canal, though several of them have been widened or otherwise altered.

3 Aqueducts

1	Haywood Mill	(Mill tail race, one arch)
2	Haywood	(River Trent, four arches)
3	Milford	(River Sow, four arches)
4	Dunstall Water Bridge	(Smestow brook, over canal)
5	Stourton	(River Stour, two arches)
6	Kidderminster	(River Stour, three arches)

These aqueducts are all contemporary with the canal and, with the exception of Nos. 3 and 4, have parapets added at a later date.

Nos. 1, 2, 5 and 6 are of identical design and are probably the
work of Brindley. No. 3 was engineered by Thomas Dadford
senior.

4 Tunnels
  1 Dunsley (No. 31)   68ft long, unlined sandstone
  2 Cookley (No. 23)   194ft long, partly unlined sand-
                              stone
  3 Kidderminster (No. 18)   Originally 68ft long (?) and re-
                              cently extended by 5ft 6in. Brick
                              lined. See page 164

The tunnels of the Staffs & Worcs are short, but important
historically. With the demolition of Armitage tunnel on the
Trent & Mersey Canal in 1971, they are the only tunnels engineered by Brindley that are still navigable. They are also unusual
in that all three have towing paths through them, as had Armitage
tunnel. It was many years after the building of the Staffs & Worcs
that towing paths became commonplace in longer tunnels.

5 Embankments
  1 Haywood   The excavations can still be seen on
                       each side where earth was obtained
                       to build the embankment
  2 Milford   Approach to the Sow aqueduct
  3 Longford   Partly obscured by approach to new
                       Wood Bank bridge
  4 Hatherton Junction Across valley of the Saredon brook

6 Cuttings
  1 Moat House
  2 Pendeford 'Rockin' Narrow excavation through Keuper
                        Sandstone
  3 Aldersley   Shallow cutting across the Trent–
                        Severn watershed
  4 Wolverley Forge

There are also several places between Botterham and Stourport
where the canal has a cliff of Bunter sandstone on the offside, the

ground falling away to the rivers Smestow and Stour on the
towpath side.

7 *Reservoirs and other Water Supplies*

1	Calf Heath Reservoir	Supply
2	Gailey New Reservoir (Upper)	Supply
3	Gailey New Reservoir (Lower)	Supply
4	Walkmill Reservoir	Supply (drained and in-filled)
5	Pottall Pool	Supply (partly drained)
6	Spring Slade Pool	Supply (no longer used, but surplus water from it enters the canal at Wood Bank)
7	Dimmingsdale Reservoir (The Pool)	Storage
8	Dimmingsdale Reservoir	Storage

The eight reservoirs of the Staffs & Worcs Canal had a total
capacity of about 265 million gallons. In addition, several small
streams ran into the canal and so also did water pumped from
Littleton colliery. Most of this water entered the canal towards
the northern end, where there was a complicated system of
feeders to compensate for the irregular heights of locks (figure
A2). The canal's main supplies at present are from the Hatherton
Branch, lockage water from the BCN and Stourbridge Canal and
the outfalls from sewage works of Wolverhampton Corporation.
An average of about 1 million gallons a day of purified effluent
enters the canal from the Coven works and the outfall from the
Barnhurst works is about 5 million gallons, soon to be increased
to about 10 million.

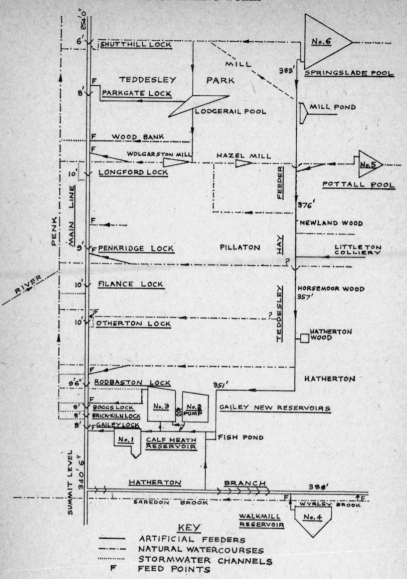

KEY

——————— ARTIFICIAL FEEDERS
— · — · — NATURAL WATERCOURSES
··············· STORMWATER CHANNELS
F   FEED POINTS

FIG. A2. STAFFS & WORCS CANAL: FORMER WATER SUPPLIES
TO NORTHERN SECTION

J.I.L. MAR/72

247

Staffs & Worcs Canal: Important Dates

1766	29 January	Wolverhampton meeting
1766	14 May	First Act of Parliament for canal
1770		Second Act of Parliament
1770	November	Canal open between Wolverhampton and and Stourport
1772	28 May	Canal opened throughout
1772	21 September	First branch—Birmingham Canal opened
1772	27 September	James Brindley died
1779	3 December	Second branch—Stourbridge and Dudley Canals opened
1781		Stourport narrow locks opened
1789	November	Thames & Severn Canal opened
1790	9 June	Staffs & Worcs Act for improving Severn Navigation
1805	1 November	Stafford Railway opened
1812	18 May	Edward C. Wallhouse, later Sir Edward Littleton, inherited Teddesley estates
1814	July	Stafford Railway dismantled and sold
1816	19 February	Sow Navigation (Stafford Branch) completed
1829	2 June	Ashwood basin and Kingswinford (Shutt End) Railway opened
1835	2 March	Birmingham & Liverpool Junction Canal opened

1835	11 May	Sir Edward Littleton created 1st Lord Hatherton
1841	April	Hatherton Branch completed
1860		South Staffordshire Railway basin opened at Churchbridge
1863		Second junction with BCN completed, via Churchbridge locks
1863	4 April	1st Lord Hatherton died
1888	3 April	3rd Lord Hatherton inherited Teddesley estates
c. 1905		Littleton Colliery basin at Otherton opened
1920s		Stafford Branch went out of use
1930	24 August	3rd Lord Hatherton died
1948	1 January	Canal passed to British Transport Commission
1948/9		Traffic ceased on Hatherton and Stour branches and from Ashwood basin
1949		Coal traffic to Stourport Power Station ceased
1959		Staffordshire & Worcestershire Canal Society formed
1963	1 January	Canal passed to British Waterways Board
1968	25 October	Transport Act: Canal became a Cruiseway

APPENDIX V

Cruising Facilities

Key to abbreviations (this appendix and route maps)

TP	Towpath side	M	Moorings (casual, road access)
OS	Offside		
BB	Boatbuilding and sales	PB	Post box
C	Chandlery	PH	Public house
CD	Disposal point, chemical toilets*	PO	Post office
		R	Repairs
DD	Dry dock	RD	Refuse disposal point
F	Fuel (usually petrol and diesel)	S	Slipway
		TB	Trip boats (usually for hire by prior arrangement)
G	Gas		
GA	Garage	TK	Telephone kiosk
GS	General store	W	Water point
H	Hirer (cruisers, unless stated otherwise)	WH	Winding hole (turning point) for 7oft boats
I	Incinerator		

* Anti-pollution regulations introduced by the Severn-Trent Water Authority require that boats with toilets shall also carry holding tanks. Disposal points will eventually be available for general use along the canal at distances not greater than can be cruised in one day.

Mooring

No attempt has been made to indicate where boats may be
moored permanently along the canal. There are several lengths
where boats can stay overnight or for a few days and these are
usually indicated by notices ([M] on route maps). In general,
casual mooring on the offside of the canal is not allowed without
the permission of the landowner. Many boatyards offer permanent
moorings and some allow boats to be moored during weekdays,
enabling owners to continue their journey at weekends. Permanent and semi-permanent moorings along the main line are
becoming congested and off-canal facilities, such as have been
available at Ashwood and Stourport for many years, are likely to
increase in the near future. Gailey Canal Cruisers are in fact constructing a marina at Calf Heath and Dawncraft plan to provide
this facility at The Paddock, Kinver.

Access

Points of access have not been included in the list of facilities,
since the towpath is readily accessible at most road bridges along
the Staffs & Worcs Canal.

While every care has been taken in compiling the information
listed, the publishers cannot be held responsible for the consequence of any inaccuracies which may have been included.

STAFFORDSHIRE & WORCESTERSHIRE CANAL:

Nearest Bridge	Location	Side of Canal	BB	C	CD	DD	F	G	GA	GS	H	I
109	HAYWOOD JUNCTION (Trent & Mersey Canal)											✓
74	HAYWOOD JUNCTION (on T. & M.)	OS										
73	HAYWOOD JUNCTION (on T. & M.) ½ ml S of Junction in Haywood Village	OS							✓			
109	HAYWOOD JUNCTION	OS			✓		✓			✓		
107	½ ml NE (Tixall Wide)	OS										
106	¾ ml S ⎱ Milford	TP						✓				
105	¾ ml, see Map 2 ⎰ Village	TP										
98	W, Radford Bank	TP						✓				
98	S, Radford Wharf	TP	✓	✓								
96	N, Hazlestrine Arm	OS										
92	E, Acton Trussell	OS										
91	S, Acton Moat	OS										
90	S, Parkgate, Teddesley	OS	✓	✓				✓			✓*	
86	W, Penkridge	TP						✓				
86	S, Penkridge Wharf	OS	✓					✓			✓	
84	S, 'Cross Keys'	TP										
84	S, 'Cross Keys'	OS										
79	S, Gailey Wharf	TP			✓							
79	S, Gailey Wharf	OS										
79	½ ml W, Gailey	TP							✓*	✓		
77	W, Four Ashes	TP										
77	½ ml W, Four Ashes	TP										
77	S, Four Ashes	OS										
—	HATHERTON JUNCTION (Calf Heath Marina)	OS	✓				✓	✓	✓		✓	✓
75	½ ml S of Deepmore Bridge	OS										
72	100 yd S of Slade Heath Bridge	OS										
71	100 yd N, Cross Green	TP							✓*			

CRUISING FACILITIES

M	PB	PH	PO	R	RD	S	TB	TK	W	WH	Notes
✓					✓				✓	✓	
							✓				'Cactus'; (Brownhills 4888)
	✓	✓	✓				✓				
					✓						Anglo Welsh (Little Haywood 711)
										✓	
	✓	✓	✓				✓				Meals at 'Barley Mow'
		✓					✓				Meals at the 'Trumpet'
					✓	✓	✓				Radford Marine (Stafford 3519)
										✓	¼ ml E
✓			✓								
										✓	
					✓						* Also Rowing & Motor Boats; Teddesley Boating Centre (Penkridge 2437 & 2477)
✓	✓										Snacks at 'Boat Inn'; All services; ½ ml
					✓			✓	✓		Bijou Line (Penkridge 2732)
	✓										Snacks
✓						✓					
✓					✓				✓		Canoe Club
										✓	
	✓						✓				* 100 yd; Meals at the 'Spreadeagle'
✓											
	✓						✓				Snacks at 'Four Ashes Inn'
										✓	
✓	✓				✓		✓	✓*	✓	✓	* At boatyard; Café; Canalware, etc; Public trips on Sundays; Gailey Canal Cruisers (Standeford 790420)
										✓	
										✓	
	✓										Meals at 'Anchor Inn'; * ¼ ml

STAFFORDSHIRE & WORCESTERSHIRE CANAL:

Nearest Bridge	Location	Side of Canal	BB	C	CD	DD	F	G	GA	GS	H	I
71	200 yd S, Cross Green	OS										
1	AUTHERLEY JUNCTION	TP			√							
1	(on Shropshire Union Canal)	TP	√				√			√	√*	
65	(66 on plate), N, Oxley Moor	TP										
65	(66 on plate), N, Oxley Moor	OS									√	
64	ALDERSLEY JUNCTION (BCN)	OS										
—	S, Hordern Road Bridge	TP	√	√			√	√		√	√	
—	W, Hordern Road (Aldersley)	TP							√			
62	N, Newbridge Wharf	OS										
61	E, Tettenhall Old Bridge	OS							√	√		
61	S, Tettenhall Old Bridge	OS	√									
59	W, Compton	TP							√	√		
57	N, above Wightwick Lock	OS										
56	W, Wightwick	TP										
56	S, Wightwick Wharf	OS	√*				√			√		
53	½ ml E, Lower Penn	OS										
53	½ ml W, Ebstree	TP										
52	Below Dimmingsdale Lock											
49	W, Aw Bridge	OS										
48	N, above Bratch Top Lock											
47	N, Bratch Bridge	TP										
47	¼ ml E, Bratch Bridge	OS								√		
45	W, Ounsdale	TP										
45	300 yd E, Ounsdale	OS										
44	N, Giggetty	OS								√*		
43	E, Brickbridge	OS										
40	W, Swindon	—										

M	PB	PH	PO	R	RD	S	TB	TK	W	WH	*Notes*
										✓	
✓					✓				✓	✓	
✓				✓			✓				* Also motor & rowing boats; Licensed boat club; Water Travel (Wolverhampton 782371)
											Canoe club
						✓	✓				Gregory's Canal Cruisers (Wolverhampton 783307)
										✓	
✓					✓	✓			✓		Double Pennant (Wolverhampton 752771)
											¼ ml, Fish & Chip Shop, Off Licence
✓							✓				Water Travel (Wolverhampton 782371)
	✓	✓	✓					✓			Meals at 'The Newbridge'
											Leisure Craft Marine (Wolverhampton 752368)
	✓	✓	✓					✓			Snacks at the 'Odd Fellows Hall'
										✓	
		✓									Snacks at 'The Mermaid'
✓					✓						* Fitting Out & Sales; Mermaid Hire Cruisers (Wolverhampton 763818)
		✓									'The Greyhound'
		✓									'The Holly Bush'
										✓	Farm Produce
✓											
					✓						
		✓									'Round Oak'
		✓									Snacks & Evening Meals at the 'Mount Pleasant'
										✓	* 400 yd E
	✓	✓									Snacks & Evening Meals at the 'Waggon & Horses'
		✓									Snacks at the 'Green Man'

Nearest Bridge	Location	Side of Canal	BB	C	CD	DD	F	G	GA	GS	H	I
40	200 yd E, Swindon	—								✓		
39	S, below Hinksford Lock	OS										
38	E, Hinksford	OS										
37	E, Greensforge	OS										
36	E, Ashwood Basin	OS	✓	✓	✓		✓	✓				
33	STOURTON JUNCTION (Stourbridge Canal)	OS										
32	N, Stewponey Wharf	TP										
32	N, Stewponey Wharf	OS	✓									
32	N, Stewponey (Stourton)	OS							✓	✓		
30	N, The Hyde	OS										
29	¼ ml N, The Paddock	TP	✓		✓		✓	✓				
29	N, Kinver Wharf	TP										
29	N, Kinver Wharf	OS										
29	N, Kinver Wharf	OS									✓	
29	E, Kinver	TP						✓	✓	✓		
28	200 yd W, Whittington Horse Bridge	TP										
28	N, Whittington Horse Bridge	OS										
27	N, above Whittington Lock	TP										
24	300 yd W (footpath from Austcliff Bridge)	TP										
23	S, Cookley	OS							✓	✓		
21	¼ ml N, World's End	OS										
20	N, Wolverley Wharf	TP										
20	E, Wolverley Lock	OS										
20	300yd W, Wolverley village	TP								✓		
19	½ ml S, Broadwaters	OS										
16	E & W, Kidderminster	—								✓		

M	PB	PH	PO	R	RD	S	TB	TK	W	WH	Notes
	✓	✓	✓					✓			Snacks at 'Old Bush' & 'Greyhound'
									✓		
	✓	✓						✓			Snacks and Light Meals at the 'Old Bush'
		✓							✓		Snacks at 'Navigation Inn'
✓						✓			✓	✓	Ashwood Marina (Kingswinford 5535) Renown Marine Services (Kingswinford 79527)
									✓		
✓											
									✓		Dawncraft (Kinver 2481)
✓	✓							✓			Café; Meals at 'Stewponey & Foley Arms'
										✓	Meals at Lock Cottage (Kinver 3244)
✓					✓	✓			✓		Dawncraft (Kinver 2363)
					✓				✓		
		✓						✓			'Bellatrix'; (021-557 7347) Snacks at 'The Vine'
											Starline Hire Cruisers (021-553 2566)
	✓		✓						✓		All services
											'Anchor Hotel', Licensed Restaurant
		✓*								✓	*¼ ml E, Meals at 'Whittington Inn'
✓											
		✓									Snacks at 'Rock Tavern'
✓	✓	✓							✓	✓	Snacks at 'The Bull'
									✓		
✓											
		✓									Snacks at 'The Lock'
✓	✓	✓						✓			
										✓	
✓	✓	✓						✓			All services

STAFFORDSHIRE & WORCESTERSHIRE CANAL:

Nearest Bridge	Location	Side of Canal	BB	C	CD	DD	F	G	GA	GS	H	I
16	¼ ml S, Kidderminster	OS										
15	W, Castle Street, Kidderminster	OS								✓		
11	S, above Falling Sands Lock	OS										
—	Pratt's Wharf Lock (disused)	OS										
8	S, Mitton Railway Basin	OS										
7	N, Mitton Chapel Bridge	TP										
4	N, above York Street Lock	OS	✓				✓				✓	
4	N, above York Street Lock	TP										
4	W, next to York Street Lock	OS								✓		
4	E, next to York Street Lock	TP										
—	Stourport Basins (Upper)	—			✓	✓						
—	Stourport Basins (Upper)	—		✓			✓	✓				
—	Stourport Basin (Upper)	—								✓		
—	Stourport (Clock Basin)	—	✓								✓	
—	Stourport Basins (Upper Barge Lock)	—										
—	JUNCTION WITH RIVER SEVERN	—										

M	PB	PH	PO	R	RD	S	TB	TK	W	WH	Notes
										✓	
		✓									'Castle Inn' & 'Old Parker's Arms'
										✓	
										✓	
										✓	
		✓									Meals at the 'Bird in Hand'
✓				✓					✓		Canal Pleasurecraft (Stourport 2970)
✓											
											Canal Ware, Books, etc at Toll Office; Stourport: All services
		✓									Café
✓					✓				✓	✓	Toilets; B.W.B. Maintenance Depot (Stourport 2838)
				✓			✓	✓*			* On River Severn; Head's Boatyard (Stourport 2044)
											Severn Valley Cruisers (Stourport 2990)
				✓							Golden Line Cruisers (Stourport 6892)
									✓		Stourport Locks; Opening times: 0800–1200; 1300–1700; 1800–2000hrs

R*

APPENDIX VI

The Staffordshire & Worcestershire
Canal Society

A feature of the age in which we live is that whenever part of our heritage is threatened with annihilation, then a group of preservationists immediately band together to save it. Canals are no exception and many have societies that were formed in this way. Once the threat of closure has been averted, the societies aim towards conservation rather than preservation and make a valuable contribution towards the life of their adopted canals. They encourage greater usage, promote interest among their members and the general public, assist towards maintenance, and act as 'watchdogs' to ensure that nothing interferes with these activities. The importance of the part played by canal societies in the recent history of our waterways cannot be underestimated and this is particularly true of the Staffs & Worcs. The story of the Staffordshire & Worcestershire Canal Society is told here by Alan T. Smith, Chairman during the period 1971 to 1974.

*   *   *

During and immediately after the Second World War, the inland navigations of this country steadily deteriorated, some becoming derelict or unnavigable and subject to Acts of Closure. The Staffs & Worcs Canal was threatened in 1959, when the Bowes Committee of Inquiry recommended that it should no longer be kept navigable. Although the Inland Waterways Association pursued an active campaign nationally to stop the decay and develop

260

waterways to the full, it was felt that a local body was needed to safeguard the future of the Staffs & Worcs. In 1959 a small group of enthusiasts from the Wolverhampton area formed the Staffordshire & Worcestershire Canal Society, a voluntary, non-profit making organisation. Its main aim, as stated in its constitution, is 'to advocate the development and maintenance of the waterway and the promotion of the waterway to its fullest usage in conjunction with other Midland navigations'. The last phrase proved to be highly significant, for some of the Society's important campaigns have been associated with adjoining waterways, whose abandonment would have seriously affected the usefulness of the Staffs & Worcs.

In order to increase membership and provide a working fund, the Society introduced various social functions, such as indoor meetings during the winter months and narrow-boat trips to places of interest, activities which have since retained their popularity. The monthly Broadsheet started as a single sheet, as its name suggests, and has grown into an illustrated magazine of many pages, though it is still produced entirely by voluntary labour. Every member receives a copy and it is also circulated widely to the Press and Public Libraries, who frequently quote from it. Since it was formed in 1959, the Society has widened its activities to include the provision of lectures to various organisations, and the establishment of a Society shop and exhibition stand that are available for public events.

The early excursions, such as one by horse-drawn narrow boat on the Cannock Extension Canal, were purely for pleasure, but these developed into trips aimed at drawing attention to canals threatened with closure. Cruises of this type were made through Toll End locks and along the Titford branch, both part of the Birmingham system. A major effort was made in 1960 when a fleet of boats started from Brades locks, Oldbury, cruised through Netherton tunnel and returned through Dudley tunnel which was then in danger of being closed. In spite of this effort, Dudley tunnel was closed to navigation the following year. However, after strong pressure was brought to bear by the Society, the British Transport Commission allowed a sight-seeing trip through the tunnel to take place. Public interest was aroused to such an extent that the Dudley Tunnel Preservation Society was formed.

This later became the Dudley Canal Trust, through whose efforts the tunnel was reopened to navigation on 21st April 1973.

In 1961 the Society was alarmed by the proposal of the Commission to close the Stourbridge Canal, a vital link between the Staffs & Worcs and the Birmingham Canal Navigations. The canal had already deteriorated to the point of being barely navigable and in October 1961 a fleet of boats attempted to reach Stourbridge town, falling short of the objective by about ½ mile, despite the strenuous efforts of their crews. The Society offered to carry out voluntary work on the canal, but the Commission refused to co-operate and the Society decided to join with the Inland Waterways Association in holding a National Rally of Boats at Stourbridge in 1962. The preparations were arduous and there was bitter antagonism between the organisers and the Commission. This came to a head with the historic incident of a dragline that had been brought to clear the canal in defiance of the Commission's ruling on the matter. Nationwide publicity resulted, there was a record attendance at the rally and the canal remained open.

Then, in January 1963, the British Transport Commission was abolished and the British Waterways Board was established with powers to command its own affairs. The different outlook of the new Board soon became apparent. In June 1963 a small fleet of boats attended a fête at Stourton on the Stourbridge Canal, and in preparation for this, the Society was given permission to carry out a moderate amount of work on the Four Locks at Stourton. This is probably the first time that such permission was given to a volunteer body and it may be said to have pioneered the widespread co-operation that exists today.

Later in the same year, two members of the Board visited Stourbridge to inspect the canal and meet officers of the Society to discuss the future of the canal. As a result, the Board invited officers of the Society to meet them in London, and it was proposed that the Stourbridge 'Sixteen' locks, by then impassible, should be restored jointly by the two bodies. This proposal was without precedent in the history of canals and was intended as a trial scheme whose outcome would influence the Board's ruling on similar projects put forward by voluntary organisations. After much hard work by the Society and other volunteer bodies, and with full co-operation from the Board, the restoration of the 'Sixteen' was completed in May 1967. The flight was reopened by the Right Honourable John Morris, MP, as part of the Society's Annual Rally, held that year at Stourton. The operation proved to be a great success and the locks have since been heavily used by pleasure craft.

Meanwhile, it was felt that the aims and activities of the Society merited its recognition as a charity, and it became registered as such by the Charity Commissioners in 1965. As a consequence of the Transport Act of 1968, the entire Staffs & Worcs Canal and the main line of the Stourbridge were included in the 'Cruiseway' system. The Society has since assisted the Board with such work as the painting of lock gates, tree felling and towpath maintenance. The condition of the canal has continued to improve and usage has increased, so that there are now about twenty boats per mile along the Staffs & Worcs, making it one of the most popular cruising canals of the entire system.

More recently the Society has been active in encouraging riparian authorities, both along the Staffs & Worcs and on neighbouring canals, to develop the adjoining land to the best advantage. Efforts have also been made to stimulate public interest in waterways and to encourage full use by the local populace for the many leisure pursuits available on canals. Social activities have increased, as has membership, and it has become necessary to meet at a larger hall in Wolverhampton. Trips by narrow boat continue to be a regular attraction and these are usually held in the early autumn, visiting parts of the system that are not readily accessible to members who do not own boats. The Annual Rally, held during the Spring Bank Holiday, is becoming increasingly popular and regularly attracts over two hundred boats and several thousands of spectators.

The activities of the Staffordshire & Worcestershire Canal Society have benefited all who use the canal and its adjoining waterways, whether they boat, fish or just walk along the towing path. Anyone interested in improving the amenities of our canals for all to enjoy would be most welcome as a member of the Society.

July 1972   Alan T. Smith, Chairman
Staffordshire & Worcestershire Canal Society

APPENDIX VII

References, Bibliography and Suggestions for Further Reading

Although most of the information contained in this book was obtained by walking along the towing path or talking to people who work or have worked on the canal, the historical framework on which the story of the Staffs & Worcs is based was taken from *The Canals of the West Midlands* by Charles Hadfield (David & Charles: 1966). Those wishing to delve deeper into the story of the Company and its relationship with neighbouring concerns should consult this authoritative work. The student of canal history will also find further information in the Acts of Parliament for the canal (6 Geo. III, C. 97 and 10 Geo. III, C. 103) and in the Company's Minute Books at the Public Record Office, London.

It is a pity that earlier commentators on life along our waterways, such as Temple Thurston and Bonthron, who wrote in the early years of this century, did not include the Staffs & Worcs in their travels. The northern section does, however, merit a chapter in L. T. C. Rolt's *Narrow Boat* (Eyre & Spottiswoode: 1944), written during the early war years, and more recently David Owen has done justice to the entire waterway in his *Water Highways* (Phoenix House: 1967).

No book deals exclusively with the Staffs & Worcs. British Waterways Board divided the canal between Nos. 4 and 13 in their series of Inland Cruising Booklets, and the Nicholson's guides that superceded the series make a similar division. The northern section is included in *Nicholson's Guide to the Canals of the Northwest* (No. 2) and the southern section is covered in No. 3, which deals with canals of the south-west.

While there are many general works on canals, canal boats and boating folk, an excellent introduction to the subject is *The Inland Waterways of England* by L. T. C. Rolt (Allen & Unwin: 1950). In addition, the authoritative and eminently readable *James Brindley: Engineer* by Cyril T. G. Boucher (Goose: 1968) includes an account of the beginnings of the Canal Era. There is also a proliferation of photographic collections, but one of the finest in so far as the Staffs & Worcs is concerned, now unfortunately out of print, is Eric de Maré's *The Canals of England* (Architectural Press: 1950). Although the Staffs & Worcs represents a very small fraction of the waterway system as a whole, 26 of the 177 illustrations are of the canal; photographs taken when it was still a commercial waterway and its buildings were intact.

Finally, those who are unfamiliar with terms used in this book which are peculiar to canals would do well to consult *Bradshaw's Canals and Navigable Rivers* by Henry de Salis (1904, reprinted by David & Charles: 1969). Aside from being the source from which many subsequent authors have taken their glossaries, it is indispensable to the armchair 'canal enthusiast'.

Maps

The Staffs & Worcs Canal is covered by the following Ordnance Survey maps:

1in. (1:63,360)

119	Stafford	Greay Haywood to Wolverhampton
130	Kidderminster	Wolverhampton to Stourport

1:50,000

127	Stafford & Telford	Great Haywood to Wolverhampton
139	Birmingham	Slade Heath to Caunsall, except Kinver
138	Kidderminster & Wyre Forest	Caunsall to Stourport & Kinver

Of more use to the towpath walker are the 2½in. (1:25,000) series and the following cover the canal.

SJ	92	Great Haywood to Hazlestrine
SJ	91	Hazlestrine to Gailey

SJ 90/80 Gailey to Newbridge, including Hatherton
Branch
SO 89 Newbridge to Swindon
SO 88 Swindon to Cookley
SO 87 Cookley to Stourport

A general account of the geology of the region surrounding the
Staffs & Worcs Canal is given in *The Central England District*, by
F. H. Edmunds and K. P. Oakley (HMSO) in the series 'British
Regional Geology'. The canal traverses the following maps pub-
lished by the Geological Survey (1in. series):

Sheet 140 Burton-on-Trent
Sheet 139 Stafford
Sheet 153 Wolverhampton
Sheet 154 Lichfield (for part of Hatherton Branch)
Sheet 167 Dudley
Sheet 182 Droitwich

A detailed description of each map is given in the accompanying
Memoir of the Geological Survey (HMSO), though Nos. 139, 153 and
154 are at present out of print. Many references to works on
specific topics are included in the memoirs, but an outstanding
paper by L. J. Wills is perhaps worth mentioning. This is the
'Pleistocene Development of the Severn from Bridgnorth to the
Sea' (*Quarterly Journal of the Geological Society*, vol. 94, 1938, pages
161 to 242). Included in this work is an excellent account of river
terraces along the Smestow and Stour valleys.

Index

Page numbers set in heavy type indicate principal references to places and items along the canal. Numbers set in italics refer to illustrations and are plate numbers not page numbers.

271

Walsall, 77, 112
Water mills, *see* Mills
Water supplies, canal, 79, 80, 85–6, 90, 92, 108, 113, 115–16, 141, 184, 190–1, 193, 197, 246–7, Fig. A2, 77, *see also* Reservoirs, Teddesley feeder; domestic, 82, 57, 114, 121, 229
Water Travel, 92, 103
Waterloo colliery, 194
Watershed, Trent/Severn, 73, 96, 105, 234, 246
Waterworks, 57, 82, 115–16, 120, 129, 134, 137–8, 151, 229
Watling Street, 71, 193, 198–9
Weaver, river, 18
Webb, J. S., author, 146
Wedge's Mill, **192–3**, 240
Wegelin, Auguste, 74
Weighbridges (weighing machines),133, 237
Weighing, of boats, *see* Gauging
Weirs, compensation, 86, 110, 123, 130; lock, 65, 68–9, 108, 111, 115–16, 118–19, 125–6, 129, 131, 135, 183, *52*; storm-water, and sluices, 28, 50, 64, 69, 79, 85, 105, 113, 126, 141, 155–6, 193, 181, *55*
Wellington, 95
Wellington Belt, 53
West Bromwich, 32, 175
West Midland Railway, 167, 170, 174
Wharfhouses, 26, 46, 71, 73, 85, 129, 135–6, 172, 185. *See also* Round houses
Wharves: adjoining roads, 70–1, 76, 84–6, 103, 112, 114–15, 125; at junctions, 24, 26, 76, 142, 144; coal, 101, 103, 112, 109–10, 163–7, 180; estate, 34–5, 51–2, 54, 58; mills, forges, ironworks, etc, 24, 26, 74, 79, 99–100, 114–15, 124, 126, 128, 130, 135–7, 148, 153, 159, 161, 163, 170, 195; pits and quarries, 58, 110, 112, 123–4, 170, 174, 176; towns and villages, 42–3, 45–6, 51, 61–4, 103, 109–10, 124, 152, 156–7, 160, 163–7, 174, 176, 186; waterworks, 82, 115, 121, 130; other, 73, 87. *See also* basins, Pratt's Wharf

Wheaton Aston, 103
Whittington, 128, 150, **153–5**, 158, 237, *54*; ironworks, 153–5, 237
Whitworth, Robert, engineer, 97
Whitworth, Sir Richard, promoter, 18
Wightwick, 104, **110–12**, 116, 118, 125, 159, 229, 238; Hall, 112; Manor, 112; mill, 111
Wilden, 172–3, 187, 236; ironworks, 171–3, 187, 236
Wilden Ferry, 18
Wilden Iron Co., 173;
Williams, J. & Co., ironworks, 154
Windmills, *see* Mills
Winding holes, 48, 74, 79, 111, 116, 129, 150, 153, 159, 175
Winsford, 18
Wolseley Bridge, 19, 22
Wolverhampton, 19, 21, 60, 85, **93–112**, 114, 145, 165, 235, 248, 263; airport, 89; race course, 99
Wolverhampton & Bridgnorth Railway, 95–6, 98, 100, 105, 112, 121–2; W'ton C., 17, 85; W'ton Canoe Club, 93; W'ton Corporation, 93–4, 103, 115, 246; W'ton Main Drainage, 94
Wolverley, 117, **158–62**, 237; forge, 159–60, 237, 246; mill, 161, 237
Wolverley Timber Co., 152
Wom brook, 121, 124
Wombourn, 27, 95, **115–25**, 229, 238
Wombourn Sailing Club, 113
Wood Bank, **58–60**, 245–6
Woodfield House, 159
Woodseaves, 88
Worcester, 174, 183, 187
Worcester & Birmingham Canal, 172
Worcestershire County Museum, 188
World's End, 158
Worsley, 18
Wrottesley Park, 105
Wrottesley, Sir John, promoter, 90; Sir Richard, promoter, 20, 104
Wyre Forest Coalfield, 227
Wyrley brook, 190, 193, 196–7

Yarranton, Andrew, engineer, 140
Young, carrier, 78